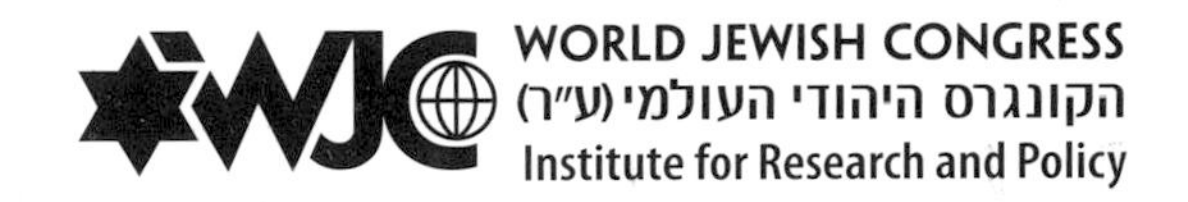

ISRAEL'S RIGHTS

as a Nation-State in International Diplomacy

Israel's Rights as a Nation-State in International Diplomacy

Jerusalem Center for Public Affairs
13 Tel Hai Street, Jerusalem, Israel
Tel. 972-2-561-9281 Fax. 972-2-561-9112
Email: jcpa@netvision.net.il
www.jcpa.org

World Jewish Congress
9A Diskin Street, 5th Floor
Kiryat Wolfson, Jerusalem 96440
Phone : +972 2 633 3000
Fax: +972 2 659 8100
Email: wjc@wjc.co.il
www.worldjewishcongress.com

Academic Editor: Ambassador Alan Baker
Production Director: Ahuva Volk
Graphic Design: Studio Rami & Jaki • www.ramijaki.co.il

Cover Photos: Results from the United Nations vote, with signatures, November 29, 1947 (Israel State Archive)
UN General Assembly Proclaims Establishment of the State of Israel, November 29, 1947 (Israel National Photo Collection)

ISBN: 978-965-218-100-8

TABLE OF CONTENTS

APPENDICES:

INTRODUCTION AND OVERVIEW

Alan Baker

The importance of this book arose in light of a concerted campaign launched some years ago and presently being waged against Israel by Palestinian, Muslim, and other non-Arab elements in the international community.

This campaign seeks to question the very legitimacy of Israel in virtually every aspect of its historical, political, and cultural life, and even extends into international organizations, international media, and the web, with the aim of questioning and undermining the very foundations of Israel's existence.

With a view to providing the international community in general, and readers, academics, parliamentarians, and others, with an authoritative exposition of Israel's basic rights as a state in international diplomacy, several world-renowned experts have been asked to write a chapter on some of the most central aspects of Israel's existence and rights.

In light of claims by Palestinian leaders questioning the very right to statehood of a Jewish state, we chose to open this book with a chapter on "The National Rights of Jews" by Prof. Ruth Gavison, recipient of the 2011 Israel Prize for Law and one of the world's experts in the field of nationalism and public law.

Addressing the issue of the right to establish a national home in Palestine, renowned historian and author Sir Martin Gilbert, who among other things has written the official biography of Sir Winston Churchill, discusses in the second chapter entitled "An Overwhelmingly Jewish State" - From the Balfour Declaration to the Palestine Mandate," issues regarding the League of Nations Mandate and the British government's understanding of the Jewish right to a national home in Palestine.

Since Israel's right to establish a Jewish state has been and still is constantly under discussion, Prof. Shlomo Avineri, one of Israel's greatest experts in political science, has written the third chapter on "Self-Determination and Israel's Declaration of Independence."

The refugee issue has tenaciously been on the international agenda since 1948, and figures in all the major international documentation. But while this was originally an issue of Jewish refugees from Arab countries, as well as of Palestinian refugees, the Jewish-refugee aspect appears to have been forgotten by the international community. Dr. Stanley A. Urman, an expert on the refugee issue who heads the international organization "Justice for Jews from Arab Countries," has written the fourth chapter, "The United Nations and Middle East Refugees: The Differential Treatment of Arabs and Jews."

Over the years, and despite developments within the peace process, the international community has formulated and insists on reiterating a sort of "accepted terminology" that defines Israel's status as an "occupying power" and determines that "settlements are illegal," without any serious attempt to review the accuracy or truth behind such terminology. In the fifth chapter, on "Israel's Rights Regarding the Territories and the Settlements in the Eyes of the International Community," I address this phenomenon and point to the inherent lack of accuracy and the way in which the international community has allowed itself to be misled by clichés.

Despite the fact that the issue of borders has been agreed between Israel and the PLO to be a subject for negotiation between them in the negotiations on the permanent status, the Palestinian leadership is persistently attempting to dictate the outcome of such negotiations through unilateral campaigning in the international community with a view to achieving recognition of the "1967 borders." Prof. Nicholas Rostow, a prominent American international lawyer and former legal counsel to the U.S. Mission to the United Nations, addresses this issue in the sixth chapter on "The Historical and Legal Contexts of Israel's Borders."

UN Security Council Resolution 242 of November 1967 serves as one of the foundations of all the peace treaties and other agreements within the Middle East peace process, as well as later UN resolutions on Middle East issues. However, considerable efforts are constantly being made to proffer interpretations of aspects of this resolution that are not compatible, neither with the text nor with the intentions of those who drafted Resolution 242. One of the key authorities on international law, and an expert on the legal documentation of the Arab-Israeli peace process, Prof. Ruth Lapidoth, who herself participated in many of the negotiations in the peace process, has written the seventh chapter and addresses the issue of "The Misleading Interpretation of Security Council Resolution 242 (1967)."

The issue of Jerusalem is perhaps one of the oldest issues on the agenda of the international community, and in one way or another has figured in historical and legal discussion for hundreds and possibly thousands of years. One of Israel's experts on Jerusalem is Dr. Dore Gold, a former ambassador to the United Nations and currently president of the Jerusalem Center for Public Affairs, who has written the eighth chapter on "Defending Israel's Legal Rights to Jerusalem."

While the principle behind the Middle East peace process, as set out both in the various UN resolutions and agreements, is premised on the assumption that all issues between the parties will be solved by negotiation, the Palestinian leadership have nevertheless developed a *modus operandi* of seeking unilateral determinations by the United Nations and other bodies for issues that are agreed to be settled by negotiation. Dan Diker, Secretary-General of the World Jewish Congress and Adjunct Fellow of the Hudson Institute in Washington, DC, addresses in the ninth chapter the issue of "Palestinian Unilateralism and Israel's Rights in Arab-Israeli Diplomacy."

Since the withdrawal of Israel's forces and civilians, and dismantling of settlements in the Gaza Strip in 2006, much has been written and discussed as to whether Israel nevertheless continues to "occupy" the area. Indeed, UN resolutions and UN rapporteurs continue to refer to Israel as the "occupying power" in the Gaza Strip notwithstanding that Israel is no longer present there and in fact the Hamas terror organization has established its own administration there. Perhaps the most fitting expert to discuss Israel's status vis-à-vis the Gaza Strip is Col. (res.) Pnina Sharvit-Baruch, lecturer in international law at Tel Aviv University and formerly head of the International Law Department of the Israel Defense Forces, who addresses in the tenth chapter the issue of "Is the Gaza Strip Occupied by Israel?"

While Israel, since the spring of 1949, has been a full-fledged member of the United Nations, to this day it is discriminated against and does not enjoy the full rights of sovereign equality guaranteed by the UN Charter in that it is not a member of the regional groups to which member states of the UN belong, and thus is unable to field its candidacy for such bodies as the Security Council and the International Court, as well as other major bodies. In the eleventh chapter, I analyze this situation under the title "The Violation of Israel's Right to Sovereign Equality in the United Nations."

Prof. Alan M. Dershowitz, the eminent U.S. jurist, addresses in the final, twelfth chapter, "Countering Challenges to Israel's Legitimacy," some of the claims persistently being made against Israel's legitimacy, such as the claim that Israel is an illegitimate "colonial" state; that it secured its statehood unlawfully; that it is an apartheid state; and the claim for a "one-state solution."

I am sure that this book will serve as a vital tool for all those who are genuinely interested in looking through the shallow and clichéd attempts by those in the international community who are determined, for whatever reason, to question Israel's legitimacy and to deny its rights.

THE NATIONAL RIGHTS OF JEWS

Ruth Gavison

INTRODUCTION

Are Jews a nation? Do they have and should they have national rights, in particular the right to state-level self-determination? Was the establishment of the state of Israel an answer to this question? How should we approach these questions now, at the beginning of the twenty-first century?

These are questions that have many dimensions – theoretical, historical, moral, political, and legal. They have been debated heatedly at least from the beginning of the Zionist movement, both among Jews and non-Jews. Recently the questions have returned to the fore due to the combination and culmination of a number of processes:

In his Bar-Ilan speech on June 14, 2009, Prime Minister Benjamin Netanyahu committed himself to the vision of "two states" but insisted that they should be "two states for two peoples."[1] He therefore demanded that Palestinians should recognize not just the independent and sovereign state of Israel, but also that Israel is the nation-state of Jews; Palestinians and other Arab leaders objected to this demand; they were also asked to do so by the representatives of the Arab citizens of Israel.[2] Palestinians explained that such a recognition may undermine the "right" of Palestinian refugees and their descendants to return to their homes in Israel if they so choose. The Arab citizens of Israel argued that such recognition would undermine their equal status within Israel, since – they claim – the Jewishness of Israel is incompatible with democracy, and Israel should be a democracy and therefore give up on its Jewish distinctness. Israel should be Israeli rather than Jewish, and this would affirm its commitment to the civic equality of all its citizens, irrespective of religion or ethnic origin.[3]

Thus questions relating to the national rights of Jews affect the prospects of the distinct but related questions of a resolution of the Israeli-Palestinian conflict as well as internal issues concerning Israel's own identity and function.

Against the background of principled challenges to the legitimacy of the idea of a Jewish nation-state, I wish to argue that the denial of national rights to Jews as Jews is neither required nor justified by any accepted norm of international law or morality. The claim that Jews have no national rights is not well founded.

The skeleton of my argument is that **Israel was established as the (ethnic) nation-state of Jews, and that it is justified that it continues to be the nation-state of Jews. As such, Israel is allowed to act in ways that promote the conditions for its ability to function as the nation-state of Jews and to maintain its Jewish distinctness so long as this does not violate the rights – personal as well as collective – of its population. Thus, the nation-state of Jews must not discriminate against its non-Jewish citizens. In addition, it cannot impose a specific conception of the Jewishness of the state on its population, Jewish or Arab. Finally, Jews in other parts of the world may have group rights as well as individual rights, but they may not claim rights to political self-determination as national minorities.**

Let me sketch some of the main theses of this argument:

- **Jews are a nation**, with cultural and ethnic characteristics, and not only a religion; this was true before Israel was established and it is true today. This is consistent with the claim that Jews are also members of the nations within which they live.

- Being a nation, **Jews are entitled to national rights**, not only to religious and cultural rights. **The strongest national right is the right to state-level self-determination.**

- Being dispersed among other nations, and living always as a minority, has throughout history proven itself harmful to Jews and has made them and continues to render them vulnerable both to persecution and to assimilation, threatening their ability to maintain their cultural identity.

- It is thus justified for Jews to have sought revival of political independence in their ancient homeland – Zion. Thus Zionism is **not** a colonial or an imperialist operation in the sense analyzed and condemned by modern political philosophy. This is true despite the fact that at the beginning of the twentieth century Jews were not a critical mass in that country. The presence of Arab population in Israel was not a conclusive reason against this move because that community never had enjoyed political independence, and Jews were at liberty to seek political revival in the only place in the world that had been their homeland.

- Israel was established to respond to the Jews' need for effective self-determination. The 1947 UN partition resolution protected the rights of Arab population of Palestine by the decision to establish an Arab state in a part of historic Palestine, and requiring both states to protect the rights – personal and cultural – of members of the other nation residing in them.

- Two wars (1947-1949 and 1967) started by the Arabs resulted in a reality under which only a Jewish state existed between the sea and the Jordan River. The "two states, two peoples" solution is designed to change that situation.
- Israel may and should maintain itself as a democratic nation-state of Jews, and should act to promote the implementation of effective self-determination for both Jews and Arabs in historic Palestine/the Land of Israel.

Advisedly, this argument does not discuss the details of present or desirable contours of the resolution of the Israeli-Palestinian conflict or the status of the Arab minority within Israel. Rather, it deals with the general constraints in these arrangements, from the starting point of examining the validity and scope of the national rights of Jews and their implications.[4]

In the body of the chapter I elaborate on some of these premises and claims.

JEWS ARE A NATION

The claim that Jews are not a nation in the context of our concerns comes from the fact that international law recognizes the right of **peoples** to self-determination, while only recognizing cultural and religious rights for other cultural groups, with a special sensitivity to the claims of national minorities.[5] If Jews are only a religion, basic elements of their claim to a right to self-determination in Zion may be undermined.[6]

We should also recall that these debates about the nature of Judaism arose before Zionism, and were made more heated by growing secularization, enlightenment, and the rise of nation-states and political emancipation in Europe.

I will argue that Jews are indeed a nation in the relevant sense, and that they have been recognized as such by the international community. Yet we should distinguish between, on the one hand, the question in terms of international law and the right to self-determination, where the answer is relatively clear and simple; and, on the other, the complex identity questions of membership in the Jewish collective and its history.[7]

It is true that for many hundreds of years Jews lived in dispersed communities all over the world, and did not share a spoken language.[8] Usually they did not enjoy political control over their fate.[9] Moreover, Jewish identity over the years was maintained and transmitted via membership in communities of faith and worship. Jews who did not observe did not remain Jews. Often Jews who integrated into host societies and agreed to the privatization of their distinct Jewish identity as a religion were not effective in transmitting it to later generations. Yet it is also quite clear that the ties among Jewish communities were not exhausted by religion even before secularization. Jews felt a community of fate and shared a history and a culture across the countries in which they lived and the languages that they used. The strength of this sense of shared fate is a central component of the amazing fact that Jews remained a distinct ethnic group despite centuries of dispersion.[10]

Nationhood and membership in nations are recognized to be based on a combination of objective and subjective characteristics. Those who remained Jews chose to do so. And they chose to do so because they felt this was an important part of their identity. The fact that this identity was not only religious became clear when many who stopped observing, some of whom defined themselves as having no religion, wanted to remain and transmit their Jewish identity to their children.

The cultural revival leading to Zionism was in fact triggered by this wish. Thus it is not surprising that Herzl, an assimilated Jew himself, affirmed clearly that "We are a People; one people." True, there are modern scholars of nationalism who doubt that Jews are a nation. But there are many others scholars, Jews and non-Jews alike, who use Zionism as a paradigm of a national liberation movement.[11]

It must be conceded that the existence of Jews before the establishment of the state could indeed raise doubts concerning their status as a nation. The doubts are raised not only by the characteristics of Jews and Judaism, but by the fact that different states treated Judaism and Jewish identity in different ways. France never saw Jews as a national group, and sought to privatize even their religious affiliation. Poland at some points was quite happy to treat Jews as a national minority. Nonetheless in World War 1 Jews fought in national armies on all sides of the battle.[12]

Be this as it may, the question of whether Jews had national rights was clearly resolved in international law by the 1922 Mandate for Palestine, in which Britain accepted the Mandate to facilitate the establishment of a "national home" for Jews in Palestine, explicitly recognizing the historical roots of Jews in the country.[13]

So while historical and sociological questions of the essence of Judaism and the Jewish collective are never settled by legal documents, the fact that Jews are seen as a nation entitled to self-determination seems to be well recognized by the international community.

Finally, there are those who claim that Zionism was a movement that sought to make Jews a "normal" people, with a territory and language. Indeed, the establishment of the state was a major achievement of Zionism. However, once the state was established, it by definition constitutes the nation of all its citizens. According to this attitude, Zionists wanted Jews to become Israelis. Once they succeeded, the collective that is now the subject of rights to self-determination is those living in the country. Israel should be an Israeli state, and the relevant collective is that of Israelis.[14] A majority of Israelis under this account are Jews by their culture. But their nationality is Israeli. Jews living in other countries are, respectively, Jews in their religion (often privatized) and English, French, or American by their nationality.

This argument ignores the distinction between ethnic national identity and civic national identity. True, all citizens of a state, irrespective of ethnic or religious identity, belong to the same "civic nation" or *demos*. But in many contexts, nationalism is not about civic identity but about the wish to gain political independence for a cultural or ethnic (national) group. If this had not been the case it would have been unintelligible to talk about "national minorities" since, by definition, no such minorities could exist in any state. True, Jews who are citizens of other countries are also affected

Theodor Herzl, 1900 (Israel National Photo Collection)

by their countries' cultural and political identity. Their ties to the country in which they live and whose citizens they are, are not exhausted by legal citizenship. It does not at all follow from this that their understanding of their Jewish identity is not deeply ethnic, historic, and cultural. By claiming that Jews are a nation I am invoking a distinction between citizenship and national-cultural identity. All Israelis, Jews and Arabs alike, share a citizenship and some cultural characteristics (such as Hebrew). Yet Arabs and Jews in Israel both want to be also recognized as members of their respective national (Jews vs. Arabs) as well as religious groups (Jews, Muslims, Druze, and Christians). Moreover, there are important cultural differences within these national and religious groups. All of these identities may have practical implications. Jews who are citizens of other countries do not seek recognition of their national rights in those countries. They may choose to immigrate and settle into the one country in the world which is the (ethnic) nation-state of Jews. This will be an exercise of their national rights. They may also choose to remain nationals of their countries of citizenship, while acknowledging their cultural ties to the nation-state of Jews.

The complexity of the relationships between citizenship, culture, religion, and ethnic heritage is highlighted in the modern world because of the scope of immigration, creating large groups of people who are citizens of one state and members of national and cultural groups whose center of life is elsewhere. Modern states now tend to recognize this complexity not only through policies of multiculturalism but also by allowing and even encouraging double citizenship.

The challenge to the fact that Jews are a nation thus fails.[15]

NOT ENJOYING EFFECTIVE SELF-DETERMINATION ANYWHERE IS BAD FOR BOTH JEWS AND JUDAISM

Some argue that even if Jews are a nation, they do not and should not have national rights because their long existence under conditions of dispersion shows that they can survive without effective political self-determination. This claim is then strengthened by invocation of the rights of Arabs in Palestine.[16]

Zionists argued that the lessons of living in dispersion showed many events of persecution, pressures to convert, expulsions, and even genocide. Moreover, they claimed that not being responsible for the whole range of matters of state created Jewish communities that were less than wholesome and a culture that was not complete. They conceded that Jews also knew periods of great affluence and creativity while in dispersion. Yet a defining mark of life in dispersion was the vulnerability of Jews, and their total dependence on the goodwill and effective defense of the rulers and elites of the countries in which they dwelt.

Finally, they argued that with secularization and emancipation, Jews would face pressures to assimilate that might threaten their power to remain Jews and transmit Jewish identity. Such pressures to assimilate might be the price for a fuller integration of Jews within their host societies. Some Zionists felt that Jews could not in fact integrate because they were considered aliens in their host communities. Others reasoned that even if assimilation might be beneficial for individual Jews, it would threaten the possibility of maintaining and transmitting Jewish identity and culture over time. Such revival of Judaism as a cultural tradition and identity required active investment in cultural creativity among Jews, which would reflect the full range of ways of being Jewish, especially ways seeking to integrate a stable Jewish identity with modernity and the achievements of science and general culture.

The Holocaust was a tragic proof that Jews could indeed become extremely vulnerable to physical danger even in host countries that were cultured and in which Jews were fully emancipated and integrated. Yet many say today that this *sui generis* event cannot support a continuing claim for political self- determination. They add that today Jews are less threatened in most parts of the world than they are in Israel. And that, in fact, Israeli policies are an important element of what endangers Jews in the world.

There are at least four responses to these claims. First, even if it is true that Jews in Israel are not safe, Jews in Israel do not depend for their safety and security on the goodwill of rulers and the societies hosting them. This is a critical element of what the Zionist revolution was all about. Second, the safety of Jews around the world may be related to the existence of Israel in complex ways. While debates and opposition to the policies of Israel may contribute to anti-Semitism, clearly anti-Semitism existed before Israel, and having a place of refuge and a state that may use diplomatic and other measures to defend Jews may be significant. Third, Zionism was also concerned with the quality of Jewish life permitted by life in the Diaspora. Israel is the only country in the world that gives Jews an opportunity to apply Judaism to the totality of their existence, including the political level. Finally, Israel is the only place in the world where a Jew can live in a public culture that is Jewish. Israel is the only place in the world where pressures to assimilate work toward Judaism rather than against it. For those who care about the continuation of Jewish identity and transmitting it, Israel provides the only place in which Jewish identity can flourish in the ways made possible by a Jewish public sphere.

Thus, the reasons which justified the thrust of Jewish nationalism before the establishment of the state are still valid and pressing today. They are even more valid now. At the beginning of the twentieth century a Jewish state was a dream. Today Israel is the home of the strongest Jewish community in the world.

Even those who think it was a terrible mistake to establish Israel as a Jewish state (the writer not included) must concede that denying Israeli Jews their national home is a very different proposition. Taking from Jews and Judaism the political base of their independence cannot be justified.

Palestinian self-determination cannot be permitted to undermine Jewish self-determination. No claim of self-determination in this context can thus be exclusive and pertain to the whole of the territory. Not surprisingly, "two states for two peoples" is the political arrangement now most popular within Israel and the international community.

LOCATION OF NATIONAL ASPIRATIONS OF JEWS: A NATIONAL HOME IN ZION

We have argued that Jews are a nation and that like all nations they are entitled to seek and exercise self-determination, which is justified by the wish to effectively gain physical and cultural security. However, for most nations or peoples, there is no special question of the **location** of this attempted exercise of independence. Usually, these peoples form the majority or at least a critical mass of the population of a territory in which they have always lived, so that territory is part of the characteristics constituting them as a people. Indeed, when there is no clear territory in which the national or ethnic group is a majority, conflicts may arise and the attempt to gain state-level self-determination may fail because of the competing interests and rights of other groups. Jews, as noted, did not constitute the majority in any territory. The only country in which they had ever exercised political sovereignty was Zion. While a small number of Jews always lived in the Land of Israel, and some Jews immigrated to it, and while Zion and Jerusalem were very central in Jewish yearnings and prayers, Jews were a very small minority in the country, which was populated – even if not very densely – by mostly Arab residents.[17]

The project of creating a national home for Jews in the Land of Israel was thus problematic not only in the sense that it was not clear that it was practicable to move large number of Jews to Zion. Palestine had not been "a country without a people waiting for a people without a country." An attempt to implement such a plan would clearly impact the local population. At a minimum, it might turn the present majority population in the country into a minority in their own country. This raised both moral and practical difficulties. One Palestinian challenge to the morality of Israel is precisely that Zionism was designed, and had to be designed, as a movement to dispossess and uproot the native population.

To overcome the claim that the country was populated and that the creation of a Jewish national home in it would infringe on the rights of the local population, Zionist leaders argued that the local residents did not enjoy political independence and were not a distinct people; that they would not be dispossessed; that they would enjoy the fruits of the progress and growth the Jewish settlement would bring; and that their civil and political rights would be secured.[18] Some among the leaders understood and expected the vehement objection of the local Arab population, but they reasoned that the combination of the Jews' urgent need and their historic ties to the land justified the movement, and that the combination of this moral force with an "iron wall" of determination might lead the Arabs to accept life as equal citizens in the Jewish state, or to a willingness to exercise their own self-determination in other territories of the region.[19]

This combination of ideas indeed contributed (together with imperialistic interests) to the Balfour Declaration of 1917 and to the British Mandate over Palestine, which was designed to facilitate the creation of a Jewish national home in Palestine while securing the rights, personal and cultural, of non-Jewish communities.[20]

Zionism was indeed unique in that it sought self-determination for Jews in a country where only a very small number of Jews lived. The logic and justification for the principle of self-determination was that of liberating people sitting on their land from the yoke of foreign rule. If all Jews had had in 1947 were the biblical promise and the historical-cultural ties, Israel would not have been founded despite the Holocaust. Zionism was successful because it created a critical mass of Jews in Palestine, who exhibited incredible powers of political, social, economic, and cultural energy and development. This achievement was based on the vigor, determination, and dedication of the Zionists, which were in fact built on their strong belief in the justice of their cause and the deep connection between Jews and the Land of Israel. The fact that the local Arab population was not well organized and did not have political control over their country was a great help.

In 1937 the Peel Commission concluded that the animosity between the two national movements was too large. They conceded that the promises Britain had made to Jews and Arabs were inconsistent. They thus recommended the partition of Mandatory Palestine into a small Jewish state and an Arab state joined with Transjordan. Jerusalem and a corridor to Jaffa were supposed to remain under international/British jurisdiction.[21]

The Jews rejected the particulars of the Peel proposals, but authorized the Jewish Agency to negotiate. They thus accepted the principle of partition. The Arabs rejected partition out of hand.

As we saw, at the beginning of the twentieth century, Jews did not have the **right** to make the local Arab population a minority in their country just because they had deep historical ties to the land and just because this was the only place in the world where they had exercised political independence. But they did have the **liberty** to try and return to their homeland. Once their wish to do this was recognized by the international community, they had **a right** to pursue their goal, without infringing on the rights of the local population. At a certain point, once the reality of the Jewish settlement had been created, Jews had national rights to effective self-determination within Palestine/the Land of Israel.[22] The need to grant Jews political independence and statehood stemmed from the fact that Jews and Arabs could not be expected to resolve peacefully their differences over immigration, security, and the identity of the state.[23]

A few points should be stressed here.

- Both the Balfour Declaration and the Mandate for Palestine recognized the national rights of **Jews** as such; not only of the Jews living at the time in the country. The Mandate explicitly addresses the need to allow for easy immigration of Jews to Palestine and their quick naturalization. Yet both documents stressed that this should not affect the existing rights of Jews in the countries in which they live; and that the promise of a national home for Jews should not be allowed to infringe the rights of non-Jews.[24]

- The Anglo-American Committee in its recommendations stressed the need to allow one hundred thousand Jews from the camps in Europe to immigrate to Palestine. Thus they clearly addressed the interests of Jews outside Palestine. At the same time, they also stated that Palestine should not be seen as providing a solution to the "Jewish problem." That committee, however, refrained from recommending a solution. Rather, it sought the continuation of an international trusteeship hoping that a peaceful agreement between Jews and Arabs could be reached.

- Partition was based on the understanding that limiting the territory of the Jewish state might give Jews the control they needed over immigration and security – while putting to rest the fears of the Arabs that Jewish immigration would create the basis for making Jews the majority in the whole of Palestine. The international community thus was willing to let Jews control immigration of Jews (and non-Jews) into the Jewish state.

- The national rights of Jews recognized by the international community were thus rights to have their own nation-state, which would be a democracy guaranteeing the individual and collective cultural rights of the non-Jewish minorities within it. The expectation was that Israel would privilege Jews in immigrating to Israel; and that individual Jews would have the liberty to choose whether to settle in Israel. Jews also had the liberty to choose to remain citizens of their own countries. It was understood that the establishment of Israel was the response to the claim of Jews that they were entitled to be like all peoples – living freely in their own homeland.

ISRAEL SHOULD REMAIN THE DEMOCRATIC NATION-STATE OF JEWS

Let us assume from now on that UN Resolution 181 of November 1947, together with other conditions and premises, established the right of Jews to a Jewish state in a part of Palestine/the Land of Israel.

In other words, Resolution 181 envisaged two ethnic nation-states, each of which would provide state-level self-determination to Jews and Arabs (now Palestinians), respectively. Specifically, it trusted that each of these countries would take the necessary steps to guarantee the majority of its own group within it. Naturally, each of these states was expected to act in ways that would guarantee its continued existence as the nation-state of its people. The United Nations demanded that this be done within the constraints of protecting the rights of members of national, religious, and linguistic minorities.

The United Nations did not envisage each of these states as a neutral state, privatizing the noncivic characteristics of its inhabitants. Most clearly, it did not envisage either of these states as a binational state, because it concluded that the two peoples could not live together within the same political unit.

Against this background it is puzzling that many now claim that Israel should abandon its definition as the nation-state of the Jewish people. The key to this challenge seems to be that the UN resolution assumed that the Jewish state would be both Jewish and democratic. But now, the challenge goes, it is quite clear that Israel cannot be both Jewish and democratic. It must therefore give up its special affiliation with Jewish self-determination.[25]

On November 29, 1947, the UN General Assembly adopted Resolution 181, also known as the Partition Plan, which called for the establishment of a Jewish state alongside an Arab state in Palestine. The resolution was accepted by the Jewish Agency. However it was rejected by the Arab Higher Committee and the Arab League. (UN Photo Library)

It should be clear that this demand also means that Israel is not permitted to act so as to secure a Jewish majority in it. Similarly, it is not allowed to promote conditions that will facilitate the continuing self-determination of Jews in it. I believe these conclusions are not warranted. Israel may promote Jewish state-level self-determination in it. In this sense, it is permitted to maintain a stance that is not neutral toward the national and cultural affiliations of its population. At the same time, the arguments supporting Jewish self-determination also support the recognition of similar rights to Palestinians in a part of their homeland. While Jews are not strangers to this country, Palestinians are longtime natives in it. They live here by right, and have not immigrated to the country. They are entitled to exercise self-determination in their homeland even if they are required to share it with Jews – the second people for which it is a homeland.

PROSPECTS

For too long, the conflict between Jews and Arabs and between Israel and Palestinians was based on rejection of the national aspirations of the other side. There are two asymmetries here. First, as I have mentioned, for historical reasons it is still the case today that only Jews enjoy state-level self-determination. This is an unstable situation both morally and politically. On the other hand, most of the Jews concede that the Arabs of Palestine have individual as well as collective and national rights in Palestine. They may differ on how this fact should be reflected in political borders. Most Arabs, however, are reluctant to concede that Jews have a right to national self-determination in any part of Palestine/the Land of Israel. At best they are willing to respect the individual rights of Jews who had lived in the country at some given time (like 1917 or 1922). Or they may concede that *de facto* an Israeli collective has been created which has a right to self-determination but not to maintaining a Jewish majority or a Jewish or Hebrew public space in Israel, nor to have the Law of Return or affective special relationships with Jewish communities abroad.

It is not my purpose here to pronounce on the question of whether the demand for recognition of Israel as a Jewish nation-state is necessary to the peace process or an obstacle to it. However, if the two parties are not both willing to accept that there are two groups here with authentic and powerful claims for national status and self-determination, it is very hard to see how a stable *modus vivendi* can be reached between Jews and Arabs in Palestine/the Land of Israel.

BIBLIOGRAPHY

Becker, Tal. "The Claim for Recognition of Israel as a Jewish State: A Reassessment." Washington Institute, February 2011.

Ben-Gurion, David, 1931. *We and Our Neighbors* (Tel Aviv: Davar Press) (Hebrew).

Ben-Israel, Hedva, 2003. "Zionism and European Nationalism," *Israel Studies* 8(1).

Berent, Moshe, 2009. *A Nation like All Nations: Towards the Birth of an Israeli Republic* (Jerusalem: Carmel) (Hebrew).

Gans, Chaim, 2008. *A Just Zionism: On the Morality of the Jewish State* (Oxford: Oxford University Press).

Gavison, Ruth, 2003. "The Jews' Right to Statehood," reprinted in Hazony et al., 2006.

Gavison, Ruth, 2010. *The Law of Return at 60: History, Ideology, Justification* (Jerusalem: Metzilah).

Gelber, Yoav, 2006. *Palestine 1948: War, Escape and the Emergence of the Palestinian Refugee Problem* (Brighton and Portland: Sussex Academic Press).

Ghanem, Asad, Nadim Rouhana and Oren Yiftahel, 1998. "Questioning Ethnic Democracy: A Response to Sammy Smooha." *Israel Studies* 3(2): 253.

Hazony, David, Yoram Hazony and Michael Oren, eds., 2006. *New Essays on Zionism* (Jerusalem: Shalem), 3.

Khalidi, Rashid, 1997. *Palestinian Identity: The Construction of Modern National Consciousness* (New York: Columbia University Press).

Kimmerling, Baruch and Joel S. Migdal, 1993. *Palestinians: The Making of a People* (New York: Free Press).

Kymlicka, Will, 2009. *Multicultural Odysseys* (Oxford: Oxford University Press).

Margalit, Avishai and Joseph Raz, 1990. "National Self-Determination." *Journal of Philosophy* 87(9): 439-461.

Morris, Benny, 2009. *2008, 1948: A History of the First Arab-Israeli War* (New Haven: Yale University Press).
Sand, Shlomo, 2009. *How the Jewish People Was Invented* (London and New York: Verso Books).
Shimoni, Gideon, 1995. *Zionist Ideology* (Waltham, MA: Brandeis University Press).
Strawson, John, 2010. *Partitioning Palestine: Legal Fundamentalism in the Israeli-Palestinian Conflict* (London: Pluto Press).
Yehoshua, Abraham B., 2008. *Homeland Grasp* (Tel Aviv: Hakibbutz Hameuhad) (Hebrew).

NOTES

1 http://www.mfa.gov.il/MFA/Government/Speeches+by+Israeli+leaders/2009/Address_PM_Netanyahu_Bar-Ilan_University_14-Jun-2009.htm. That Israel be recognized explicitly as the nation-state of Jews has been an Israeli demand at least from the time of Israel's response to the roadmap in 2003.

2 For a comprehensive analysis of the positions of Palestinian negotiators and the views of representatives of the Israeli Arab citizens, see, e.g., Becker (2011).

3 See, e.g., Becker (2011), next to note 102. See also the Democratic Constitution proposed by Adala.

4 This paper concerns the national rights of Jews and not how they should be protected in view of the fact that the situation in Palestine/the Land of Israel is one of competing claims to self- determination, and that under some accounts these claims are inconsistent in principle, or cannot be accommodated in any practical way. These are serious arguments which may have political implications. My argument is limited to the claims that Jews do have national rights to state-level self-determination in at least a part of Zion.

5 In fact, the post-World War II international regime provided limited protection to group rights under section 27 of the *International Covenant on Civil and Political Rights*, and explicitly excluded national minorities from that protection. This resulted from the fact that many believed national and ethnic conflicts were major contributors to the onset of World War II. With time, however, this attitude changed somewhat. For a comprehensive analysis, see Kymlicka (2009).

6 I will not discuss the claim that Jews are not a nation because the amended Law of Return defines "a Jew" in terms of Jewish religious law. For details of the definition of the Law of Return, see Gavison (2010).

7 Indeed, in a classical article on self-determination Margalit and Raz suggest that the right to self-determination should be analyzed and justified without aspiring to give a definite answer to the question of what groups are "peoples" or "nations." Rather, they talk of "all-encompassing groups" who have characteristics which justify claims for self-determination.

8 There is a fascinating debate about the relationships between modern Hebrew and the language of Jewish texts. Yet it seems clear that Hebrew, maintained in the teaching and culture of all Jewish communities, was a central element of the affinity among Jews everywhere.

9 There were places and times in which Jews enjoyed effective cultural and religious autonomy, while being allowed to integrate into the host society. Yet even in those times and places Jews as such did not exercise political independence. In this sense, the Jewish element was "privatized" in their lives.

10 While at certain times one talked about "people" and "race" as interchangeable, today we distinguish between race in the narrow sense in terms of genetic connections and race in a more general sense of identifying a distinct group. Jews were at times persecuted as a race, but they were also persecuted as a community of faith and a distinct nation.

11 For detailed discussions of these issues, see Shimoni (1995); and the writings of Hedva Ben-Israel, e.g., Ben-Israel (2003), where the positions of Anderson, Smith, Gellner, and Hobsbawm are discussed concerning the question of whether Zionism is the national liberation movement of Jews.

12 This situation persists today. While Jews are not recognized as a national minority anywhere, Jews do enjoy collective rights in some countries. E.g., Sweden recognized Yiddish (as well as Roma) as an official minority language. In some countries Jewish schools are recognized as denominational public schools by the state.

13 Since I concentrate here on the national rights of Jews, I will not discuss the question of the national rights of Palestinians, which is quite intricate for different reasons. Yet I should mention that the Arabs of Palestine resisted the fact that in the early

international documents on Palestine they were described as "the non-Jewish communities" with a stress on religion and not on national status. There is a debate as to whether Palestinians are a distinct nation or a part of the Arab nation. Politically there are many Arabs who then saw and still see Palestine as a natural part of Greater Syria. It is significant that some claim that Palestinian national identity was only developed as a counterweight to Zionism. Others (Khalidi [1997], Kimmerling and Migdal [1993]) find evidence of Palestinian identity from the end of the nineteenth century. At this stage this debate is not important because clearly the Arab population of Palestine sees itself as forming a distinct nation and they are entitled as such to some collective recognition. But the history is important as it shows that the competing narratives are in some ways very symmetrical. There is a question concerning the identity of the Palestinian collective that is not less complex than that concerning the Jewish one. This fact does influence the status of claims to mutual recognition.

14 This view is expressed clearly by Berent (2009). A. B. Yehoshua (2008) advocates a similar notion.

15 I want to stress that my conclusion stands even if there is some truth in some of the claims made by, e.g., Sand (2009). Jews are not a nation only by blood ties. They are a nation through long and complex historical, religious, cultural, and social processes. The fact that some aspects of Jewish identity are "invented" or "mobilized" by national liberation movements does not weaken the validity of claims of national self-determination.

16 Some add that Israel will inevitably turn into a theocracy and that this too is an argument against its justification. There is a struggle about the meaning of the Jewishness of Israel and at present a majority of Jews, including many Orthodox Jews, insist that Israel should remain a democracy. However, theocracies in the world are not denied their right to exist as states.

17 Debates abound about the numbers and the nature of the mid-nineteenth-century population of Palestine, including hypotheses that at least some of the longstanding Arab population are in fact Islamized Jews. It appears that claims that most of the Arab population moved to Palestine after the onset of Zionist settlement are misguided, although it is true that parts of Palestinian population still connect themselves to origins in other Arab countries.

18 See, e.g., the collection of essays by Ben-Gurion (1931). He describes the question as a "tragic fateful" one, and stresses that the Zionist project seeks to help the Arab population of Palestine flourish.

19 Even if agreements such as the Faisal-Weizmann understandings had been implemented, the local Palestinian population might have objected. Some Zionist thinkers did not expect understanding and agreement, and sought only to justify the fact that Zionism might weaken or undermine political self-determination for the Palestinian Arabs. Among those some thought that the combination of progress and civil rights with self-determination in other Arab countries were enough (like Jabotinsky), while others concluded that in Palestine itself, Jews should seek to become many but not the majority, so that a binational state could be formed (like Brit Shalom). Arabs had rejected all ideas of Jewish political independence in any part of Palestine.

20 For short historical accounts of these events, see Morris (2009), ch. 2; Strawson (2010), chs. 1-3.

21 Under Resolution 181 of 1947, Palestine itself was partitioned into two states, one Jewish and one Arab, enjoying economic union. The Jewish state was larger than under the Peel proposal, and Jerusalem was designated to be a separate entity under international jurisdiction.

22 I develop this argument in Gavison (2003). I follow here the argument made by Gans (2008). Ironically, had the Arabs not objected by force to the growth of the Jewish population, and to their autonomy, it may well be the case that the national rights of Jews in Palestine would be exhausted by rights to cultural and linguistic autonomy. Most of the Jews would have found that solution unacceptable, but the compelling necessity to grant them independence might have been weaker. In this sense, Arab rejectionism strengthened, and it still strengthens, the claim of Jews to state-level self-determination.

23 One could see the logic of partition in both the Peel report and in the analysis of the majority of the *United Nations Special Committee on Palestine* (UNSCOP). Both took the arguments of the Arabs seriously, but concluded that the physical and cultural security of Jews could not be guaranteed without the establishment of a state in which there would be a Jewish majority.

24 The Arabs were right to object to the fact that while Jews were described as a people, the local communities were described as "non-Jews" in religious terms!

25 See, e.g., Ghanem, Rouhana, and Yiftahel (1998).

"AN OVERWHELMINGLY JEWISH STATE" - FROM THE BALFOUR DECLARATION TO THE PALESTINE MANDATE

Martin Gilbert

On 22 July 1922, when the League of Nations announced the terms of Britain's Mandate for Palestine, it gave prominence to the Balfour Declaration. '**The Mandatory should be responsible,**' the preamble stated, '**for putting into effect the declaration originally made on November 2nd, 1917, by the Government of His Britannic Majesty...in favor of the establishment in Palestine of a national home for the Jewish people...**'[1] The preamble of the Mandate included the precise wording of the Balfour Declaration.

Nothing in the Balfour Declaration dealt with Jewish statehood, immigration, land purchase or the boundaries of Palestine. This essay examines how British policy with regard to the 'national home for the Jewish people' evolved between November 1917 and July 1922, and the stages by which the Mandate commitments were reached.

In the discussions on the eve of the Balfour Declaration, the British War Cabinet, desperate to persuade the Jews of Russia to urge their government to renew Russia's war effort, saw Palestine as a Jewish rallying cry. To this end, those advising the War Cabinet, and the Foreign Secretary himself, A.J. Balfour, encouraged at least the possibility of an eventual Jewish majority, even if it might – with the settled population of Palestine then being some 600,000 Arabs and 60,000 Jews – be many years before such a majority emerged. On 31 October 1917, Balfour had told the War Cabinet that while the words 'national home...did not necessarily involve the early establishment of an independent Jewish State', such a State 'was a matter for gradual development in accordance with the ordinary laws of political evolution'.[2]

How these laws were to be regarded was explained in a Foreign Office memorandum of 19 December 1917 by Arnold Toynbee and Lewis Namier, the latter a Galician-born Jew, who wrote jointly: 'The objection raised against the Jews being given exclusive political rights in Palestine on a basis that would be undemocratic with regard to the local Christian and Mohammedan population,' they wrote, 'is certainly the most important which the anti-Zionists have hitherto raised, but the difficulty is imaginary. Palestine might be held in trust by Great Britain or America until there was a sufficient population in the country fit to govern it on European lines. Then no undemocratic restrictions of the kind indicated in the memorandum would be required any longer.'[3]

On 3 January 1919 agreement was reached between the Zionist leader Chaim Weizmann and the Arab leader Emir Feisal. Article Four of this agreement declared that all 'necessary measures' should be taken 'to encourage and stimulate immigration of Jews into Palestine on a large scale, and as quickly as possible to settle Jewish immigrants upon the land through closer settlement and intensive cultivation of the soil'. In taking such measures, the agreement went on, 'the Arab peasant and tenant farmers shall be protected in their rights, and shall be assisted in forwarding their economic development.'[4]

The Weizmann-Feisal agreement did not refer to Jewish statehood. Indeed, on 19 January 1919, Balfour wrote to his fellow Cabinet Minister Lord Curzon: 'As far as I know, Weizmann has never put forward a claim for the Jewish Government of Palestine. Such a claim is, in my opinion, certainly inadmissable and personally I do not think we should go further than the original declaration which I made to Lord Rothschild.'[5]

Scarcely six weeks later, on February 27, in Balfour's presence, Weizmann presented the essence of the Weizmann-Feisal Agreement to the Allied Supreme Council in Paris, telling them that the nation that was to receive Palestine as a League of Nations Mandate must first of all 'Promote Jewish immigration and closer settlement on the land', while at the same time ensuring that 'the established rights' of the non-Jewish population be 'equitably safe-guarded'.

During the discussion, Robert Lansing, the American Secretary of State, asked Weizmann for clarification 'as to the meaning of the words "Jewish National Home." Did that mean an autonomous Jewish Government?' Weizmann replied, as the minutes of the discussion record, 'in the negative'. The Zionist Organisation, he told Lansing – reiterating what Balfour had told Curzon – 'did not want an autonomous Jewish Government, but merely to establish in Palestine, under a Mandatory Power, an administration, not necessarily Jewish, which would render it possible to send into Palestine 70,000 to 80,000 Jews annually.' The Zionist Organisation wanted permission 'to build Jewish schools where Hebrew would be taught, and to develop institutions of every kind. Thus it would build up gradually a nationality, and so make Palestine as Jewish as America is American or England English.'

The Supreme Council wanted to know if such a 'nationality' would involve eventual statehood? Weizmann told them: 'Later on, when the Jews formed the large majority, they would be ripe to establish such a Government as would answer to the state of the development of the country and to their ideals.'[6]

British Foreign Secretary Arthur James Balfour, 1917 (Israel National Photo Collection)

The British Government supported the Weizmann-Feisal Agreement with regard to both Jewish immigration and land purchase. On June 19 the senior British military officer in Palestine, General Clayton, telegraphed to the Foreign Office for approval of a Palestine ordinance to re-open land purchase 'under official control'. Zionist interests, Clayton stated, 'will be fully safeguarded'.[7]

Clayton's telegram was forwarded to Balfour, who replied on July 5 that land purchase could indeed be continued 'provided that, as far as possible, preferential treatment is given to Zionist interests'.[8]

The Zionist plans were thus endorsed by both Feisal and Balfour. But on 28 August 1919 a United States commission, the King-Crane Commission, appointed by President Woodrow Wilson, published its report criticising Zionist ambitions and recommending 'serious modification of the extremist Zionist programme for Palestine of unlimited immigration of Jews, looking finally to making Palestine distinctly a Jewish State'.[9]

The King-Crane Commission went on to state that the Zionists with whom it had spoken looked forward 'to a practically complete dispossession of the present non-Jewish inhabitants of Palestine, by various forms of purchase'. In their conclusion, the Commissioners felt 'bound to recommend that only a greatly reduced Zionist programme be attempted'; a reduction that would 'have to mean that Jewish immigration should be definitely limited, and that the project for making Palestine a distinctly Jewish commonwealth should be given up'.[10]

The United States was in a minority at the Supreme Council. On September 19 the Zionists received unexpected support from *The Times*, which declared: 'Our duty as the Mandatory power will be to make Jewish Palestine not a struggling State, but one that is capable of vigorous and independent national life.'[11]

Winston Churchill, then Secretary of State for War, and with ministerial responsibility for Palestine, took a more cynical view of Zionist ambitions. On October 25, in a memorandum for the Cabinet, he wrote of 'the Jews, whom we are pledged to introduce into Palestine and who take it for granted that the local population will be cleared out to suit their convenience.'[12]

Churchill's critical attitude did not last long. Fearful of the rise of Communism in the East, and conscious of the part played by individual Jews in helping to impose Bolshevik rule on Russia, he soon set his cynicism aside. In an article entitled 'Zionism versus Bolshevism: the Struggle for the Soul of the Jewish People', he wrote in the *Illustrated Sunday Herald* on 8 February 1920 that Zionism offered the Jews 'a national idea of a commanding character'. Palestine would provide 'the Jewish race all over the world' with, as Churchill put it, 'a home and a centre of national life'. Although Palestine could only accommodate 'a fraction of the Jewish race', but 'if, as may well happen, there should be created in our own lifetime by the banks of the Jordan a Jewish State under the protection of the British Crown which might comprise three or four millions of Jews, an event will have occurred in the history of the world which would from every point of view be beneficial, and would be especially in harmony with the truest interests of the British Empire.'

Churchill's article ended with an appeal for the building up 'with the utmost rapidity' of a 'Jewish national centre' in Palestine; a centre, he asserted, which might become 'not only a refuge to the oppressed from the unhappy lands of Central Europe', but also 'a symbol of Jewish unity and the temple of Jewish glory'. On such a task, he added, 'many blessings rest'.[13]

Former British Prime Minister David Lloyd George, January 16, 1943 (AP Photo)

On 24 April 1920, at the San Remo Conference, the British Prime Minister, David Lloyd George accepted a British Mandate for Palestine, and that Britain, as the Mandatory Power, would be responsible for giving effect to the Balfour Declaration. The Chief of the Imperial General Staff, Field Marshal Sir Henry Wilson, noted in his diary that there had been a 'two-hour battle' among the British and French delegates, 'about acknowledging and establishing Zionism as a separate State in Palestine under British protection'.[14]

In January 1921, Lloyd George appointed Churchill to be Secretary of State for the Colonies, charged with drawing up the terms of the Mandate and presenting them to the League of Nations. In March 1921, at the Cairo Conference, Churchill agreed to the establishment of a Jewish gendarmerie in Palestine to ward off local Arab attacks (Churchill preferred a Jewish Army). He also agreed that Transjordan, while part of the original Mandated Territory of Palestine, would be separate from it, and under an Arab ruler. This fitted in with what Britain had in mind as the wider settlement of Arab claims. On 17 January 1921, T.E. Lawrence had reported to Churchill that Emir Feisal 'agreed to abandon all claims of his father to Palestine' in return for Mesopotamia (Iraq) – where Churchill agreed at the Cairo Conference to instal him as King – and Transjordan, where Feisal 'hopes to have a recognised Arab State with British advice'.[15]

From Cairo, Churchill went to Jerusalem, where he was given a petition from the Haifa Congress of Palestinian Arabs, dated 14 March 1921, which began: '1. We refuse the Jewish Immigration to Palestine. 2. We energetically protest against the Balfour Declaration to the effect that our Country should be made the Jewish National Home.'[16] Churchill rejected the Arab arguments. 'It is manifestly right,' he announced publicly on March 28, 'that the Jews, who are scattered all over the world, should have a national centre and a National Home where some of them may be reunited. And where else could that be but in the land of Palestine, with which for more than 3,000 years they have been intimately and profoundly associated? We think it would be good for the world, good for the Jews, and good for the British Empire.'[17]

After Churchill's visit, Arab violence in Jaffa led the British High Commissioner in Palestine, a British Jew, Sir Herbert Samuel, to order an immediate temporary suspension of Jewish immigration. This did not find favour in the Colonial Office. A telegram drafted for Churchill by one of his senior advisers, Major Hubert Young, who during the war had played his part in the Arab Revolt, was dispatched to Samuel on May 14. 'The present agitation', the telegram read, 'is doubtless engineered in the hope of frightening us out of our Zionist policy... We must firmly maintain law and order and make concessions on their merits and not under duress.'

On June 22 Churchill explained the British position on Zionism at a meeting of the Imperial Cabinet. The Canadian Prime Minister, Arthur Meighen, questioned Churchill about the meaning of a Jewish 'National Home'. Did it mean, Meighen asked, giving the Jews 'control of the Government'? To this Churchill replied: 'If, in the course of many years, they become a majority in the country, they naturally would take it over.'[18]

Winston Churchill, Britain's wartime prime minister, arrives at the White House in Washington on March 11, 1946. (AP Photo/William J. Smith)

Churchill was asked about this sixteen years later by the Palestine Royal Commission. 'What is the conception you have formed yourself,' he was asked, 'of the Jewish National Home?' Churchill replied: 'The conception undoubtedly was that, if the absorptive capacity over a number of years and the breeding over a number of years, all guided by the British Government, gave an increasing Jewish population, that population should not in any way be restricted from reaching a majority position.' Churchill went on to tell the Commission: 'As to what arrangement would be made to safeguard the rights of the new minority' – the Arab minority – 'that obviously remains open, but certainly we committed ourselves to the idea that some day, somehow, far off in the future, subject to justice and economic convenience, there might well be a great Jewish State there, numbered by millions, far exceeding the present inhabitants of the country and to cut them off from that would be a wrong.' Churchill added: 'We said there should be a Jewish Home in Palestine, but if more and more Jews gather to that Home and all is worked from age to age, from generation to generation, with justice and fair consideration to those displaced and so forth, certainly it was contemplated and intended that they might in the course of time become an overwhelmingly Jewish State.'[19]

Whether the Jews could form a majority – the *sine qua non* of statehood – was challenged publicly by Herbert Samuel on 3 June 1921, when he said that 'the conditions of Palestine are such as not to permit anything in the nature of mass immigration'.[20] But at a meeting in Balfour's house in London on July 22, Lloyd George and Balfour had both agreed 'that by the Declaration they had always meant an eventual Jewish State'.[21]

Churchill's adviser, Major Young, likewise favoured a policy that, he wrote to Churchill on August 1, involved 'the gradual immigration of Jews into Palestine until that country becomes a predominantly Jewish State'. Young went on to argue that the phrase 'National Home' as used in the Balfour Declaration implied no less than full statehood for the Jews of Palestine. There could be 'no half-way house', he wrote, between a Jewish State and 'total abandonment of the Zionist programme'.[22]

When the Cabinet met on August 17 there was talk of handing the Palestine Mandate to the United States, but Lloyd George rejected this. The official minutes noted: 'stress was laid on the following consideration, the honour of the government was involved in the Declaration made by Mr Balfour, and to go back on our pledge would seriously reduce the prestige of this country in the eyes of the Jews throughout the world'.

On 3 June 1922 the British Government issued a White Paper, known as the Churchill White Paper, which stated: '**So far as the Jewish population of Palestine are concerned it appears that some among them are apprehensive that His Majesty's Government may depart from the policy embodied in the Declaration of 1917. It is necessary, therefore, once more to affirm that these fears are unfounded, and that that Declaration, re-affirmed by the Conference of the Principal Allied Powers at San Remo and again in the Treaty of Sèvres, is not susceptible of change.**'

The White Paper also noted: '**During the last two or three generations the Jews have recreated in Palestine a community, now numbering 80,000... it is essential that it should know that it is**

in Palestine as of right and not on the sufferance. That is the reason why it is necessary that the existence of a Jewish National Home in Palestine should be internationally guaranteed, and that it should be formally recognized to rest upon ancient historic connection.'[23]

To reinforce this concept of 'right', Churchill had granted the Zionists a monopoly on the development of electrical power in Palestine, authorising a scheme drawn up by the Russian-born Jewish engineer, Pinhas Rutenberg, to harness the waters of the Jordan River. To stop what critics were calling the 'beginning of Jewish domination', a debate was held in the House of Lords demanding representative institutions that would enable the Arabs to halt Jewish immigration. In the debate, held on June 21, sixty Peers voted against the Mandate as envisaged by the White Paper, and against the Balfour Declaration. Only twenty-nine Peers voted for it.

On July 4 it fell to Churchill to persuade the House of Commons to reverse this vote. He staunchly defended the Zionists. Anyone who had visited Palestine recently, he said, 'must have seen how part of the desert have been converted into gardens, and how material improvement has been effected in every respect by the Arab population dwelling around.' Apart from 'this agricultural work – this reclamation work – there are services which science, assisted by outside capital, can render, and of all the enterprises of importance which would have the effect of greatly enriching the land none was greater than the scientific storage and regulation of the waters of the Jordan for the provision of cheap power and light needed for the industry of Palestine, as well as water for the irrigation of new lands now desolate.' The Rutenberg concession offered to all the inhabitants of Palestine 'the assurance of a greater prosperity and the means of a higher economic and social life'.

Churchill asked that the Government be allowed 'to use Jews, and use Jews freely, within limits that are proper, to develop new sources of wealth in Palestine'. It was also imperative, he said, if the Balfour Declaration's 'pledges to the Zionists' were to be carried out, for the House of Commons to reverse the vote of the House of Lords. Churchill's appeal was successful. Only thirty-five votes were cast against the Government's Palestine policy, 292 in favour.[24]

The way was clear for presenting the terms of the Mandate to the League of Nations. On July 5, Churchill telegraphed Sir Wyndham Deedes, who was administering the Government of Palestine in Samuel's absence, that 'every effort will be made to get terms of Mandate approved by Council of League of Nations at forthcoming session and policy will be vigorously pursued'.[25]

On 22 July 1922 the League of Nations approved the Palestine Mandate (it came into force on 29 September 1923). One particular article, Article 25, relating to Transjordan, disappointed the Zionists, who had hoped to settle on both sides of the Jordan River. **'In the territories lying between the Jordan and the eastern boundary of Palestine as ultimately determined', Article 25 stated, 'the Mandatory shall be entitled, with the consent of the Council of the League of Nations, to postpone or withhold application of such provisions of this mandate as he may consider inapplicable to the existing local conditions, and to make such provision for the administration of the territories as he may consider suitable to those conditions, provided that no action shall be taken which is inconsistent with the provisions of Articles 15, 16 and 18.'**

The Zionists pointed out that Article 15 was clearly inconsistent with not allowing a Jewish presence in Transjordan, for it stated clearly, with regard to the whole area of Mandatory Palestine, west and east of the Jordan, that '**The Mandatory shall see that complete freedom of conscience and the free exercise of all forms of worship, subject only to the maintenance of public order and morals, are ensured to all. No discrimination of any kind shall be made between the inhabitants of Palestine on the ground of race, religion or language. No person shall be excluded from Palestine on the sole ground of his religious belief. The right of each community to maintain its own schools for the education of its own members in its own language, while conforming to such educational requirements of a general nature as the Administration may impose, shall not be denied or impaired.**'

The rest of the Mandate was strongly in support of Zionist aspirations. Article 2, while making no reference to the previous four and a half years' debate on statehood, instructed the Mandatory to secure '**the development of self-governing institutions**'. In a note to the United States Government five months later, the Foreign Office pointed out that 'so far as Palestine is concerned' Article 2 of the Mandate 'expressly provides that the administration may arrange with the Jewish Agency to develop any of the natural resources of the country, in so far as these matters are not directly undertaken by the Administration'. The reason for this, the Foreign Office explained, 'is that in order that the policy of establishing in Palestine a national home for the Jewish people could be successfully carried out, it is impractical to guarantee that equal facilities for developing the natural resources of the country should be granted to persons or bodies who may be motivated by other motives'.[26] It was on this basis that the Rutenberg electrical concession had been granted as a monopoly to the Zionists, and on which representative institutions had been withheld for as long as the Arabs were in a majority.

Article 4 recognised the Zionist Organization as the 'appropriate Jewish Agency', to work with the British Government 'to secure the co-operation of all Jews who are willing to assist in the establishment of a Jewish national home'. Article 6 instructed the Palestine Administration both to 'facilitate' Jewish immigration, and to 'encourage' close settlement by Jews on the land, 'including State lands and waste lands not required for public purposes'.[27]

On the evening of 22 July 1922, Eliezer Ben Yehuda, the pioneer of modern spoken Hebrew, went to see his friend Arthur Ruppin. It was more than forty years since Ben Yehuda had come to live in Palestine. He had just seen a telegram announcing that the League of Nations had just confirmed Britain's Palestine Mandate. 'The Ben Yehudas were elated,' Ruppin recorded in his diary, with Ben Yehuda telling Ruppin, in Hebrew, 'now we are in our own country.' Ruppin himself was hesitant. 'I could not share their enthusiasm,' he wrote. 'One is not allocated a fatherland by means of diplomatic resolutions.' Ruppin added: 'If we do not acquire Palestine economically by means of work and if we do not win the friendship of the Arabs, our position under the Mandate will be no better than it was before.'[28]

NOTES

1 Council of the League of Nations, League of Nations Permanent Mandates Commission, 22 July 1922: *League of Nations – Official Journal.*

2 War Cabinet minutes, 30 October 1917; Cabinet Papers, 23/4.

3 Foreign Office papers, 371/3054.

4 The text of the Weizmann-Feisal Agreement was quoted in *The Times*, 10 June 1936.

5 Curzon papers, India Office Library.

6 Supreme Council minutes: *Event 4651: Zionist presentation to the Supreme Council of the Paris Peace Conference.*

7 Foreign Office papers, 371/4171.

8 ibid.

9 Henry C. King was a theologian and President of Oberlin College, Ohio. Charles R. Crane was a prominent Democratic Party contributor who had been a member of the United States delegation at the Paris Peace Conference.

10 *Report of American Section of Inter-Allied Commission of Mandates in Turkey: An official United States Government report by the Inter-allied Commission on Mandates in Turkey. American Section. First printed as 'King-Crane Report on the Near East,' Editor & Publisher*: New York, 1922, Editor & Publisher Co., volume 55.

11 *The Times*, London, 9 September 1919.

12 Churchill papers, 16/18.

13 *Illustrated Sunday Herald*, 8 February 1920.

14 Field Marshal Sir Henry Wilson, diary (unpublished).

15 Churchill papers, 17/20.

16 ibid.

17 ibid.

18 Minutes of the Imperial Cabinet: Lloyd George papers.

19 Palestine Royal Commission, notes of evidence, 12 March 1937: Churchill papers: 2/317.

20 Samuel papers.

21 Weizmann papers.

22 Colonial Office papers, 733/10.

23 *Statement of British Policy in Palestine*, Command Paper 1700 of 1922, 3 June 1922.

24 *Hansard*, Parliamentary Debates, 4 July 1922.

25 Colonial Office papers, 733/35.

26 Communication dated 29 December 1921, Command Paper 2559 of 1926.

27 Council of the League of Nations, League of Nations Permanent Mandates Commission, 22 July 1922: *League of Nations – Official Journal.*

28 Arthur Ruppin diary, Ruppin papers.

SELF-DETERMINATION AND ISRAEL'S DECLARATION OF INDEPENDENCE

Shlomo Avineri

The history of the Zionist movement is fraught with paradoxes and ambiguities regarding its ultimate political aim. Theodor Herzl's foundational document *Der Judenstaat* (1896) referred explicitly to statehood, yet the Basel Declaration issued at the First Zionist Congress in 1897 judiciously avoided such explicit language: after much discussion it settled on stating that "Zionism aims at achieving in Palestine a Jewish homeland, secured by public law." And in Herzl's utopian novel *Altneuland* (1902), which described how a Jewish society in the Land of Israel would look in 1923, its precise status within and vis-à-vis the Ottoman Empire is left somewhat nebulous – though Herzl's clarion call in Basel ("We are a nation") clearly suggested where Zionism was ultimately heading.

The reasons for this ambiguity were obvious: while the fundamental subtext of Zionism was to aim at a Jewish state, the geopolitics of the period and the region called for a careful approach. Herzl's aim, despite numerous disappointments, was to try to obtain from the Ottoman Sultan a charter for Jewish immigration, settlement, and practical self-government. The diplomatic contacts of the Zionist movement – not only with the Sublime Porte in Constantinople but also with the German Kaiser, the British government, Russian ministers, and numerous other statesmen – were aimed at achieving such a de facto control of Palestine, regardless of the exact legal formula – a chartered company, autonomy or the like.

This ambiguity continued also when Britain became the hegemonic power in the region. The Balfour Declaration was the first major international victory for Zionism, but its careful language spoke merely of "establishing in Palestine a national home for the Jewish people," hedging this with an assurance that this would "not prejudice the civil and religious rights of the non-Jewish communities" in the country. These formulations were incorporated in 1922 into the text of the League of Nations Mandate to Great Britain, and consequently were naturally interpreted in different ways by Zionists, various British administrations, and of course the Arabs in Palestine.

In the first decade and a half of the British Mandate, official Zionist policies, despite some noisy internal debates, were mainly focused on immediate activities – immigration, purchase of land, establishing settlements, institution building – rather than on final goals. That Jewish immigration to Palestine in the 1920s was minimal, and with the economic crisis toward the end of the decade emigrants outnumbered immigrants, only accentuated the need for pragmatic rather than declaratory politics. The League of Nations concept of "mandates" was crafted around the idea of eventual self-determination (as in Syria, Lebanon, and Iraq), but this was viewed as a long-term process, not an immediate challenge. The final goal (*Endziel* in Zionist parlance) was always there, but there were more immediate and pressing needs.

The rise of Nazism in Germany and the darkening clouds gathering over European Jewry in the 1930s changed the agenda. The dramatic increase in Jewish immigration, which more than doubled the population of the Yishuv from 1933 to 1936, transformed the politics on all sides. The Palestinian Arab leadership, which until then had viewed Zionism as an irritant but not a serious national threat, for the first time realized that developments could turn the Jews into a majority in the country – and the Arab Revolt of 1936-1939, aimed at Britain but accompanied by terror attacks against the Jews, had a twofold aim: pressuring Britain to curb Jewish immigration and, at the same time, making life for Jews dangerous, thus deterring Jews fleeing Europe from seeking a safe haven in Palestine. The Zionist leadership also realized that given the changed circumstances, deferring Zionism's final goals was no longer feasible. And the British government, which until then believed in muddling through by balancing Jewish and Arab claims under the vague umbrella of the League of Nations Mandate, came to the conclusion that a more decisive approach would be necessary.

This was the background to the appointment in 1936 of the Royal Commission on Palestine (the Peel Commission), which for the first time addressed the final status of Palestine. At its base was the realization that the Mandate as originally devised could not be carried out, given changed circumstances as well as the positions of the two communities in Palestine. Hence the Peel Commission Report suggested the partition of Mandatory Palestine into two states – Jewish and Arab – with Jerusalem and a corridor to Jaffa remaining under British control.

After World War II and the Holocaust, and the pressure of Jewish survivors to reach Palestine despite the British ban on immigration and the incarceration of fifty-three thousand illegal immigrants in detention camps in Cyprus, Britain handed over its Mandate to the United Nations. On November 29, 1947, the UN General Assembly, after having sent an inquiry commission of its own to the region (UNSCOP), followed the principles of the Peel Commission – though with a different map – and recommended partition and the setting up of two independent states, a Jewish and an Arab one (with Jerusalem as an international *corpus separatum*). In the final vote, thirty-three countries voted in favor, thirteen against, ten abstained, and one was absent. That both the United States and

UNITED NATIONS GENERAL ASSEMBLY November 29, 1947.

VOTING SHEET

Country	Yes	No	Abstain	Absent
AFGHANISTAN		X		
ARGENTINA			*	
AUSTRALIA	/			
BELGIUM	/			
BOLIVIA	/			
BRAZIL	/			
BYELORUSSIAN S.R.	/			
CANADA	/			
CHILE			*	
CHINA			*	
COLOMBIA			*	
COSTA RICA	/			
CUBA		X		
CZECHOSLOVAKIA	/			
DENMARK	/			
DOMINICAN REPUBLIC	/			
ECUADOR	/			
EGYPT		X		
EL SALVADOR			*	
ETHIOPIA			*	
FRANCE	/			
GREECE		X		
GUATAMALA	/			
HAITI	/			
HONDURAS			*	
ICELAND	/			
INDIA		X		
IRAN		X		
IRAQ		X		
LEBANON		X		
LIBERIA	/			
LUXEMBOURG	/			
MEXICO			*	
NETHERLANDS	/			
NEW ZEALAND	/			
NICARAGUA	/			
NORWAY	/			
PAKISTAN		X		
PANAMA	/			
PARAGUAY	/			
PERU	/			
PHILIPPINES	/			
POLAND	/			
SAUDI ARABIA		X		
SIAM				X
SWEDEN	/			
SYRIA		X		
TURKEY		X		
UKRANIAN S.R.	/			
UNION OF SOUTH AFRICA	/			
UNION OF SOVIET SOCIALIST REPUBLICS	/			
UNITED KINGDOM			*	
UNITED STATES OF AMERICA.	/			
URUGUAY	/			
VENEZUELA	/			
YEMEN		X		
YUGOSLAVIA.			*	

Yes 33 No 13 Abstain 10 Absent 1

— PALESTINE PARTITION PLAN —

Results from the United Nations vote, with signatures, November 29, 1947 (Israel State Archive)

the Soviet Union voted in favor of partition, despite the darkening clouds of the Cold War, suggested how deep and wide was international support for such a compromise solution: there cannot be shown any other issue on which the two superpowers agreed in 1947, and while there were obvious realpolitik reasons for this unusual convergence, the basic acceptance of the fundamental rights of Jews – as well as of Palestinian Arabs – to live under their own governments was clearly visible in this decision. After all, this was also the period in which the newly established United Nations dealt with many other issues of decolonization in the same spirit.

It is the reaction of the two communities – Jewish and Arab – to the partition idea, endorsed first by the Peel Commission and then by the United Nations, which has determined to a large extent the history of the country and the region as well as the principles and language underlining Israel's 1948 Declaration of Independence.

Initially, both Jews and Arabs were shocked by the idea of partition. The Zionist movement viewed the whole of Eretz Yisrael as a Jewish patrimony, and the effort – not very successful until 1939, but becoming more pressing and feasible after 1945 – to reach a Jewish majority was aimed at giving this claim international support and legitimacy. And the emerging Palestinian national movement, supported by neighboring Arab states then already organized in the Arab League, viewed Falastin as integral a part of the great Arab homeland as all other lands from Morocco to Iraq. Yet the responses of the two national movements to the very idea of partition developed in different ways.

The decade of 1937-1947 represents the darkest hours in Jewish history, and it was in this context that the searing debate which divided the Zionist movement and the Yishuv in its reaction to the idea of partition took place: local geopolitics, as well as the enormity of the Holocaust, made it impossible to defer discussing the Zionist *Endziel*. With hundreds of thousands of Holocaust survivors viewing Palestine as their only destination, and with the Arab total refusal to entertain *any* Jewish immigration to the country, the debate about partition became the major agenda of the political discourse in the Jewish community in Palestine and the Zionist movement all over the world. Innumerable articles, books, speeches, pamphlets, and election manifestos appeared in those fateful years: political parties split, families were divided, paramilitary organizations were formed and re-formed with this issue at the center of debate in an extremely contentious and agitated political discourse. Eventually, the majority of the Yishuv and the Zionist moment accepted – with mixed feelings, one has to admit – partition. It is therefore extremely interesting to follow the arguments raised and used by the supporters of partition – the liberal and social-democratic wings of the Zionist movement.

Two sets of arguments could be discerned – one hailing from universalistic, humanist moral values, the other from considerations of realpolitik. Since these two sets of arguments usually lead to contradictory conclusions, it is both historically and intellectually intriguing to follow them when, as in this case, they led to the same conclusion of accepting the idea of partition.

The universalist, humanist, and moral argument ran along the following lines: the Jewish claim to independence, statehood, and sovereignty is based on the idea of self-determination, on the notion that Jews have a right to govern themselves and not be subject to foreign rule. This idea, however, based on the heritage of the Enlightenment, is a universal idea; hence if you claim this right to yourself, you cannot deny it to others. Specifically, if Zionism claims that Jews have a right not to be ruled by Arabs, it follows that Arabs have the same right not to be ruled by Jews. Ergo, a compromise is needed, and partition is the vehicle which will grant the right of self-determination – and not living under foreign rule – to both Jews and Arabs. This approach was perhaps best encapsulated by a saying attributed to Chaim Weizmann, the elder statesman of Zionism and later the first president of Israel: when asked, after enumerating the depth of the Jewish attachment to Eretz Yisrael and the Jewish rights to the land, if the Arabs have no rights in Palestine, he is said to have replied: "Of course they have rights: the conflict in Palestine is not between right and wrong, it is between right and right."

The second set of arguments is from realpolitik: clearly in order to establish a Jewish state, Zionism would need international support – moral, political, diplomatic, perhaps also military. Nobody in the world would support Zionism if it claimed that 600,000 Jews in Palestine had a right to rule over 1,100,000 Arabs. Such international support could be achieved only if the Zionist movement accepted the idea of partition and limited its claim to a territory where there was a Jewish majority.

These two sets of arguments were proposed sometimes as distinct, sometimes as overlapping. But the combination of ethical considerations with the reality of power politics endowed them with enormous appeal, which cut across party lines and could bring together left-wingers and right-wingers, secularists and religious people, hardheaded realists and idealistic dreamers: this became the bedrock of the powerful resilience which helped propel the Yishuv in the difficult years of the struggle for independence.

Tragically, a parallel debate did not occur within the Arab community. Here an absolutist position – we have all the rights, the Jews don't have *any* right – continued to be the foundation of their response to the idea of partition. Not only that: the Arabs of Palestine, and Arab states (some of them members of the United Nations) went to war not only against the emerging Jewish state, but also against a UN resolution: the only case known to me when member states of the UN not only did not abide by a UN resolution, but went to war against it.

But it could have been different: there was nothing deterministic, or preordained, in the Arab refusal. It could be imagined that the Arab community, just like the Jewish community, would have gone through a profound internal debate and come out of it – as did the Jewish community – with an acceptance, however reluctant, of the compromise idea of partition, be it on moral or realistic grounds, or both.

This could have happened – but it did not. Had it happened – and the responsibility, moral and political, that it did not rests on the shoulders of the Arab side – history would have been different: on May 15, 1948, two states – Israel and Palestine – would have been established. There would have been no 1948 war, no Palestinian refugees, no *nakba*, no further Arab-Israeli wars, no terrorism, no Israeli reprisals. The Palestinian Arabs, and the countries of the Arab League, had they chosen this path, would have made the Middle East a region of prosperity, mutual respect and recognition, progress and abundance for all its peoples.

For the Jewish community in Palestine and the Zionist movement, the UN partition plan was a vindication of the Jewish people's right to self-determination and sovereignty. This endorsement of its historical legitimacy by the international community was achieved, however, at the price of accepting a painful – yet necessary – compromise, which was perhaps most difficult because Jerusalem, with all of its significance in Jewish history and religion, was left outside the future Jewish state. Yet Jews viewed this as an almost messianic breakthrough, especially coming just two years after the end of World War II which had entailed the almost complete annihilation of European Jewry. In its deliberations, the United Nations noted as one of the reasons for the historical need for the establishment of a Jewish state the dire distress of survivors of the Holocaust – many of them cramped into displaced persons' (DP) camps in the western occupation zones of defeated Germany: this was one of the reasons for allotting the largely uninhabited Negev to the Jewish state, so as to enable it to absorb as many immigrants as possible.

The debates at the United Nations, as well as the partition plan itself (UN General Assembly Resolution 181) showed the international community's awareness of the complexity of the issues involved in any decision about the future of British Mandatory Palestine. The drawing of the borders of the two planned nation-states tried to incorporate as many Jews and Arabs as possible in their own respective future states, and this was responsible for the somewhat unusual shape both states were to have. But at the same time, the United Nations was aware of the fact that in whichever way borders were to be drawn, there would remain Arab and Jewish minorities in the titular states of the other nation. In was for this reason that Resolution 181 took extra care to guarantee minority rights and went into great detail to specify the rights each of the national minorities should be entitled to while living in the titular nation-state of the other community: what the United Nations mandated were not only equal citizenship and voting rights but also guarantees for language, freedom of religious worship, education, landholding, and so on. This, like the very recognition of the rights of both nations to self-determination, expressed the best ideals of the young United Nations as inspired by its San Francisco founding Charter.

It is interesting to note that an alternative proposal was submitted to the United Nations and rejected: a complex plan for a federal – or really confederal – binational state. This was proposed by the Yugoslav member of UNSCOP, and was obviously inspired by the post-World War II model of the Federative Socialist Republic of Yugoslavia, then under the leadership of the heroic Marshal Tito. It was an appealing model, and Yugoslavia was at that time rather popular not only in the communist bloc but also among many Western liberals and social democrats, who viewed its multinational structure as a creative historical achievement. But most UN members realized that it would not be accepted by either of the two contending parties in Palestine, as both sides would feel frustrated in their aims at self-determination. In retrospect one can only comment today that this appealing model of Yugoslavia eventually turned out to be sustained only by the Communist Party dictatorship headed by Tito and that ultimately it failed horrendously, causing the worst post-1945 set of atrocities in Europe: when Yugoslavia imploded in the 1990s, the consequences were a series of ethnic/religious wars entailing near-genocidal atrocities, including mass murder, ethnic cleansing, mass rapes, concentration camps, and causing international military intervention.

David Ben-Gurion flanked by the members of his provisional government reading the Declaration of Independence at the Tel Aviv Museum, May 14, 1948 (Israel National Photo Collection)

With all its goodwill toward both national movements in Palestine, the United Nations found itself powerless to confront the Arab refusal to accept the compromise idea of partition. The Palestinian Arabs, and the neighboring Arab states organized in the Arab League, translated their opposition to the partition plan into military terms: first various Palestinian Arab militias, and after the termination of the British Mandate on May 15, 1948, the neighboring Arab states of Egypt, Syria, Jordan, Lebanon, and even distant Iraq went to war against the Jewish community and the international legitimacy expressed in the partition plan, sending their armies to crush the emerging Jewish state. The Arab refusal was almost universal: only the small groups of Arab communists (in Palestine as well as in Egypt and Iraq) opposed Arab military intervention, with the consequence of their members being jailed by the Arab regimes going to war. The Arab communists supported partition mainly because this was the Soviet position, but it also went well with their internationalist ideology which accepted national self-determination for all peoples. The small group of Palestinian Arab communists chose to remain in Israel and became instrumental in forming the Israel Communist Party, which for decades held two unusual distinctions: in Israel it was the only truly Jewish-Arab party, and in the region it turned out to be the only legal communist party, as communists were banned, persecuted, and imprisoned by all Arab regimes, whether conservative monarchies or revolutionary nationalistic republics.

At the end of the day, and despite the UN endorsement of the establishment of a Jewish state in part of Palestine, the Jews were left to fend for themselves. The United Nations held numerous debates and emergency sessions in the face of the Arab assault, condemning unambiguously the Palestinian Arab refusal to accept partition and the Arab states' invasion after May 15, 1948. Yet ultimately the Jewish community, and the nascent Israel, survived because they were able to defend themselves by force of arms: not for the last time the United Nations proved unable to live up to its mission and to put into practice, in the real world and not in deliberative chambers, its own ideals, decisions, and vision.

Israel's Declaration of Independence of May 14, 1948, attempted to take into account this extremely complex reality: on the one hand, the newly established state was sustained by the international legitimacy of the United Nations; on the other, independence was achieved not as hoped through peaceful means where both Jews and Arabs would gain a place in the sun, albeit in only a part of what each group perceived as its homeland, but in the middle of a war waged against the very existence of a Jewish homeland.

The challenge imposed by these contradictory developments is clearly evident in the carefully crafted language of the Declaration of Independence, which enumerates the various historical levels from which Israel derives its legitimacy. It starts with the role of the Land of Israel in forming and constructing the Jewish nation; it mentions the yearning of generations for a return to the ancestral land, translated into the historical realm through the Zionist movement and the waves of immigration to the country since the late nineteenth century and the transformations wrought by these developments. It goes on to refer to the Holocaust and the attempt of multitudes of Jewish survivors to reach Palestine despite British exclusionary legislation. It culminates in the UN partition plan as being the vindication of the Jewish nation's "natural and historical right" to a state in its ancestral land. Despite the war situation, it reaches out to the Arab neighbors, in the country and in the region, and hopes to live in peace and mutual prosperity with them.

True to the founding ideas of Zionism, as well as to the stipulations of the UN partition plan, the Declaration guarantees equal citizenship rights to all the inhabitants of the country without discrimination and assures the cultural and religious rights of all communities. And – in what had been crucial to the Zionist fight against British rule – it declares that the newly established state will be open to Jewish immigration – a principle later to be enshrined in one of the foundational pieces of Israeli legislation, namely, the Law of Return, which guarantees the right of immigration and citizenship to every Jewish person willing to immigrate to Israel. As viewed within the Israeli and Zionist discourse, this is a law based on solidarity with the downtrodden and persecuted; it is also the most encompassing piece of affirmative-action legislation ever enacted anywhere: never again would persecuted Jews be exposed to a situation – as had happened during World War II when many had been trying to flee Nazi-occupied Europe – where they would not have a place of refuge and asylum which would be willing to take them in and which they could call their home.

Yet beyond the principles enunciated in the Declaration, the practical steps taken by the newly established, independent state of Israel reflected, despite the difficult war situation, both the country's willingness to abide by obligations inherent in the UN partition plan as well as the basic tenets of the liberal version of Zionism. Perhaps the best way to assess these steps is to consider decisions that Israel did not take.

In British Mandatory legislation there had been three official languages – English, Arabic, and Hebrew. Israel immediately abolished the status of English as an official language, but kept the two others, meaning that Arabic was declared the second official language of the Jewish state – a status it maintains to this very day, as is evident from the bilingual inscriptions on its stamps, currency, and so on. Moreover – and much more significant for the Arab minority in the country – Israeli Arabs have the right to send their children to state schools which teach in Arabic, with the curriculum tailored to the cultural differences involved. Yet Israel could have decided differently; following democratic countries like Britain, France, or Germany, it could have decided on a uniform, Hebrew-language curriculum in all its state schools, perhaps leaving the option for the Arab community to set up private schools in their language if they so wished. Without using the term – in 1948 not yet in existence – Israel adopted a multicultural approach toward its Arab minority; it could have done differently. Israel's decision to maintain the status of Arabic as an official language – with all the consequences flowing from it – was not demanded by the stipulations of the UN partition plan.

Furthermore, on holding its first parliamentary elections in January 1949, when the war was still going on, Israel extended voting rights to those Arabs who had remained in the country and they participated in the elections on an equal basis. Yet because Israel was still at war, it could have decided that so long as a status of war prevailed between it and Palestinian Arabs and the surrounding Arab countries, Arabs living in Israel would not be entitled to the vote. Such an option was not followed, and was not even raised in the discussion in the Provisional Government or the Provisional State Council. Had such a step been taken, it could have been construed as in contravention of the UN partition plan, but could also have been conceivably justified by reference, in international law, to the state of war. But Israel decided on an inclusive policy – inspired, at least in part, by the Jewish memory of what it meant to be a minority and by decades of Jewish efforts in the Diaspora to ensure equal citizenship and voting rights for members of Jewish communities.

The Arab minority in Israel obviously finds itself in a difficult and complex situation, exacerbated by the continuing conflict in which Israel finds itself; one should not idealize its situation. But Israel could have taken decisions which would not have been divergent from what other democracies have followed, especially in war or emergency situations (the American treatment in World War II of its own citizens of Japanese ancestry comes to mind). It is to Israel's credit that on this issue, the newly established country, despite having been attacked and besieged, did not adopt a harsher policy.

The possible tensions between Israel as a Jewish nation-state and its commitments to liberal values of equal citizenship continue to surface in some of the current political discourse in the country; decades of war and enmity have not made those issues disappear, and in some cases have exacerbated them. But the political system developed in Israel, based on the Jewish right of self-determination, was combined, at the same time, with respect not only for the minority population's equal civil rights but also for their language rights. For Israel, its claim for Jewish self-determination has always been viewed within a wider, universalist context, and has assured, in a difficult situation, its adherence to the basic norms of a liberal democracy.

Nevertheless, it is clear that so long as there is no final peace agreement between Israel and all its neighbors, and so long as the future of the Palestinians has not been settled through negotiations with Israel, some of these issues have not yet found their satisfactory solution. Consequently, peace for Israel is not just an issue of international relations, but also an imperative necessary for the maintenance and further development of its own democratic, liberal and pluralist society. The acceptance by most Israelis today of a two-state solution – of two nation-states, a Jewish and a Palestinian one – living in peace with each other, is a testimony to the fact that despite decades of war and siege, the fundamental decision adopted by the Jewish community in 1947 continues to guide, despite all difficulties, the moral compass of the Jewish state.

THE UNITED NATIONS AND MIDDLE EAST REFUGEES: THE DIFFERENTIAL TREATMENT OF ARABS AND JEWS

Stanley A. Urman

INTRODUCTION

For over half a century, seminal issues in the Arab-Israeli conflict have defied resolution. Negotiations over security, Jerusalem, refugees, borders, settlements, and so on engender passionate, entrenched demands and expectations.

There are few international arenas that provide a balanced platform for the discussion of these contentious issues and in particular, the issue of refugees. This especially applies to the United Nations and its affiliated entities, where the predominant focus has been on Palestinian refugees.

Emanating as a result of the 1948 conflict in the Middle East, Palestinians are considered by some as the world's longest-standing extant refugee population. They continue to require international assistance. On the political level, the United Nations has addressed – and continues to address annually – the issue of Palestinian refugees exclusively, even though Palestinians were not the only Middle East refugees.

Their continuing needs, however, do not supersede the fact that, during the twentieth century, two refugee populations emerged as a result of the conflict in the Middle East – Arabs as well as Jews. Neither the mass violations of the human rights of Jews in Arab countries, nor their displacement from their countries of birth, has ever been adequately addressed by the international community.

Asserting rights and redress for Jewish refugees is intended neither to argue against any claimed Palestinian refugee rights nor to negate any suffering. It is a legitimate call to recognize that Jewish refugees from Arab countries, as a matter of law and equity, possess the same rights as all other refugees.

While asserting equal rights for all Middle East refugees, there is no parallel history, geography, nor demography that could allow for any just comparison between the fate of Palestinian refugees and the plight of Jewish refugees from Arab countries. Moreover, there is a fundamental distinction between these two narratives:

- The newly established state of Israel, under attack from six Arab armies, with scant and scarce resources, opened its doors to hundreds of thousands of Jews displaced from Arab countries, granted them citizenship, and tried, as best it could, under very difficult circumstances, to absorb them into Israeli society.
- By contrast, the Arab world, with the sole exception of Jordan, turned their backs on displaced Palestinian Arabs, sequestering them in refugee camps to be used as a political weapon against the state of Israel for the last sixty-three years.

While there is no symmetry between these two narratives, there is one important factor that applies to both; namely, the moral imperative to ensure that the rights of all bona fide refugees are fully acknowledged, respected, and addressed within any putative resolution of the conflict in the Middle East.

JEWS AS AN INDIGENOUS PEOPLE OF THE MIDDLE EAST

Jews and Jewish communities have lived in parts of the Middle East, North Africa, and the Gulf region for more than 2,500 years.[1]

HISTORICAL JEWISH PRESENCE IN THE REGION

COUNTRY/REGION	DATE OF JEWISH COMMUNITY[2]
Iraq	6th century BCE
Lebanon	1st century BCE
Libya	3rd century BCE
Syria	1st century CE
Yemen	3rd century BCE
Morocco	1st century CE
Algeria	1st-2nd century CE
Tunisia	3rd century CE

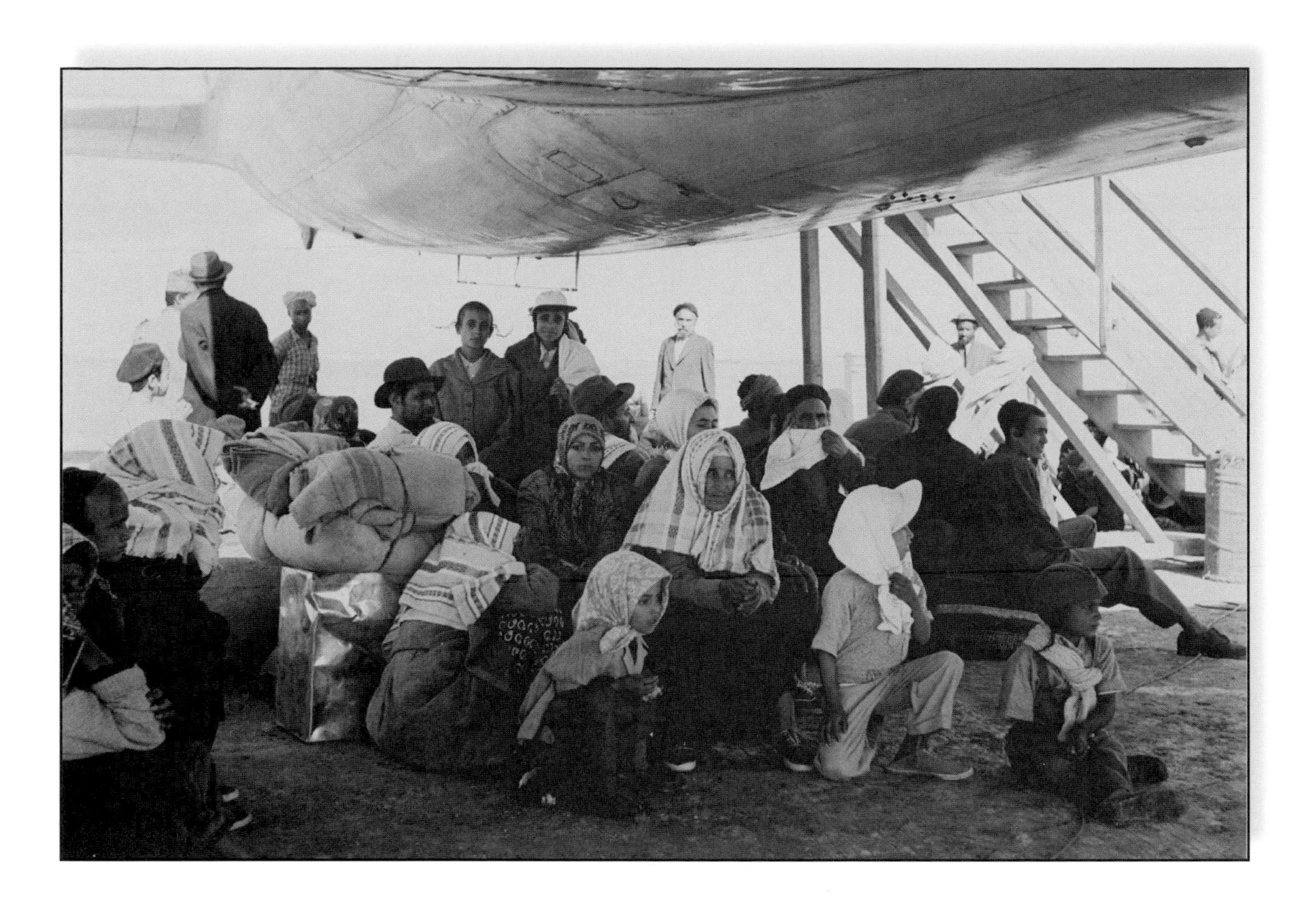

Jewish refugees, bound for Israel, wait for an airplane with their belongings as they escape persecution in Yemen, 1949. (Israel National Photo Collection/David Eldan)

This historical record is important as today, its detractors claim that Israel is an illegitimate state made up of Jews who are foreign to the region – insinuating that this is the root cause of the Arab-Israeli conflict. For example, Iranian President Mahmoud Ahmadinejad has stated that Jews in Israel "have no roots in Palestine," and "If the Europeans are honest they should give some of their provinces in Europe – like in Germany, Austria or other countries – to the Zionists and the Zionists can establish their state in Europe."[3] In another speech, Ahmadinejad cited the events in Europe as the reason Jews left there, stating that "then the Jews must return to where they came from… If there really had been a Holocaust, Israel ought to be located in Europe, not in Palestine."[4]

The allegation that Israel is made up solely of latter-day immigrants is a distortion of history. The long and proud legacy of Jews and Jewish communities in North Africa, the Middle East, and the Gulf region proves this claim false. In fact, Jews are an indigenous people of the Middle East, and were resident in the region over one thousand years before the advent of Islam. Their descendants make up a significant portion of Israel's population and their presence there demonstrates the historical connection of Jews to Israel, for thousands of years, as the homeland of the Jewish people.

With the beginning of Islam in the seventh century CE, Jews were ruled under the legal status of *dhimmi*, a "protected" people, a status assigned to Christians and Jews. *Dhimmi*s were extended some degree of legal protection, while relegated to being second-class citizens.[5]

Upon the declaration of the state of Israel in 1948, the status of Jews in Arab countries worsened dramatically as many Arab countries declared war, or backed the war against Israel. Jews were either uprooted from their countries of longtime residence or became subjugated, political hostages of the Arab-Israeli conflict. Jews were often victims of murder, arbitrary arrest and detention, torture, and expulsions. Official decrees and legislation enacted by Arab regimes denied human and civil rights to Jews and other minorities, expropriated their property, and stripped them of their citizenship and other means of livelihood. For example:

In Iraq:

- Law No. 1 of 1950, entitled "Supplement to Ordinance Canceling Iraqi Nationality," in fact deprived Jews of their Iraqi nationality. Section 1 stipulated that "the Council of Ministers may cancel the Iraqi nationality of the Iraqi Jew who willingly desires to leave Iraq for good" (official Iraqi English translation).[6]

- Law No. 5 of 1951, entitled "A law for the Supervision and Administration of the Property of Jews who have Forfeited Iraqi Nationality," also deprived them of their property. Section 2(a) "freezes" Jewish property.[7]

In Egypt:

- A mass departure of Jews was sparked when Egypt, in 1956, amended the original Egyptian Nationality Law of 1926. Article 1 of the Law of November 22, 1956, stipulated that "Zionists" were barred from being Egyptian nationals.[8] Article 18 of the 1956 law asserted that "Egyptian nationality may be declared forfeited by order of the Ministry of Interior in the case of persons classified as Zionists." Moreover, the term "Zionist" was never defined, leaving Egyptian authorities free to interpret the law as broadly as they wished.

In Libya:

- On August 8, 1962, the Council of Ministers announced a Royal Decree amending Article 10 of the law of citizenship, which provided, inter alia, that a Libyan national forfeited his nationality if he had had any contact with Zionism. The retroactive effect of this provision, which covered the preceding period commencing with Libyan independence on December 24, 1951, enabled the authorities to deprive Jews of Libyan nationality at will.

As a result of these and similar measures adopted by Arab regimes throughout the region, many Jews concluded that their situation had become untenable and decided to leave. The difficulty in doing so varied greatly from country to country. During the twentieth century, in some countries, Jews were forbidden to leave (e.g., Syria); in others, Jews were displaced en masse (e.g., Iraq); in some places, Jews lived in relative peace under the protection of Muslim rulers (e.g., Tunisia, Morocco); while in other states, they were expelled (e.g., Egypt). However, the final result was the same – the mass displacement of some 856,000[9] Jews from some ten Arab countries – in a region overwhelmingly hostile to Jews.

Hundreds of thousands of Jewish refugees from Arab states arrive in Israel. Initially they live in refugee camps, but are shortly integrated into Israeli society. (International Center of Photography/ Magnum Photos/ Robert Capa)

WERE JEWS DISPLACED FROM ARAB COUNTRIES REALLY REFUGEES?

The internationally accepted definition for the term "refugee" derives from the Statute of the United Nations High Commissioner for Refugees that was established by United Nations General Assembly Resolution 319 (IV) on December 3, 1949. The Convention Relating to the Status of Refugees was adopted on July 28, 1951, by the United Nations Conference of Plenipotentiaries on the Status of Refugees and Stateless Persons, which was convened under General Assembly Resolution 429 (V) of December 14, 1950, and entered into force on April 22, 1954. Article 1 states the following:

> For the purposes of the present Convention, the term "refugee" shall apply to any person who:
>
> (2) As a result of events occurring before 1 January 1951 and owing to well-founded fear of being persecuted for reasons of race, religion, nationality, membership of a particular social group or political opinion, is outside the country of his nationality and is unable, or owing to such fear, unwilling to avail himself of the protection of that

> country; or who, not having a nationality and being outside the country of his former habitual residence as a result of such events, is unable or, owing to such fear, unwilling to return to it...[10]

Clearly, this definition applied to many Jews who fled Arab countries who had, as described earlier, a "well-founded fear of being persecuted." Moreover, on two separate occasions, the United Nations High Commissioner for Refugees (UNHCR) specifically declared that Jews fleeing from Arab countries were indeed refugees "who fall under the mandate" of the UNHCR. The first recognition pertained to Jews fleeing Egypt:

> "Another emergency problem is now arising: that of refugees from Egypt. There is no doubt in my mind that those refugees from Egypt who are not able, or not willing to avail themselves of the protection of the Government of their nationality fall under the mandate of my office."
>
> — Mr. Auguste Lindt, UN High Commissioner for Refugees,
> Report of the UNREF Executive Committee, Fourth Session –
> Geneva 29 January to 4 February, 1957.

The second recognition came eleven years later:

> "I refer to our recent discussion concerning Jews from Middle Eastern and North African countries in consequence of recent events. I am now able to inform you that such persons may be considered prima facie within the mandate of this Office."
>
> — Dr. E. Jahn, Office of the UN High Commissioner, United Nations
> High Commissioner for Refugees, Document No. 7/2/3/Libya,
> July 6, 1967.

The significance of this second ruling was twofold:

- Unlike the first statement by the High Commissioner that merely referred to "refugees," this letter referred specifically to "Jews"; and
- Unlike the first determination that limited UNHCR involvement to refugees from Egypt, this statement constituted a ruling that Jews who had left *any* of the Middle Eastern and North African countries concerned, namely: Algeria, Egypt, Lebanon, Libya, Morocco, Syria, and Tunisia, fell within the mandate of the Office of the UNHCR.

So in fact, both populations were recognized as bona fide refugees by the relevant UN Agencies – Palestinian Arabs by UNRWA[11] and Jewish refugees by the UN High Commissioner for Refugees.[12]

THE RESPONSE OF THE INTERNATIONAL COMMUNITY TO MIDDLE EAST REFUGEES

The United Nations, through statute and precedent, has developed international standards and mechanisms for the protection, resettlement, and rehabilitation of refugees around the world. These rights are well enshrined in international law.

There is no statute of limitations on the rights of refugees. Therefore, both refugee populations still retain rights, albeit each according to different internationally accepted definitions and statutes.

As far as the United Nations was concerned, the symmetry ended there. There was an anomaly in the way the United Nations responded to the two, different Middle East refugee populations.

The record provides a damning indictment of the United Nations and the international community. Extensive research into voting patterns and UN meeting transcripts reveals that there was no equity in the United Nations' response to the respective plights of Palestinian and Jewish refugees. The following criteria were used to arrive at this conclusion:

- *United Nations Resolutions*

Resolutions of the United Nations, either binding or nonbinding, reflect the thinking of the majority of nations on the seminal issues of the day; and become the consensus – indeed the "policy" – of the international community on these issues.

- *United Nations Agencies*

The involvement of its affiliated agencies reflects the UN decision to take action on these concerns.

- *United Nations Resources*

The provision of financial assistance gives UN agencies the capacity to act upon and implement the will of the international community.

RESOLUTIONS OF THE UNITED NATIONS SECURITY COUNCIL

The **United Nations Security Council (UNSC)**, one of the principal and most powerful organs of the United Nations, is charged with the maintenance of international peace and security – from politics to peacekeeping; from wars to the environment.

Since its inception, the Security Council has been seminally involved in Middle East affairs. From 1946 to 2009 inclusively, the total number of Security Council resolutions on the Middle East in general, and on Palestinian and Jewish refugees in particular, is as follows:[13]

UN body	Resolutions on Middle East	Resolutions on Palestinian refugees	Resolutions on Jewish refugees
Security Council	288	9	0

The primary preoccupation of the Security Council by far, among all the other Middle East problem areas, was Lebanon with 102 resolutions. Well back is the issue of Palestinian refugees with nine resolutions, not a predominant number but still dealt with by the Security Council. During this same period, there was not one resolution that even mentions Jewish refugees from Arab countries.

RESOLUTIONS OF THE UNITED NATIONS GENERAL ASSEMBLY

The **UN General Assembly (UNGA),** established in 1945 under the Charter of the United Nations, also occupies a central position as the chief deliberative, policymaking, and representative organ of the United Nations. Comprising all 192 members of the United Nations, it is intended to provide a unique forum for multilateral discussion of any and all international issues.

UN body	Resolutions on Middle East	Resolutions on Palestinian refugees	Resolutions on Jewish refugees
General Assembly	800	163	0

From 1949 to 2009, General Assembly resolutions focused much greater attention on the issue of Palestinian refugees – some 20 percent – than on any other Middle East issue.[14]

There were never any General Assembly resolutions that specifically addressed the issue of Jewish refugees, nor any resolutions on other topics that even mention Jewish refugees from Arab countries.

Moreover, other primary UN entities are also guilty of this same omission.

Since its founding in 1968, the **UN Human Rights Commission** (now **Council**) has adopted 132 resolutions on the plight of Palestinians, alleging violations of their human rights, and calling for compensation for Palestinian losses. No resolutions ever dealt with those same human rights of Jewish refugees.[15]

Since 1974, the **UN Economic and Social Council (ECOSOC)** has adopted 122 resolutions on the plight of Palestinian refugees including on "Living Conditions in Occupied Territory" (twenty-two resolutions), "Violations of Human Rights" (twenty-one resolutions), and "Assistance to Palestinian People" (fifteen resolutions).[16]

The lack of any UN attention to Jewish refugees was not due to a lack of trying. On numerous occasions, governmental and nongovernmental officials alerted the United Nations, its leadership, and affiliated agencies to the problem of Jewish refugees and sought its intervention, to no avail. The United Nations proceeded to deal solely with Palestinian refugees. This UN pattern of exclusivity, focusing only on Palestinian refugees, has continued up to today.[17]

There are at least ten identifiable UN entities that have been specifically created, or charged, with addressing issues affecting Palestinian refugees. These include: the United Nations Conciliation Commission for Palestine (UNCCP); the United Nations Relief and Works Agency for Palestine Refugees in the Near East (UNRWA); the Special Rapporteur on the Situation of Human Rights in the Palestinian Territories Occupied since 1967; the Committee on the Inalienable Rights of the Palestinian People; the United Nations Division for Palestinian Rights; the United Nations Development Programme of Assistance to the Palestinian People (UNDP); the United Nations Economic and Social Commission for Western Asia (ESCWA); the United Nations Office for the Coordination of Humanitarian Affairs (OCHA); the Office of the Special Coordinator of the Middle East Peace Process; and the Arab International Forum on Rehabilitation and Development in the Occupied Palestinian Territory, sponsored by the ESCWA, the Arab League, and the Palestinian National Authority Ministry of Planning.

No UN entities were especially created or specifically instructed to address issues affecting Jewish refugees from Arab countries.

ALLOCATION OF UN RESOURCES TO MIDDLE EAST REFUGEES

There is a huge disparity in the UN resources provided to the two Middle East refugee populations – Arabs and Jews.

Since 1947, billions of dollars have been spent by the international community – by the UN, its affiliated entities, and member states – to provide relief and assistance to Palestinian refugees. In 2007 prices, UNRWA has spent $13.7 billion since its inception in 1950.[18] During that same period, the UNHCR did not provide any comparable financial assistance to Jewish refugees. The international resources provided Jewish refugees from Arab countries were negligible.[19]

Moreover, Palestinian refugees receive disproportionate UN financial assistance as compared to all other refugees. The current, respective UNHCR and UNRWA expenditures for services to refugee populations reveal the differential treatment accorded Palestinian refugees. With a 2008 budget of $1,849,835,626, the UNHCR spends approximately $56 on each of the 32,900,000 persons under its mandate.[20] By comparison, with a 2008 budget of $548,603,000, UNRWA spends more than double what the UNHCR does – approximately $117 on each of the 4,671,811 (December 2008) registered Palestinian refugees.[21]

MANIPULATION OF THE UN

Whenever the subject of Jews in Arab countries was raised in the United Nations, a variety of tactics were used by member states to ensure that the United Nations never formally, nor properly, dealt with the issue of Jewish refugees. There are many such examples. Here are but a few:

USING THREATS IN AN ATTEMPT TO INFLUENCE UN DECISION-MAKING

For example, in the 1947 debate on whether the United Nations should adopt the partition plan, Heykal Pasha (Egypt) stated:

> The United Nations…should not lose sight of the fact that the proposed solution might endanger a million Jews living in the Moslem countries… If the United Nations decides to partition Palestine, it might be responsible for the massacre of a large number of Jews.[22]

Further, he contended:

> If the United Nations decides to amputate a part of Palestine in order to establish a Jewish state, no force on earth could prevent blood from flowing there… If Arab blood runs in Palestine, Jewish blood will necessarily be shed elsewhere in the Arab world…[23]

A few days later Iraq's Foreign Minister Fadil Jamali warned that "any injustice imposed upon the Arabs of Palestine will disturb the harmony among Jews and non-Jews in Iraq; it will breed inter-religious prejudice and hatred."[24] The threat was clear and real.

Misleading the United Nations: Treatment of Jewish Populations

When allegations were raised against the ill-treatment of Jews in their countries, Arab delegates asserted that there was no discrimination against Jews; that they were well treated. For example:

- In 1970, the Saudi representative to the Human Rights Commission stated that "The Arab Jews were quite happy in their own countries and did not wish to go to Israel."[25]
- Mr. Kelani (Syrian Arab Republic) contended in 1974 that "In the Syrian Arab Republic the Jews are treated as Syrian citizens."[26]

- At the UN General Assembly, on October 1, 1991, Syrian Foreign Minister Farouk al-Shara denied that the Arabs had ever discriminated against Jews, stating:

  > The Arabs have never adopted measures of racial discrimination against any minority, religious or ethnic, living among them. For hundreds of years Jews have lived amidst Moslem Arabs without suffering discrimination. On the contrary, they have been greatly respected.[27]

Misleading the United Nations: Jews Left Freely and Were Not Refugees

In 1970, the UN representative from Morocco claimed that Jews had left Arab countries for economic reasons, not as a result of racial discrimination:

> It had been said that many Jews had left Arab states because discriminatory pressure had been exerted on them. Although many Jews had indeed left those countries, the explanation given for their departure was wrong. Such emigration formed part of a general world pattern, as did the movement of population from the developing countries to the developed countries for the purpose of seeking better working conditions and greater economic well-being.[28]

Misleading the United Nations: On Statistics

Sometimes figures provided by Arab delegates on the numbers of Jews leaving their countries were disputed by others. One such interchange occurred on June 5, 1957, at a meeting of the Executive Committee of the United Nations Refugee Fund. Mr. Safouat (Egypt) tried to differentiate between Egyptians who had a specific nationality and those who were "stateless":

> Those Egyptian nationals included 35,000 Jews, none of whom had been expelled. They in fact enjoyed the same rights and privileges as other citizens. Among those [possessing a foreign nationality], there were 11,046 British and 7,013 French subjects. Some of them, to wit 800 British and 684 French subjects, had been asked to leave Egyptian territory because the Egyptian Government had considered their activities to be harmful to the interest of the State... With regard to the category of stateless persons, they numbered 7,000 and only 280 of them had been requested to leave the country in the public interest or for reasons of state security.[29]

The representative of France, Mr. Monod, similarly disputed the Egyptian representative's report that only 280 stateless persons had been asked to leave Egyptian territory: He "too was obliged to enter reservations about the accuracy of the figures cited by the Observer for the Government of Egypt. France alone had received nearly 2,300 stateless persons from that country."[30]

Using Procedural Maneuvers to Divert Attention Away from Jewish Refugees

There are recorded instances when procedural maneuvers were used in an attempt to divert attention away from Jewish refugees from Arab countries.

- On March 5, 1948, Item 37 on the agenda of a meeting of ECOSOC was to address, inter alia, "Reports of the NGO Committee," including Document E/710 containing two memos from the World Jewish Congress (WJC) warning that "all Jews residing in the Near and Middle East face extreme and imminent danger." The meeting was presided over by Dr. Charles H. Malik (Lebanon) who, through a procedural maneuver, passed over Agenda Item 37 that included the WJC reports. Six days later, on March 11, 1948, when the Council was ready to resume its deliberations, Mr. Katz-Suchy (Poland) rose on a "point of order concerning the consideration of Item 37 of the Agenda" and objected to the fact that it had not been addressed. Concurring was Mr. Kaminsky (Byelorussian Soviet Socialist Republic) who declared that "he could not condone a practice whereby items on the agenda were allowed to disappear from the agenda." Nonetheless, after discussion, the matter was referred back to the NGO Committee and the danger facing Jews in Arab countries never made it back to the ECOSOC table.[31]
- In the aftermath of the 1967 Arab-Israeli war, the Security Council adopted Resolution 237, which called for the "scrupulous respect of the humanitarian principles governing the treatment of prisoners of war and the protection of civilian persons in time of war." The United Nations then sent an emissary to examine the plight of Palestinians as well as Jewish civilians in Arab countries. One year later, to prevent this dual focus on both Palestinians and Jews, the Security Council adopted Resolution 259, which recalled "its resolution 237 (1967) of 14 June 1967" while limiting the United Nations' focus only to "the safety, welfare and security of the inhabitants of the Arab territories under military occupation by Israel" – eliminating the previous generic reference to "civilian persons in times of war," which included Jews in Arab countries.

At the UN Human Rights Commission, on January 27, 1969, then-Israeli Ambassador Zeltner raised the issue of the public lynching of nine Jews that had occurred in Baghdad. The Egyptian representative, Ambassador Khallaf, contended that the discussion was procedurally out of order:

> In light of the Commission's decision to confine its attention to the question of the violations of human rights in the territories occupied by Israel, the whole of the statement made by the representative of Israel at the previous meeting was out of order.[32]

Moroccan Ambassador Kettani supported the Egyptian position, saying that the Israeli statement "was quite alien to the agenda" and inappropriate "as if the State of Israel was competent to speak on behalf of all Jews throughout the world."[33]

The matter was subsequently not dealt with by the Human Rights Commission.

Challenging UN Authority to Deal with the Issue

In 1967, the United Nations' envoy Mr. Gussing reported to the General Assembly that he had been rebuffed by government officials in his efforts to determine the condition of Jews in Egypt since the June war. He further reported that the Egyptian government had "expressed the firm opinion that the Security Council resolution [237] did not apply to the Jewish minority."[34]

In 1969, at the Human Rights Commission, the Soviet Union described the Baghdad lynching of nine Iraqi Jews as "a purely internal matter."[35]

* * *

Individually, none of the above incidents would have a significant impact on the United Nations' decision-making. However, together, these manipulative tactics can be seen as the reflection of a much larger collaborative assault on Israel at the United Nations.

Israel has long complained about what it perceives as the anti-Israel bias of the United Nations. Abba Eban, Israel's first ambassador to the world body, once quipped: "If Algeria introduced a resolution declaring that the earth was flat and that Israel had flattened it, it would pass by a vote of 164 to 13 with 26 abstentions."[36]

The United Nations was and continues to be politically and numerically dominated by a consortium of political alliances. Together, they provide a voting bloc that assures overwhelming majorities of all Middle East resolutions and prevents the recognition of the rights of Jewish refugees from Arab countries.[37] The only common denominator among these vastly different and politically diverse factions is their anti-Israel stance on virtually every issue. The following (somewhat overlapping) multilateral organizations demonstrate this pattern: the Organization of the Islamic Conference (OIC – including the Arab League) has fifty-seven members;[38] the communist bloc, led by the former Soviet Union, included seven Warsaw Pact members[39] and fifteen other countries;[40] and the Organization of African Unity (OAU) has fifty-three members,[41] while additional support for anti-Israel resolutions could be counted on from the 118-member Non-Aligned Movement (NAM).[42]

LEGAL AND POLITICAL BASIS FOR THE RIGHTS OF JEWISH REFUGEES

As detailed earlier, all resolutions and other declaratory examples of UN recognition are restricted to Palestinian refugees.

Notwithstanding this lack of formal recognition, under international law, the rights of Jewish refugees from Arab countries are compelling, and their recognition finds expression in numerous legal and political declarations.

Coincidently, one of the most seminal resolutions recognizing Jewish refugees emanated from the United Nations in a resolution that never even mentions "Jewish refugees."

UN Resolution 242 (1967)

On November 22, 1967, the UN Security Council unanimously adopted Resolution 242, laying down the principles for a peaceful settlement in the Middle East. Resolution 242, still considered by many as a primary blueprint for resolving the Arab-Israel conflict, stipulates, inter alia, that a comprehensive peace settlement should necessarily include "a just settlement of the refugee problem" (Art.2 (b)).

Prior to the Security Council's consideration of Resolution 242, on Thursday, November 16, 1967, the United Kingdom submitted its draft of Resolution 242 (S/8247) to the Council. The UK version of 242 was not exclusive, and called for a just settlement of "the refugee problem." Just four days after the United Kingdom's submission, the Soviet Union's UN delegation submitted their own draft of 242 to the Council. This version (S/8253) restricted the "just settlement" only to "Palestinian refugees" (para. 3 (c)).

On Wednesday, November 22, 1967, the Security Council gathered for its 1,382nd meeting in New York. At that time, the United Kingdom's draft of Resolution 242 was voted on and unanimously approved.[43] Immediately thereafter, the Soviet delegation advised the Security Council that "it will not insist, at the present stage of our consideration of the situation in the Near East, on a vote on the draft Resolution submitted by the Soviet Union" – which would have limited 242 to Palestinian refugees only. Even so, Ambassador Kuznetsov of the Soviet Union later stated: "The Soviet Government would have preferred the Security Council to adopt the Soviet draft Resolution."[44]

Thus the attempt by the Soviet delegation to restrict the "just settlement of the refugee problem" merely to "Palestinian refugees" was not successful. The Security Council's adoption of the United Kingdom's inclusive version can be seen as the intention of its supporters to ensure that Resolution 242 include a *just solution* for all Middle East refugees – Arabs as well as Jews.

Moreover, Justice Arthur Goldberg, the United States' Chief Delegate to the United Nations, who was instrumental in drafting the unanimously adopted Resolution 242, has pointed out that:

> A notable omission in 242 is any reference to Palestinians, a Palestinian state on the West Bank or the PLO. The resolution addresses the objective of "achieving a just settlement of the refugee problem." This language presumably refers both to Arab and Jewish refugees, for about an equal number of each abandoned their homes as a result of the several wars...[45]

* * *

Buttressing the legal argument supporting rights for Jewish refugees is the fact that, in all relevant international bilateral or multilateral agreements, the reference to "refugees" is generic, allowing for the recognition and inclusion of all Middle East refugees – Jews, Christians, and other minorities. By way of example:

The Madrid Peace Conference

The 1991 Madrid Peace Conference launched historic, direct negotiations between Israel and many of its Arab neighbors. The mandate of the Refugee Working Group made no distinction between Palestinian refugees and Jewish refugees: "The refugee group will consider practical ways of improving the lot of people throughout the region who have been displaced from their homes."[46]

***

Israel and some of its Arab neighbors – Egypt, Jordan, and the Palestinians – have signed bilateral agreements affirming that a comprehensive solution to the Middle East conflict will require a "just settlement" of the "refugee problem." The case can be made that this language, consistent with UN Resolution 242, pertains to both Middle East refugee populations – Arabs and Jews:

Israel-Egypt Agreements

The Camp David Framework for Peace in the Middle East of 1978 (the "Camp David Accords") includes, in paragraph A(1)(f), a commitment by Egypt and Israel to "work with each other and with other interested parties to establish agreed procedures for a prompt, just and permanent resolution of the implementation of the refugee problem."

Israel-Jordan Peace Treaty

Article 8 of the Israel-Jordan Peace Treaty (1994), entitled "Refugees and Displaced Persons," recognizes (para. 1) "the massive human problems caused to both Parties by the conflict in the Middle East."

Israeli-Palestinian Agreements

Israeli-Palestinian agreements often use the generic term "refugees," without qualifying which refugee community is at issue, including the Declaration of Principles of 13 September 1993 (Article V (3)) and the Interim Agreement of September 1995 (Article XXXI (5)), both of which refer to "refugees" as a subject for permanent status negotiations, without qualifications.

The 2003 Roadmap to Middle East Peace

Performance-Based Roadmap to a Permanent Two-State Solution to the Israeli-Palestinian Conflict. The roadmap to Middle East peace currently being advanced by the Quartet (the United Nations, the European Union, and United States, and Russia) also refers, in Phase III, to an "agreed, just, fair and realistic solution to the refugee issue," language applicable both to Palestinian and Jewish refugees.

U.S. Resolution HR 185

On April 1, 2008, the U.S. House of Representatives unanimously adopted *H.Res.185* which, for the first time, recognizes the rights of Jewish refugees from Arab countries.

In a rare display of bipartisanship, congressmen from both political parties joined in cosponsoring this landmark resolution on the rights of Jewish refugees from Arab countries. While underscoring the fact that Jews living in Arab countries suffered human rights violations, the resolution recognizes that Jews were subsequently uprooted from their homes in Arab countries, and were made refugees. Congressional Resolution *H.Res.185* affirms that all victims of the Arab-Israeli conflict must be treated with equality, including Jewish, Christian, and other refugees from countries in the Middle East and urges the president to instruct U.S. officials participating in Middle East discussions:

> 2 (A) ...to ensure that any resolutions relating to the issue of Middle East refugees, and which include a reference to the required resolution of the Palestinian refugee issue, must also include a similarly explicit reference to the resolution of the issue of Jewish refugees from Arab countries; and
>
> 2 (B) make clear that the United States Government supports the position that, as an integral part of any comprehensive Arab-Israeli peace, the issue of refugees from the Middle East, North Africa, and the Persian Gulf must be resolved in a manner that includes recognition of the legitimate rights of and losses incurred by all refugees displaced from Arab countries, including Jews, Christians, and other groups.[47]

Seeking a just solution for the "losses incurred by all refugees" may not as problematic as many people assume. Indeed, some contend that Israel will never allow itself to be held singularly responsible for the losses incurred by Palestinian refugees. Similarly, few believe that Arab leaders would agree to compensate Jewish refugees for their losses as a result of their displacement from Arab countries. In the face of this seemingly intractable deadlock, in a fitting irony, the United

Nations has established an international precedent for a Compensation Commission which might ultimately prove a useful model in the provision of equitable compensation for both Jewish and Arab refugees.

AN INTERNATIONAL FUND

During two important Palestinian-Israeli negotiations, discussion took place on the need to create an International Fund as part of any comprehensive Middle East peace.

In July 2000, immediately after the Camp David summit, it was President Bill Clinton who first introduced the notion of an International Fund during an interview on Israeli television:

> There will have to be some sort of international fund set up for the refugees. There is, I think, some interest, interestingly enough, on both sides, in also having a fund which compensates the Israelis who were made refugees by the war, which occurred after the birth of the State of Israel. Israel is full of people, Jewish people, who lived in predominantly Arab countries who came to Israel because they were made refugees in their own land.
>
> That's another piece of good news I think I can reveal out of the summit. The Palestinians said they thought those people should be eligible for compensation, as well. So we'll have to set up a fund and we will contribute...[48]

The idea of an International Fund was again raised during the Palestinian-Israeli negotiations in Taba, Egypt, in January 2001. The following is an excerpt from the report on those Taba negotiations by EU Middle East Envoy Miguel Moratinos:

> 3.3 Compensation
>
> Both sides agreed to the establishment of an International Commission and an International Fund as a mechanism for dealing with compensation in all its aspects. Both sides agreed that "small-sum" compensation shall be paid to the refugees in the "fast-track" procedure, [and] claims of compensation for property losses below [a] certain amount shall be subject to "fast-track" procedures.[49]

It was intended that such a fund, to provide compensation for both populations of refugees, would be endowed by the international community. Multilateral involvement would also provide support and legitimacy for any comprehensive Middle East agreement. During the abovementioned interview on Israeli television, Clinton reported that he had approached the G-8 members and others on contributing to an International Fund:

> So we'll have to set up a fund and we will contribute. I went to the G-8 in Okinawa in part to give them a report, and I asked the Europeans and the Japanese to contribute, as well.

That was in July 2000. The report on the Taba negotiations prepared six months later by Moratinos indicated that by then Israel had already agreed to contribute to the International Fund:

> 3.3 ...There was also progress on Israeli compensation for material losses, land and assets expropriated including agreement on a payment from an Israeli lump sum or proper amount to be agreed upon that would feed into the International Fund.

Some believe it illogical that such an International Fund should be created, with a mandate to provide compensation to all parties involved in the same conflict. In fact, only a decade ago, the United Nations established just such a precedent for a Compensation Commission that can serve as a model for providing restitution equitably to both Jewish and Palestinian refugees.

The United Nations Compensation Commission (UNCC) Fund was established by Resolution S/RES/687, adopted by the Security Council at its 2987th meeting on May 20, 1991. It assigns liability to Iraq for losses, damages, and injuries directly caused by its unlawful invasion of Kuwait and created a fund to pay compensation to the aggrieved parties.[50] Since its inception, the UNCC has been able to resolve roughly 2.6 million claims[51] totaling an estimated $320 billion.[52] Among those who received compensation for losses suffered as a result of the Iraqi Scud attacks were Kuwaitis, Saudi Arabians, and Israelis.

So after neglecting the rights of Jewish refugees for over half a century, the United Nations – even inadvertently – may have identified an appropriate mechanism to provide recognition of rights, and compensation, to all Middle East refugees.

For the United Nations or other international entities to continue to ignore, or reject, the rights of Jewish refugees from Arab countries is to validate past and continuing injustice.

The first injustice was the mass violations of the human rights of Jews in Arab countries.

The second injustice was the absence of any credible UN response to the plight of over 850,000 Jews displaced from Arab countries.

Today it would constitute a third injustice to allow any continuing UN recognition of the rights of one population – Palestinian Arabs – without recognizing equal rights for other victims of the very same conflict, namely, Jewish refugees from Arab countries.

NOTES

1 Carole Basri, "The Jewish Refugees from Arab Countries: An Examination of Legal Rights – A Case Study of the Human Rights Violations of Iraqi Jews," *Fordham International Law Journal* 26:3, article 6 (2002): 659.

2 Cecil Roth, ed., *Encyclopedia Judaica*, 1971.

3 On December 8, 2005, Ahmadinejad gave a speech at a summit for Muslim nations in Saudi Arabia , as reported in http://www.politics.ie/foreign-affairs/4463-iranian-president-why-cant-europe-take-israel.html. Also reported in "Iran's President Says Move Israel," BBC News, December 8, 2005.

4 Interview with Iranian President Mahmoud Ahmadinejad, *Der Spiegel*, May 28, 2006, http://www.spiegel.de/international/spiegel/0,1518,418660,00.html.

5 Bat Ye'or, *Islam and Dhimmitude: Where Civilizations Collide* (Madison, NJ: Fairleigh Dickinson University Press, 2001), 21.

6 Law No. 1 of 1950, entitled "Supplement to Ordinance Canceling Iraqi Nationality," *Official Iraqi Gazette*, March 9, 1950.

7 Law No. 5 of 1951, entitled "A Law for the Supervision and Administration of the Property of Jews who have Forfeited Iraqi Nationality," *Official Iraqi Gazette*, March 10, 1951 (English version), 17.

8 Law No. 391 of 1956, Section 1(a), *Revue Egyptienne de Droit International*, vol. 12, 1956, p. 80.

9 Maurice Roumani, *The Jews from Arab Countries: A Neglected Issue* (New York: WOJAC, 1983), 2; *WOJAC'S Voice* 1:1 (January 1978).

10 United Nations High Commissioner for Refugees (UNHCR), "Convention Relating to the Status of Refugees of 28 July, 1951," Article 1(A), 2.

11 Stanley A. Urman, chapter on UNWRA in *The United Nations and Middle East Refugees: The Differing Treatment of Palestinians and Jews*, PhD dissertation, Rutgers University, 2010, 189-198.

12 Stanley A. Urman, chapter on UNHCR in ibid., 200-224.

13 Analysis derived from *United Nations Information System on the Question of Palestine* (UNISPAL), Security Council Resolutions, http://unispal.un.org/unispal.nsf/vCouncilRes? Open View.

14 *United Nations Information System on the Question of Palestine* (UNISPAL), General Assembly Resolutions, http://unispal.un.org/unispal.nsf/vGARes?OpenView.

15 *United Nations Information System on the Question of Palestine* (UNISPAL), UNHRC Resolutions, http://unispal.un.org/unispal.nsf/vCHRRes?OpenView.

16 *United Nations Information System on the Question of Palestine* (UNISPAL), ECOSOC Resolutions, http://unispal.un.org/unispal.nsf/vECOSOCRes?OpenView.

17 Urman, *United Nations and Middle East Refugees*, 131-135. Currently, in a continuing pattern, there are four UN resolutions adopted annually by huge majorities that reinforce rights and redress only for Palestinian refugees. They are entitled: "Assistance to Palestinian Refugees," "Persons displaced as a result of the June 1967 and subsequent hostilities," "Operations of the United Nations Relief and Works Agency for Palestine Refugees in the Near East," and "Palestine refugees' properties and their revenues."

18 Based on compilation of individual years from UNRWA reports with each year increased to 2007 prices using the U.S. Consumer Price Index. See Sidney Zabludoff, "The Palestinian Refugee Issue: Rhetoric vs. Reality," *Jewish Political Studies Review* 20:1-2 (Spring 2008): 7.

19 Urman, *United Nations and Middle East Refugees*, 217-222.

20 UNHCR "Financial Figures," http://www.unhcr.org/pages/49c3646c1a.html.

21 http://www.unrwa.org/etemplate.php?id=253.

22 United Nations General Assembly, Second Session, Official Records, Ad Hoc Committee on the Palestinian Question, Summary Record of the Thirtieth Meeting, Lake Success, New York, November 24, 1947 (A/AC.14/SR.30).

23 Ibid.

24 UN General Assembly, Second Session, Official Records, Verbatim Record of the Plenary Meeting, November 28, 1947, p. 1391.

25 UNHRC, Human Rights Commission, Document E/CN.4/SR.1080, 1970.

26 United Nations 2283rd, General Plenary Meeting Assembly, Twenty-Ninth Sessions on 13 Wednesday, November 1974, New York, A/PV, p. 2283.

27 Ya'akov Meron, "The Expulsion of the Jews from the Arab Countries: The Palestinians' Attitude toward It and Their Claims," in Malka Hillel Shulewitz, ed., *The Forgotten Millions: The Jewish Exodus from Arab Lands* (New York: Cassell, 1999), 83.

28 UNHRC, Human Rights Commission, Document E/CN.4/SR.1081, 1970.

29 United Nations Refugee Fund (UNREF) Executive Committee, UNREF "Summary Record" of June 5, 1957 meeting, p. 4.

30 Ibid., p. 5.

31 UN Economic and Social Council, One Hundred and Seventy-Fourth Meeting, Held at Lake Success, New York, March 11, 1948, p. 485.

32 Human Rights Commission, Document E/CN.4/SR.1010, February 27, 1969.

33 Human Rights Commission, Document E/CN.4/SR.1011, February 27, 1969.

34 General Assembly, 5th Emergency Special Session, Agenda item 5, "The Question of the Treatment of Minorities," A/6797, Article 218, September 15, 1967.

35 Human Rights Commission, Document E/CN.4/SR.1011, February 27, 1969.

36 Alan M. Dershowitz, *Chutzpah* (Boston: Touchstone, 1992), 224.

37 Analysis of UN Security Council and General Assembly Resolutions, charts. Appendices A & B, in Urman, Stanley A. *The United Nations and Middle East Refugees: the Differing Treatment of Palestinians and Jews.* (Ph.D. Thesis) New Brunswick, NJ: Rutgers University, 2010.

38 Afghanistan, Algeria, Chad, Egypt, Guinea, Indonesia, Iran, Jordan, Kuwait, Lebanon, Libya, Malaysia, Mali, Mauritania, Morocco, Niger, Pakistan, Palestine, Saudi Arabia, Senegal, Somalia, Sudan, Tunisia, Turkey, Yemen, Bahrain, Oman, Qatar, Syrian Arab Republic, United Arab Emirates, Sierra Leone, Bangladesh, Gabon, Gambia, Guinea-Bissau, Uganda, Burkina Faso, Cameroon, Comoros, Iraq, Maldives, Djibouti, Benin, Brunei Darussalam, Nigeria, Azerbaijan, Albania, Kyrgyzstan, Tajikistan, Turkmenistan, Mozambique, Kazakhstan, Uzbekistan, Suriname, Togo, Guyana, Côte d'Ivoire.

39 Albania, Bulgaria, Czechoslovakia, East Germany, Hungary, Poland, Romania.

40 Armenia, Azerbaijan, Belarus, Estonia, Georgia, Kazakhstan, Kyrgyzstan, Latvia, Lithuania, Moldova, Russia, Tajikistan, Turkmenistan, Ukraine, Uzbekistan.

41 Algeria, Angola, Benin, Botswana, Burkina Faso, Burundi, Cameroon, Cape Verde, Central African Republic, Chad, Comoros, Democratic Republic of the Congo, Republic of the Congo, Côte d'Ivoire, Djibouti, Egypt, Equatorial Guinea, Eritrea, Ethiopia, Gabon, Ghana, Guinea, Guinea-Bissau, Kenya, Lesotho, Liberia, Libya, Madagascar, Malawi, Mali, Mauritania, Mauritius, Mozambique, Namibia, Niger, Nigeria, Rwanda, Sahrawi Arab Democratic Republic, Senegal, Seychelles, Sierra Leone, Somalia, South Africa, Swaziland, São Tomé and Príncipe, Sudan, Tanzania, The Gambia, Togo, Tunisia, Uganda, Zambia, Zimbabwe.

42 Afghanistan, Algeria, Angola, Antigua and Barbuda, Bahamas, Bahrain, Bangladesh, Barbados, Belarus, Belize, Benin, Bhutan, Bolivia, Botswana, Burma (Myanmar), Brunei, Burkina Faso, Burundi, Cambodia, Cameroon, Cape Verde, Central African Republic, Chad, Chile, Colombia, Comoros, Congo, Côte d'Ivoire, Cuba, Democratic Republic of the Congo, Djibouti, Dominica, Dominican Republic, Ecuador, Egypt, Equatorial Guinea, Eritrea, Ethiopia, Gabon, Gambia, Ghana, Grenada, Guatemala, Guinea, Guinea-Bissau, Guyana, Haiti, Honduras, India, Indonesia, Iran, Iraq, Jamaica, Jordan, Kenya, Kuwait, Laos, Lebanon, Lesotho, Liberia, Libya, Madagascar, Malawi, Malaysia, Maldives, Mali, Mauritania, Mauritius, Mongolia, Morocco, Mozambique, Namibia, Nepal, Nicaragua, Niger, Nigeria, North Korea, Oman, Pakistan, Palestine, Panama, Papua New Guinea, Peru, Philippines, Qatar, Rwanda, Saint Lucia, Saint Kitts and Nevis, Saint Vincent and the Grenadines, São Tomé and Príncipe, Saudi Arabia, Senegal, Seychelles, Sierra Leone, Singapore, Somalia, South Africa, Sri Lanka, Sudan, Suriname, Swaziland, Syria, Tanzania, Thailand, Timor-Leste, Togo, Trinidad and Tobago, Tunisia, Turkmenistan, Uganda, United Arab Emirates, Uzbekistan, Vanuatu, Venezuela, Vietnam, Yemen, Zambia, Zimbabwe.

43 UN Security Council, S/PV.1382, para. 67.

44 Security Council Official Records, November 22, 1967, S/PV.1382, para. 117.

45 Arthur J. Goldberg, "Resolution 242: After 20 Years," *Security Interests*, National Committee on American Foreign Policy, April 2002.

46 Remarks by Secretary of State James A. Baker, III, before the Organizational Meeting for Multilateral Negotiations on the Middle East, House of Unions, Moscow, January 28, 1992, Dept. of State.

47 H. Res. 185, House of Representatives, http://www.govtrack.us/congress/billtext.xpd?bill=hr110-1851, 2008.

48 Interview on Israel Television, July 28, 2000 (excerpt from White House transcript).

49 First published in *Haaretz*, February 14, 2002, and by Arab Gateway, http://www.al-bab.com/arab/docs/pal/taba2001.htm.

50 S.C. Res. 687, U.N. SCOR, 46th Sess., 2981st mtg. P 16, U.N. Doc. S/RES/687 (1991).

51 A Wiser Peace: An Action Strategy for a Post-Conflict Iraq, Supplement I: Background Information on Iraq's Financial Obligations CSIS, 2003, http://www.csis.org/isp/wiserpeace_I.pdf.

52 UNCC website: http://www.unog.ch/uncc/theclaims.htm.

ISRAEL'S RIGHTS REGARDING TERRITORIES AND THE SETTLEMENTS IN THE EYES OF THE INTERNATIONAL COMMUNITY

Alan Baker

For over fifty years, in countless United Nations resolutions adopted virtually *verbatim* year after year on various aspects of the Middle East problem, and specifically on issues regarding the territories, the reference to Israel is almost exclusively couched in terms of "*Israel, the occupying Power*" and the reference to the territories is termed "*the occupied Palestinian territories*." Similarly, reference to Israel's settlement policy consistently includes the element of illegitimacy or illegality.

These general and all-embracing terms have become the "*lingua franca*" of the United Nations – accepted phrases that neither generate nor attract any thought or discussion as to their legal, historical, or political accuracy. Nor do they connect with ongoing developments in the region. They are merely accepted as part of the reality of the UN General Assembly and other organs within the UN system.

As an illustration, one need merely refer to fourteen of the resolutions on the Middle East issue that were adopted at the recent 65th General Assembly in 2010,[1] to grasp the repetitiveness and the automatic usage of the above phrases in their various clauses. If one multiplies this number by over fifty years of constant repetition and brainwashing in UN resolutions, one may well perceive how the phrases "Israel, the occupying Power" and "occupied Palestinian territories" have indeed become accepted, standard UN terminology.

Strangely enough, this description is not limited to Israel's status in the West Bank areas of Judea and Samaria, but, despite removal by Israel of all its forces and civilians from the Gaza Strip in

2005, including the dismantling of its settlements, these phrases are still used by UN bodies, in reports, other documentation, and in resolutions, to describe Israel's status in the Gaza Strip.[2]

In light of the developments over the years, including the signing of agreements between Israel and the PLO, the support and affirmation of such agreements by the United Nations, and the changes in the status of the respective parties vis-à-vis the territories that such agreements generated, one may well ask whether the continued usage of this standard terminology is accurate or relevant, and if it indeed reflects international realities, or rather the ongoing and blind "wishful thinking" of the initiators of the resolutions and those member states that blindly and unthinkingly support them.

Israel's status vis-à-vis the respective territories has indeed evolved over the years and has been accompanied by constant discussion as to its nature.

Following the 1967 Six Day War, the views as to Israel's status veered between a predominant section of the international community that considered, for whatever reason, that it was a classical occupation, as affirmed in the UN General Assembly resolutions, and others, predominantly Israel itself, that considered that Israel had come into control of the territories following a legitimately fought defensive war.[3] Another very significant historical and legal viewpoint regards Israel's presence in the West Bank areas of Judea and Samaria as emanating from the historical rights granted in Palestine to the Jewish people by the Balfour Declaration and affirmed by resolution of the League of Nations in 1922, granting to the Jewish people a national home in all parts of Mandatory Palestine and enabling "close settlement on the land." The continued validity of this resolution, beyond the days of the League of Nations, was in fact maintained by Article 80 of the UN Charter, according to which rights granted to peoples by international instruments remain unaltered, and hence still valid.[4]

However Israel's status might have been perceived, up to the signing of the Oslo accords between Israel and the PLO in 1993, the legal and political nature of both the Gaza Strip and the West Bank has undergone a critical change. The fact that the international community has failed, and consistently fails to acknowledge this change, and repeats inaccuracies and absurdities in UN resolutions that are utterly disconnected from reality, is perhaps indicative of the selective blindness vis-à-vis Israel, and the extent to which the international community is being manipulated by the Arab and Muslim states.

While each of the various viewpoints set out above as to Israel's status in the territories has had, and in some cases continues to have its respective merits, no one in the international community – not even the United Nations – can negate the fact that with the signature by Israel and the Palestinian leadership of the Israel-Palestinian Interim Agreement of 1995,[5] signed and witnessed by the United States, the European Union, Egypt, Jordan, Russia, and Norway, the status of the territory changed, and the status of each of the parties to the agreement vis-à-vis the territory changed as well.

THE UNIQUE CIRCUMSTANCES OF THE TERRITORY AND THE SPECIAL NATURE OF THE ISRAELI-PALESTINIAN RELATIONSHIP

The agreements and memoranda between the Palestinian leadership and the government of Israel, affirmed and recognized by the United Nations both in its signature as witness to the 1995 agreement, as well as in resolutions acknowledging the agreements,[6] have produced a special regime – a *lex specialis* – that governs all aspects of the relationship between them, the relationship of each one of the parties to the territory under its responsibility and control, and its rights and duties in that territory.[7]

These documents[8] cover all the central issues between them including governance, security, elections, jurisdiction, human rights, legal issues, and the like. In this framework, when referring to the rights and duties of each party in the territory that remains under its jurisdiction pending the outcome of the permanent status negotiations, there is no specific provision either restricting planning, zoning, and continued construction by either party, of towns, settlements, and villages, or freezing such construction. Article 27 of Annex III (Civil Affairs Annex) to the 1995 agreement sets out the agreed terms for planning and zoning, and construction powers in the territories, and places no limitation on either side to build in the areas under its respective jurisdiction.[9]

The central legal and political change brought about by the agreement is the fact that the two sides agreed pending the outcome of the negotiations on a permanent status agreement between them, to divide their respective jurisdictions in the West Bank into Areas A and B (Palestinian jurisdiction) and Area C (Israeli jurisdiction).[10]

They defined the respective powers and responsibilities of each side in the areas under its control. In Area A (the major cities and towns and highly populated areas) Israel completely transferred all powers and responsibilities to the Palestinian Authority including security and police powers. In Area B Israel transferred all powers and responsibilities except for security, over the villages that predominantly constituted Area B. Area C, without Palestinian villages and population centers, includes the Israeli settlements and military installations. Thus Israel's powers and responsibilities in Area C include all aspects regarding Israeli residents of settlements and military installations – all this pending the outcome of the permanent status negotiations.

This division of control, powers, and responsibilities was accepted and agreed upon by the Palestinians in the 1995 agreement and even acknowledged by the United Nations. As such it constitutes a radical change in the status and nature of the territory. Israel's continued presence in Area C, pending the outcome of the permanent status negotiations, enjoys the sanction of the PLO. It cannot, by any measure of political manipulation or legal acrobatics, be considered "occupied territory," and hence, Israel cannot be termed "the occupying Power." Israel's presence in the territory of the West Bank is with the full approval of the Palestinian leadership composing the PLO.

THE SETTLEMENTS ISSUE

In a similar vein, the legal nature of Israel's settlements, which has also become a cliché in UN terminology as being illegal, is equally part and parcel of this *lex specialis* regime based on the Oslo Accords. The Palestinian leadership cannot present this as an alleged violation by Israel of the 1949 Fourth Geneva Convention, in order to bypass their acceptance of the rights and responsibilities pursuant to the Interim Agreement as well as the international community's acknowledgment of that agreement's relevance and continued validity.

In fact, even in the 1993 Israeli-PLO Declaration of Principles, and as repeated in all the ensuing agreements including the 1995 Interim Agreement, the settlement issue is one of the core issues determined by the parties to be negotiated in the permanent status negotiations.[11] This is a mutually agreed-upon component of the accords between Israel and the Palestinian leadership. That Palestinian leadership has accepted and is committed to the fact that it does not exercise jurisdiction regarding permanent status issues, settlements included, in Area C pending the outcome of the permanent status negotiation.

As such, the Oslo Accords contain no requirement that prohibits, limits, or freezes construction by Israel in Area C.

In fact, during the course of the negotiations on the Interim Agreement in 1995, the Palestinian delegation requested that a "side letter" be attached, the text of which would be agreed upon, whereby Israel would commit to restricting settlement construction in Area C during the process of implementation of the agreement and the ensuing negotiations. Several drafts of this "side letter" passed between the negotiating teams until Israel indeed agreed to a formulation restricting construction activities on the basis of a government decision that would be adopted for that purpose. Ultimately, the Palestinian leadership withdrew its request for a side letter.

THE LEGALITY OF ISRAEL'S SETTLEMENTS

The issues of the legality of Israel's settlements and the rationale of Israel's settlement policy have for years dominated the attention of the international community. This has been evident in countless reports of different UN bodies, rapporteurs, and resolutions,[12] as well as in political declarations and statements by governments and leaders. In varying degrees, they consider Israel's settlements to be in violation of international law, specifically Article 49 of the Fourth Geneva Convention relative to the Protection of Civilian Persons in Time of War, of August 12, 1949.[13]

But apart from the almost standardized, oft-repeated, and commonly accepted clichés as to the "illegality of Israel's settlements," or the "flagrant violation" of the Geneva Convention, repeated even by the International Court of Justice,[14] there has been little genuine attempt to elaborate and consider the substantive legal reasoning behind this view. Yet there are a number of very relevant factors that inevitably must be considered when making such a serious accusation against Israel.

President Bill Clinton, Israeli Prime Minister Yitzhak Rabin, and PLO leader Yasser Arafat sign the Oslo II Interim Agreement, September 28, 1995, at the White House. (AP Photo/Doug Mills)

These factors include:

- the text of the sixth paragraph of Article 49 of the Fourth Geneva Convention and the circumstances of, and reasons for, its inclusion in the Convention in December 1949;
- the unique circumstances of the territory and the context of the Israeli-Palestinian relationship that, as set out above, has developed since 1993 through a series of agreements between them. These agreements have created the *sui generis* framework that overrides any general determinations unrelated to that framework.

IS ARTICLE 49 OF THE FOURTH GENEVA CONVENTION APPLICABLE TO ISRAEL'S SETTLEMENTS?

Immediately after the Second World War, the need arose to draft an international convention to protect civilians in times of armed conflict in light of the massive numbers of civilians forced to leave their homes during the war, and the glaring lack of effective protection for civilians under any of the then valid conventions or treaties.[15] In this context, the sixth paragraph of Article 49 of the Fourth Geneva Convention states:

> The Occupying Power shall not deport or transfer parts of its own civilian population into the territory it occupies.[16]

The authoritative and official commentary by the governing body of the International Red Cross movement, the International Committee of the Red Cross (ICRC), published in 1958 in order to assist "Governments and armed forces...called upon to assume responsibility in applying the Geneva Conventions,"[17] clarifies this provision as follows:

> It is intended to prevent a practice adopted during the Second World War by certain Powers, which transferred portions of their own population to occupied territory for political and racial reasons or in order, as they claimed, to colonize those territories. Such transfers worsened the economic situation of the native population and endangered their separate existence as a race.

In other words, according to the ICRC commentary, Article 49 relates to deportations, meaning the *forcible* transfer of an occupying power's population into an occupied territory. Historically, over forty million people were subjected to forced migration, evacuation, displacement, and expulsion, including fifteen million Germans, five million Soviet citizens, and millions of Poles, Ukrainians, and Hungarians.

The vast numbers of people affected and the aims and purposes behind such a population movement speak for themselves. There is nothing to link such circumstances to Israel's settlement policy. The circumstances in which Article 49(6) of the Geneva Convention was drafted, and specifically the meaning attached by the International Committee of the Red Cross itself to that article, raise a serious question as to the relevance of linkage to and reliance on the article by the international community as the basis and criterion for determining Israel's settlements as illegal. One may further ask if this is not a misreading, misunderstanding, or even distortion of that article and its context.

The international lawyer Prof. Eugene V. Rostow, a former dean of Yale Law School and Under Secretary of State, stated in 1990:

> [T]he Convention prohibits many of the inhumane practices of the Nazis and the Soviet Union during and before the Second World War – the mass transfer of people into and out of occupied territories for purposes of extermination, slave labor or colonization, for example... The Jewish settlers in the West Bank are most emphatically volunteers. They have not been "deported" or "transferred" to the area by the Government of Israel, and their movement involves none of the atrocious purposes or harmful effects on the existing population it is the goal of the Geneva Convention to prevent.[18]

Ambassador Morris Abram, a member of the U.S. staff at the Nuremburg Tribunal and later involved in the drafting of the Fourth Geneva Convention, is on record as stating that the convention:

Ariel, an Israeli settlement in the central West Bank

> was not designed to cover situations like Israeli settlements in the occupied territories, but rather the forcible transfer, deportation or resettlement of large numbers of people.[19]

Similarly, international lawyer Prof. Julius Stone, in referring to the absurdity of considering Israeli settlements as a violation of Article 49(6), stated:

> Irony would...be pushed to the absurdity of claiming that Article 49(6), designed to prevent repetition of Nazi-type genocidal policies of rendering Nazi metropolitan territories *judenrein,* has now come to mean that...the West Bank...must be made *judenrein* and must be so maintained, if necessary by the use of force by the government of Israel against its own inhabitants. Common sense as well as correct historical and functional context excludes so tyrannical a reading of Article 49(6).[20]

Article 49(6) uses terminology that is indicative of governmental action in coercing its citizens to move. Yet Israel has not forcibly deported or mass-transferred its citizens into the territories. It has consistently maintained a policy enabling people to reside voluntarily on land that is not privately owned. Their continued presence is subject to the outcome of the negotiation process on the status of the territory, and without necessarily prejudicing that outcome.

In some cases Israel has permitted its citizens who have for many years owned property or tracts of land in the territory, and who had been previously dispossessed and displaced by Jordan, to return to their own properties. The presence in these areas of Jewish settlement from Ottoman and British Mandatory times is totally unrelated to the context of, or claims regarding, the Geneva Convention.

Israel has never expressed any intention to colonize the territories, to confiscate land, nor to displace the local population for political or racial reasons, nor to alter the demographic nature of the area.

As stated above, the agreements signed with the Palestinian leadership have in fact placed the entire issue of the status of the territory, as well as Israel's settlements, on the negotiating table – a factor that proves the lack of any intention to colonize or displace. The fact that Israel chose unilaterally to dismantle its settlements and remove its citizens from the Gaza Strip in 2005 is further evidence of this.

During the negotiation on the 1998 Rome Statute of the International Criminal Court,[21] Arab states initiated an alteration in the text of the court's statute listing as a serious violation of the laws of armed conflict the war crime of "transferring, *directly or indirectly,* parts of the civil population into the occupied territory."[22] The deliberate addition of the phrase "directly or indirectly" to the original 1949 text was intended by them to adapt the original 1949 Geneva Convention language in order to render it applicable to Israel's settlement policy. This in itself is indicative of the proponents' and the international community's acknowledgment of the fact that Article 49(6) as drafted in 1949 was simply not relevant to the circumstances of Israel's settlements.

CONCLUSION

The propensity of the international community, whether through constant, parrot-like repetition in UN documentation and annual resolutions or other means, to label Israel as the "occupying Power," and the West Bank and Gaza territories as the "occupied Palestinian territories," as well as the automatic labeling of Israel's settlements as "illegal," are indicative of a stubborn refusal to face the realities of the situation in the Middle East.

In permitting themselves to be driven by certain states with a clear political agenda, to ignore vital and serious agreements between the PLO and Israel in which the status of the Gaza Strip and West Bank territories is mutually redefined; and to ignore the legislative history and logic behind the Fourth Geneva Convention provision regarding forcible transfer of peoples, those member states of the United Nations supporting such resolutions and determinations are damaging the UN as a credible body in international law and society, and undermining the Middle East peace process.

The international community cannot seriously continue to bury its head in the sand and ignore these factors. It is high time that responsible and likeminded states endeavor to restore the credibility of the international community in general and the United Nations in particular, and bring it back into reality as a viable body capable of fulfilling the purposes for which it was established.

NOTES

1 See, for example, those resolutions most recently adopted in the 65th Session of the General Assembly in 2010 including A/RES/65/202 on "The right of the Palestinian People to Self-Determination" (in the 7th and 9th preambular paragraphs); A/65/179 on "Permanent sovereignty of the Palestinian people in the Occupied Palestinian Territory, including East Jerusalem, and of the Arab population in the occupied Syrian Golan over their natural resources" (in virtually all the preambular and substantive paragraphs); Resolution A/65/134 on "Assistance to the Palestinian people"; Resolution A/65/105 on "Israeli practices affecting the human rights of the Palestinian people in the Occupied Palestinian Territory, including East Jerusalem"; Resolution A/65/104 on "Israeli practices affecting the human rights of the Palestinian people in the Occupied Palestinian Territory, including East Jerusalem"; Resolution A/65/103 on "Applicability of the Geneva Convention relative to the Protection of Civilian Persons in Time of War, of 12 August 1949, to the Occupied Palestinian Territory, including East Jerusalem, and the other occupied Arab territories"; A/65/102 on "Work of the Special Committee to Investigate Israeli Practices Affecting the Human Rights of the Palestinian People and Other Arabs of the Occupied Territories"; A/65/100 on "Operations of the United Nations Relief and Works Agency for Palestine Refugees in the Near East"; A/65/98 on "Assistance to Palestine refugees"; A/65/17 on "Jerusalem"; A/65/16 on "Peaceful settlement of the question of Palestine"; A/65/15 on "Special information programme on the question of Palestine of the Department of Public Information of the Secretariat"; A/65/14 on "Division for Palestinian Rights of the Secretariat"; A/65/13 on "Committee on the Exercise of the Inalienable Rights of the Palestinian People."

2 For a full analysis of Israel's status in the Gaza Strip, see the chapter in this book by Pnina Sharvit Baruch, "Is the Gaza Strip Occupied by Israel?"

3 For a full analysis of Israel's status following the 1967 war, see the chapter of this book by Nicholas Rostow, "The Historical and Legal Contexts of Israel's Borders."

4 See the chapter in this book by Martin Gilbert, "'An Overwhelmingly Jewish State' from the Balfour Declaration to the Palestine Mandate."

5 http://www.mfa.gov.il/MFA/Peace+Process/Guide+to+the+Peace+Process/THE+ISRAELI-PALESTINIAN+INTERIM+AGREEMENT.htm. See also UN General Assembly Resolutions A/RES. 50/21, A/RES.50/29 and A/RES.50/84 of December 1995, in which the UN welcomed and expressed support for the Interim Agreement.

6 See annex to UN document A/48/486-S/26560 dated 11 October 1993.

7 See the Israeli-Palestinian Interim Agreement on the West Bank and Gaza Strip, Sept. 28, 1995, at Article XVIII, para. 1, http://www.mfa.gov.il/MFA/Peace+Process/Guide+to+the+Peace+Process/THE+ISRAELI-PALESTINIAN+INTERIM+AGREEMENT.htm.

8 Israel-Palestinian Declaration of Principles, September 13, 1993, Exchange of Letters between Prime Minister Rabin and Chairman Arafat of September 9-10, 1993, Agreement on the Gaza Strip and the Jericho Area, May 4, 1994, Interim Agreement between Israel and the Palestinians, September 28, 1995, Agreement on Temporary International Presence in Hebron, May 9, 1996, The Wye River Memorandum, October 23, 1998, The Sharm el-Sheikh Memorandum on Implementation Timeline of Outstanding Commitments of Agreements Signed and the Resumption of Permanent Status Negotiations, September 4, 1999, Protocol Concerning Safe Passage between the West Bank and the Gaza Strip, October 5, 1999. All these documents are referenced in http://www.mfa.gov.il/mfa/peace%20process/reference%20documents.

9 http://www.mfa.gov.il/MFA/Peace+Process/Guide+to+the+Peace+Process/Gaza-Jericho+Agreement+Annex+II.htm.

10 Id., Article IV (Land).

11 Israel-Palestinian Declaration of Principles on Interim Self-Government Arrangements of Sept. 13, 1993, Article V, para. 3, as well as Article XXXI, para. 5 of the Interim Agreement, http://www.mfa.gov.il/MFA/Peace+Process/Guide+to+the+Peace+Process/Declaration+of+Principles.htm.

12 Extending from General Assembly Resolution A/RES/3005/(XXVII) of December 15, 1972, through Security Council Resolutions 446 (1979), 452 (1979), 465 (1980), to the most recent General Assembly resolution of December 10, 2010, A/RES/65/105.

13 United Nations, Treaty Series, vol. 75, No. 973, p. 287.

14 The International Court of Justice in its 2004 Advisory Opinion on Israel's Security Fence. See http://www.icj-cij.org/docket/files/131/1671.pdf at paragraph 120.

15 See *ICRC Commentary to the Fourth Geneva Convention*, edited by Jean S. Pictet (1958), at pp. 3-9, for an extensive summary of the reasoning behind the drafting of the convention.

16 Id., p. 278.

17 Foreword to the ICRC Commentary, at n. 13 above.

18 *American Journal of International Law*, Vol. 84, 1990, p. 719.

19 Ambassador Morris Abram, in a discussion with Arab ambassadors in Geneva, February 1, 1990.

20 Quoted in David M. Phillips, "The Illegal Settlements Myth," *Commentary*, December 2009.

21 U.N. Doc. A/CONF.183/9*.

22 The relevant part of Article 8, paragraph 2(b)(viii), listing the various war crimes, reads as follows: "The transfer, *directly or indirectly*, by the Occupying Power of parts of its own civilian population into the territory it occupies" (emphasis not in the original).

THE HISTORICAL AND LEGAL CONTEXTS OF ISRAEL'S BORDERS[1]

Nicholas Rostow

INTRODUCTION

More than sixty years after the admission to the United Nations of the state of Israel with no internationally recognized boundaries,[2] a central question remains: what legal rights to territory does Israel have and, assuming such rights exist, how far do they reach, that is, what are Israel's rightful borders? These questions in turn are connected to others: how might Israel's legal rights inform an Israeli-Palestinian peace agreement and perhaps even a general Arab-Israeli peace agreement? The reverse of these questions is relevant too: what are the sources of Arab rights, and how might these rights inform a peace agreement?

This chapter examines these issues because a viable lasting peace depends on reliability and mutual satisfaction (or at least not too great dissatisfaction) among the parties, not just strength of arms alone. In short, the law is a necessary ingredient of reliability and also may provide a common language for negotiators.

The first step is to "find" the law. Therefore, this chapter begins with the legal sources of Israel's rights: the League of Nations Mandate for Palestine, the establishment, recognition, and admission of the state of Israel to the United Nations, and the 1949 Armistice Agreements. The chapter examines the border question and the impact of UN Security Council resolutions and ongoing negotiations that have resulted in agreements, not treaties establishing peace. The resulting conclusion is that Israel's boundaries for the most part are set as a matter of law. Final boundaries between Israel and any Palestinian state that may be established should reflect what the parties agree to – and, after numerous agreements, they are or should be close to being able to define a boundary. To Israel's north, if there is peace, not just a stable frontier, Syria and Israel need to agree on a boundary. It may involve full, partial, or conditional (with demilitarized zones, for example) restoration to Syria of the Golan Heights. The chapter ends by suggesting a way of analyzing the legal context that might help negotiators seeking a formal Israeli-Palestinian peace agreement.

I. ISRAEL'S RIGHTS UNDER INTERNATIONAL LAW TO TERRITORY IN THE MIDDLE EAST

From 1511 to 1917, "Palestine" was part of the Ottoman Empire, although the term did not denote a defined people or area. What today is understood as Palestine was never geographically a single sovereign entity, state, or internationally recognized sovereign. In fact, geographically the area called Palestine was not administered in Ottoman times as a single unit. World War I resulted in the end of the Ottoman Empire and Turkish claims to far-flung Ottoman territories. More important was the establishment of the League of Nations, the first global international organization and the predecessor of the United Nations. While it ultimately failed as a vehicle for maintaining international peace, the League of Nations nonetheless constituted a forum in which states could make authoritative decisions and establish norms. What the Covenant of the League of Nations promised, and what the League did, have continuing political and legal significance.

The League of Nations Covenant established the Mandate system of trusteeships to dispose of territory of the defeated Central Powers.[3] Thus, the geographical area called Palestine covering what now are Israel, Jordan, the West Bank, and Gaza became a Mandate of the League of Nations. Britain was the Mandatory Power. Syria/Lebanon also became a League of Nations Mandate with France as the Mandatory Power. Boundaries, if any, were set by agreement between Britain and France. As a general matter, the Mandate system redefined colonialism as a public trust for indigenous peoples. The Mandate for Palestine contained a variation on this theme.

A. THE LEAGUE OF NATIONS MANDATE AND THE ESTABLISHMENT OF ISRAEL

On July 24, 1922, the League of Nations adopted and the British government accepted the Mandate:

> Whereas recognition has thereby been given to the historical connection of the Jewish people with Palestine and to the grounds for reconstituting their national home in that country. ... The Mandatory shall be responsible for placing the country under such political, administrative, and economic conditions as will secure the establishment of the Jewish national home, as laid down in the preamble, and the development of self-governing institutions, and also for safeguarding the civil and religious rights of all the inhabitants of Palestine, irrespective of race and religion.[4]

MANDATE FOR PALESTINE

AND MEMORANDUM BY THE BRITISH GOVERNMENT RELATING TO ITS APPLICATION TO TRANSJORDAN, APPROVED BY THE COUNCIL OF THE LEAGUE OF NATIONS ON SEPTEMBER 16TH, 1922.

Whereas recognition has thereby been given to the historical connection of the Jewish people with Palestine and to the grounds for reconstituting their national home in that country;

The British Mandate for Palestine was a binding treaty between Great Britain and the League of Nations that recognized "the historic connection of the Jewish people with Palestine."

By the terms of the Mandate, the British Palestine administration was to facilitate both Jewish immigration and "close settlement by Jews on the land, including State lands and waste lands not required for public purposes."[5] Notably, the League's use of the language "for reconstituting their national home in that country" indicated recognition of a preexisting Jewish right, derived from the Jews' three-thousand-year-old historical connection to the land.

The Mandate for Palestine therefore had as its principal purpose the implementation of the 1917 Balfour Declaration, which in fact the Mandate incorporated in almost identical language.[6] In 1920, at San Remo, the Mandate territory had been defined as running from the Mediterranean Sea, including the Gaza Strip, to Iraq and Saudi Arabia. In September 1922, Britain requested, and the League of Nations approved, a division of the territory with respect to Jewish "close settlement" of the land, separating what is now Jordan from the Mandate territory – 75 percent – dedicated to the creation of the Jewish national home.[7] Thus, the League of Nations granted Jews rights to territory in Palestine west of the Jordan River without limitation. Article 80 of the UN Charter – the "Palestine" article – affirmed the ongoing validity of this grant by the League and the international instruments embodying them.[8] By virtue of its consistent articulation of peoples' rights, the League of Nations also laid a legal foundation, which the United Nations has carried forward, for eventual assertions – for example, by the Palestinians of today – of a right to territory and to have it recognized.

B. ISRAEL BECOMES A STATE, MAY 1948

On May 14, 1948, Israel declared itself a state. Boundaries were uncertain. Repeated proposals further to partition the area of the Mandate west of the Jordan River into Jewish and Arab states had come to nothing. The Zionists had accepted the 1947 UN General Assembly recommendation set forth in Resolution 181 (II) (1947).[9] The resolution proposed to the Mandatory Power and to the UN Security Council a Jewish and an Arab state with an international city of Jerusalem. The Arab states at the United Nations voted against the recommendation and threatened to use force to prevent it coming into effect. When Israel declared itself a state, five Arab armies – Egypt, Iraq, Saudi Arabia, Syria, and Transjordan (now Jordan) – attacked.

The war ended with armistice agreements. Israel occupied more territory than the 1947 General Assembly resolution had recommended for the Jewish state but less than the Mandatory territory open to Jewish settlement.[10] Armistice agreements between Israel and Egypt, Israel and Jordan, Israel and Lebanon, and Israel and Syria, concluded in 1949, demarcated boundaries. Unlike the Israel-Lebanon Line and parts of the Israel-Syria Line, which tracked the international boundary between the Syria/Lebanon and Palestine Mandates, the Armistice Demarcation Lines that did not follow recognized international boundaries contained the common thought (as expressed in the agreement between Israel and Jordan) that such lines were "without prejudice to future territorial settlements or boundary lines or claims of either Party related thereto."[11] The Jordanians insisted on this language to preserve future diplomatic and, it is reasonable to assume, military options.

The expectation or hope in 1949 was that peace treaties would replace armistice agreements. For that reason, the United Nations admitted Israel to membership after the Armistice Agreements were concluded, giving Israel a definable, if not finally demarcated, territorial extent. Sixty years later, two peace treaties and a multiplicity of lesser agreements among the parties in fact have been concluded. Also in the mix have been a number of UN Security Council resolutions, which have constituted the parties' agreed framework for peace negotiations and brought the demarcation of boundaries closer to completion.

C. THE SIX-DAY WAR AND THE OCCUPIED TERRITORIES

From 1949 to June 1967, Israel's Arab neighbors were engaged more or less in continuous guerrilla warfare against Israel. Israel's armed forces contended with attacks aimed indiscriminately at military and civilian targets. At some periods in the 1950s, for example, the risk of attacks on Israeli civilian automobile traffic reached a point where the names of the occupants of motor vehicles were recorded so that if cars were blown up, the corpses could be identified. In the wake of the Suez Crisis of 1956, which, because of Egypt's nationalization of the Suez Canal, Egyptian support for Algerian rebellion against France, and the ongoing attacks on Israel, resulted in Anglo-French-Israeli military operations against Egypt, the United Nations established a peacekeeping force in the Sinai Peninsula to separate Israeli and Egyptian forces. This step, together with political agreements articulated in interlocking speeches at the UN General Assembly in 1957, laid the basis for uneasy peace until 1967.

In the spring of 1967, with the United States mired in Vietnam, Egypt, Syria, and Jordan were tempted to try their strength with Israel. The Soviet Union encouraged them, although it is perhaps excessive to blame Moscow entirely for Egyptian, Syrian, and Jordanian behavior.

At Egypt's request, UN Secretary-General U Thant withdrew the UN peacekeeping force from the Sinai Peninsula. Egypt blockaded the Straits of Tiran, Israel's route to the Red Sea, which it had promised not to do in 1957. Weeks of intense diplomacy to head off war accomplished little except to persuade the international community that Israel was left with no nonmilitary options to defend itself against threats, military buildups, and the uniting of Arab armies under Egyptian command.[12] Israel struck on June 5. Within six days, its forces had pushed the Arab armies back to the Suez Canal, the Jordan River, and across the Golan Heights. Israel took control of, and eventually purported to annex, East Jerusalem, which had been outside the territory awarded Israel in 1949. The UN Security Council repeatedly condemned such annexation measures as null and void.[13]

This history is legally relevant because it provides the backdrop for the subsequent forty years of Arab-Israeli diplomacy. Regrettably, this important historical context rarely appears in UN statements or Arab-Israeli peacemaking or diplomacy.

Yet the events of 1967 form the context of the most important of UN Security Council resolutions on the Arab-Israeli conflict, Resolution 242 (1967) adopted November 22, 1967. The United States, mindful that Israel had withdrawn from Sinai in 1957 at U.S. insistence without a peace agreement, was determined that the aftermath of the 1967 war not repeat the 1957 experience. This history is critically important to understand why Israel took control of the West Bank, Gaza Strip, Sinai Peninsula, and Golan Heights in 1967, and why it has not withdrawn from every inch of these disputed territories without peace agreements (Israel, of course, withdrew its civilians and forces from Gaza in 2005). UN Security Council Resolution 242 (1967), subsequently strengthened in legal terms by Resolution 338 (1973), established the framework for ensuing diplomatic steps and for consideration of legal rights. More than forty years later, Resolution 242 remains the most important framework, accepted by the parties, for Arab-Israeli peace and has been applied in every agreement Israel has reached with its neighbors.

Resolution 242 (1967) provides in part:

> ... *Emphasizing* the inadmissibility of the acquisition of territory by war and the need to work for a just and lasting peace in which every State in the area can live in security, ...
>
> 1. Affirms that the fulfillment of Charter principles requires the establishment of a just and lasting peace in the Middle East which should include the application of both the following principles:
>
> (i) Withdrawal of Israeli armed forces from territories occupied in the recent conflict;
>
> (ii) Termination of all claims or states of belligerency and respect for and acknowledgement of the sovereignty, territorial integrity and political independence of every State in the area and their right to live in peace within secure and recognized boundaries free from threats or acts of force.[14]

Resolution 242 used the term "territories occupied," not "*the* territories occupied." The resolution left open for negotiation where Israel's final boundaries would be in exchange for withdrawal from Egyptian, Jordanian, Syrian, and disputed territory, rather than requiring a restoration of the 1949 Armistice Demarcation Lines as the international boundary of Israel; the resolution thus treated that boundary only as marking a minimum Israeli territory. Resolution 242 arguably entitled Israel to more territory than that. Adjustments were contemplated, as implied by the requirement for "secure and recognized boundaries." The U.S. ambassador to the United Nations, Arthur Goldberg, stated in November 1967 that the 1949 Armistice Demarcation Lines did not meet this standard. In 1967, minor adjustments of the borders, together with the establishment of demilitarized zones, as Resolution 242 suggested, seemed the way to achieve a secure peace. The expectation was not realized, at least not in the short run.

In the wake of the Yom Kippur War of 1973, the Security Council used even stronger language:

> 2. *Calls* upon the parties concerned to start immediately after the cease-fire the implementation of Security Council resolution 242 (1967) in all of its parts;
>
> 3. *Decides* that, immediately and concurrently with the cease-fire, negotiations shall start between the parties concerned under appropriate auspices aimed at establishing a just and durable peace in the Middle East.[15]

These documents framed the conclusion of the Israel-Egypt Peace Treaty of 1979 and the Israel-Jordan Peace Treaty of 1994. And while the Palestinians were not a state party included in Resolution 242 in 1967, 242 would become the framework within which Israel concluded agreements with the Palestine Liberation Organization (PLO) and its newly created Palestinian Authority in 1993 on principles and steps designed to lead to a peace treaty between Israel and the Palestinians. These agreements formed the basis for UN Security Council Resolution 1397 (2002) in which the Security Council "affirm[ed] a vision of a region where two States, Israel and Palestine, live side by side within secure and recognized borders."[16]

Ongoing diplomacy so far has failed to realize every aspect of the vision of Resolution 242. It has resulted, however, in the formal agreement between Israel and the PLO to resolve "remaining issues, including: Jerusalem, refugees, security arrangements, borders, relations and cooperation with other neighbors, and other issues of common interest relating to permanent status. . .through negotiations."[17]

II. RIGHTS AND PEACE

By 2011, Israel's borders had been finalized on three fronts: with Egypt and the Gaza Strip, with Lebanon, and with Jordan. The frontier with Egypt was established by the Israel-Egypt treaty of 1979 just as the Israel-Jordan boundary was set by the 1994 treaty. Israel's boundaries with the Gaza Strip have been established de facto by Israel's withdrawal of armed forces and civilians in 2005 and relinquishment of any territorial claim there. Israel's border with Lebanon always has tracked the internationally recognized boundary between the Mandate for Palestine and the Mandate for Syria/Lebanon.

Israel's borders with the Palestinian Authority and Syria remain uncertain. The 1993 Oslo Agreements and their progeny have gone far toward recognizing a Palestinian state and toward demarcating boundaries, but the process has not reached an end. Indeed, one may argue that the remaining issues, principally how Jerusalem can remain united while serving as capital of two countries, territorial adjustments here and there, and even whether a prospective state of Palestine and its peace with Israel should be policed by international peacekeepers to prevent violence, while important, are hardly issues that pose within their resolution existential threats to Israel or to a Palestinian state. Those who harbor the wish to destroy either Israel or a Palestinian state exist and may yet achieve their ambitions. That fact should act as pressure to reach final agreement. So far, it has not done so.

Israel still holds the Golan Heights, which it captured from Syria in 1967. Offers to return the Heights as part of a peace agreement between Israel and Syria have not led to agreement. So, Israel's borders are recognized on a number of fronts; two unsettled areas remain. As far as the Palestinian border is concerned, one may say that all that remains is to define the distribution of the hitherto undefined remainder of the territory of the League of Nations Mandate for Palestine: those parts of the West Bank not yet distributed by means of agreement between Israel and the Palestinian Authority.

III. CONCLUSION

The question of Jewish/Israeli rights to territory in the Middle East is important to any complete resolution of the Arab-Israeli conflict. In entering political and territorial agreements with Israel, Egypt, Jordan, and the Palestinian Authority have recognized such rights and determined all but the Israel-Palestine and Israel-Syria borders. Israel's territorial rights do not derive from, or depend on, such agreements. Rather, to the extent they do not derive from claims rooted in ancient historical connections to the territory and religious belief, they come from the most important parts of contemporary international law – the authoritative legal and political decisions of the first global international organization, the League of Nations, as reaffirmed by the United Nations. Too much of the world's minimum public order and too many of peoples' international-law rights derive from the same sources for them to be dismissed as crucially important foundations of Israel's right to territory but otherwise irrelevant. That international law, carried forward to today, affirmed that Israel too has a right to self-determination in its territory. For all its flaws,[18] including its slighting of the history and documentation of Israel's legal rights, the International Court of Justice Advisory Opinion on the Israeli security "wall" assumes, by not challenging it, that Israel has a right to exist on territory in the Middle East.[19] The court's assertions of Palestinian rights to self-determination do not undermine this reading of the opinion.[20]

The diplomacy of the past sixty years has gone far to establishing final boundaries for Israel within and outside the 1949 Armistice Demarcation Lines. Within those boundaries, Israelis enjoy self-determination. Outside them, others enjoy it. Voting and other civil, political, and human rights depend on it.

Recognition of rights to land is a necessary but not sufficient condition for peace in the region. Rights are based in law, the same law in which international agreements are rooted and from which they gain their strength. Rights do not need to be exercised and may be waived. And they may be affected by conduct. Thus, an aggressor may lose standing in a contest of legal claims by lacking "clean hands."[21] But if a state or people are to benefit from the rule of law that creates their rights, they must accept that the same law grants others rights. Israelis and Palestinians have taken that step in the various agreements already signed between them. It remains for them to take the other measures necessary to complete the process of formalizing peace. Through their negotiations, Israelis and Syrians and Israelis and Lebanese have taken the same step as well. They all need to take the process to conclusion if the Middle East is to know peace.

NOTES

1 The views expressed are the author's own and do not necessarily reflect the views of the U.S. Department of Defense, the National Defense University, or any other entity with which I am or have been associated.

2 Israel's application for membership and the General Assembly decision to admit Israel said nothing about borders. The General Assembly accepted the application in 1949 after the Armistice Agreements between Israel and Egypt, Jordan, Lebanon, and Syria demarcated armistice lines. UN Docs. UN Gen. Ass. Res. 273 (III), May 11, 1949, S.C.Res. 69 (1949), Mar. 4, 1949, S/1093, 1/1267 (none of these documents discussed borders).

3 This system also implicitly called into question all colonial regimes not based on the consent of the governed.

4 Mandate for Palestine, Preamb. and Art. 2.

5 *Id.* Art. 6.

6 *See* Balfour to Rothschild, Nov. 2, 1917, http://avalon.law.yale.edu/20th_century/balfour.asp.

7 David Fromkin, *A Peace to End All Peace* (New York: Avon, 1989), 514.

8 According to Paul S. Riebenfeld, Article 80 was drafted as a result of Zionist representations at the San Francisco conference in order to protect, in addition to the existing rights of any states, also those of "any peoples or the terms of existing international instruments to which Members of the United Nations may respectively be parties." It mentions "peoples." The rights referred to were in particular those of the *Jewish people* as the beneficiary of the Palestine Mandate, in an international system based on the membership of *states*.

Paul S. Riebenfeld, "The Legitimacy of Jewish Settlement in Judea, Samaria and Gaza," in Edward M. Siegel, ed., *Israel's Legitimacy in Law and History* (New York: Center for Near East Policy, 1993), 41-42.

9 GA Res. 181 (II), Nov. 29, 1947.

10 The Mandate and the resolution are of different character. The Mandate set forth the obligations of the Mandatory power. By its terms, the resolution was a recommendation.

11 Israel-Jordan Armistice, Apr. 3, 1949, Art. V1 (9). See also Israel-Egypt Armistice, Feb. 24, 1949, Art. V (2); Israel-Lebanon-Armistice, Mar. 23, 1949, Art. V; Israel-Syria Armistice, Jul. 20, 1949, Art. V (1), (3). Reprinted in John Norton Moore, ed., *The Arab-Israeli Conflict*, vol. 3 (Princeton: Princeton University Press, 1974), Documents 401, 383, 393, 410.

12 *See, e.g.,* Dennis Ross, *The Missing Peace* (New York: Farrar, Straus & Giroux, 2004), 21-22 and works cited therein.

13 *E.g.,* S. Res. 252 (1967), May 21, 1968; 267 (1968), Jul. 3, 1968; 298 (1971), Sept. 25, 1971. These resolutions, firm as they are in tone and tint, are not by their terms decisions binding on the international community under Article 25 of the UN Charter ("The Members of the United Nations agree to accept and carry out the decisions of the Security Council in accordance with the present Charter"). While some would argue on behalf of a contextual analysis to determine if a resolution meets the test of Article 25, the Permanent Five Members of the United Nations have agreed that the word "decides" must appear in that portion of a resolution intended to bind the international community. Thus, even at this stage in the historical development of Security Council practice under the UN Charter, the presence or absence of the word "decides" in a Security Council resolution determined whether all or part of such resolution constituted a decision for purposes of Article 25. See a more nuanced discussion in Jost Delbrück, "Article 25," in Bruno Simma, ed., *The Charter of the United Nations: A Commentary* (New York: Oxford University Press, 2002), 453-464.

The international law of occupation makes occupation irrelevant to title to territory. *See, e.g.,* Nicholas Rostow, "Gaza, Iraq, Lebanon: Three Occupations under International Law," 37 Israel Yearbook on Human Rights 205 (2007).

14 S. Res. 242 (1967), Nov. 22, 1967.

15 S. Res. 338 (1973), Oct. 22, 1973.

16 S. Res. 1397 (2002), Mar. 12, 2002.

17 http://www.mfa.gov.il/MFA/Peace%20Process/Guide%20to%20the%20Peace%20Process/Declaration%20of%20Principles.

18 *See, e.g.,* Eli Hertz, *Reply to the Advisory Opinion of 9 July 2004 in the Matter of the Legal Consequences of the Construction of a Wall in the Occupied Palestinian Territory*, 2nd ed. (New York: Myths and Facts, Inc., 2006); Nicholas Rostow, "Wall of Reason: Alan Dershowitz v. the International Court of Justice," 71 Albany L. Rev. 953 (2008), and works cited therein.

19 Legal Consequences of the Construction of a Wall in the Occupied Palestinian Territory, Advisory Opinion, 2004 I.C.J. 136 (Jul. 9), *available at* http://www.icj_cij.org/docket/files/131/1671.pdf (hereinafter cited as ICJ Opinion). The court does not specify where Israel may exercise those rights, a point noted by Judge Al-Khasawneh, Concurring opinion, paras. 8-10.

20 ICJ Opinion, paras. 70, 88 *et seq.*

21 Stephen M. Schwebel, "What Weight Conquest?," 64 Am. J. Int'l. L. 344 (1970).

THE MISLEADING INTERPRETATION OF SECURITY COUNCIL RESOLUTION 242 (1967)

Ruth Lapidoth

INTRODUCTION

Among the UN resolutions concerning the Middle East that are quite often mentioned and referred to is Security Council Resolution 242 (1967).[1] It has even been considered the building block of peace in the Middle East.[2] Unfortunately, however, it has often been misunderstood or misrepresented. This chapter will deal with two of these misleading interpretations. First, I will show that, contrary to certain opinions,[3] the resolution does *not* request Israel to withdraw from *all* the territories occupied in the 1967 Six Day War. Second, I will show that, contrary to certain opinions, the resolution does not recognize that the Palestinian refugees have a right to return to Israel. It will be shown that the resolution recommends that the parties negotiate in good faith in order to reach an agreement based on certain principles, including an Israeli withdrawal to recognized and secure (i.e., agreed) borders, and a just settlement of the refugee problem reached by agreement. The resolution also mentions several other principles that will not be dealt with in this chapter.[4]

TEXT OF THE RESOLUTION

Since not all readers of this chapter may remember the wording of the resolution, it is here reproduced:

> *The Security Council,*
>
> *Expressing* its continuing concern with the grave situation in the Middle East,
>
> *Emphasizing* the inadmissibility of the acquisition of territory by war and the need to work for a just and lasting peace in which every State in the area can live in security,
>
> *Emphasizing further* that all Member States in their acceptance of the Charter of the United Nations have undertaken a commitment to act in accordance with Article 2 of the Charter,
>
> 1. *Affirms* that the fulfillment of Charter principles requires the establishment of a just and lasting peace in the Middle East which should include the application of both the following principles:
>
> (i) Withdrawal of Israel armed forces from territories occupied in the recent conflict;[5]
>
> (ii) Termination of all claims or states of belligerency and respect for and acknowledgment of the sovereignty, territorial integrity and political independence of every State in the area and their right to live in peace within secure and recognized boundaries free from threats or acts of force;
>
> 2. *Affirms further* the necessity
>
> *(a)* For guaranteeing freedom of navigation through international waterways in the area;
> *(b)* For achieving a just settlement of the refugee problem;
> *(c)* For guaranteeing the territorial inviolability and political independence of every State in the area, through measures including the establishment of demilitarized zones;
>
> 3. *Requests* the Secretary-General to designate a Special Representative to proceed to the Middle East to establish and maintain contacts with the States concerned in order to promote agreement and assist efforts to achieve a peaceful and accepted settlement in accordance with the provisions and principles in this resolution;
>
> 4. *Requests* the Secretary-General to report to the Security Council on the progress of the efforts of the Special Representative as soon as possible.[6]

U.S. Ambassador to the United Nations Arthur Goldberg addresses the emergency session of the UN General Assembly in New York on June 19, 1967. (AP Photo)

THE LEGAL EFFECT OF THE RESOLUTION

Although it is also authorized to adopt binding decisions, in particular when dealing with "threats to the peace, breaches of the peace, and acts of aggression" (under Chapter VII of the Charter), it is well known that in most cases the Security Council adopts resolutions in the nature of recommendations. The effect of this particular resolution was discussed by the UN Secretary-General in a press conference given on March 19, 1992. Replying to a question, the Secretary-General said that "[a] resolution not based on Chapter VII is non-binding. For your information, Security Council Resolution 242 (1967) is not based on Chapter VII of the Charter." In a statement of clarification it was said that "the resolution is not enforceable since it was not adopted under Chapter VII." [7]

Thus it would seem that the resolution was a mere recommendation, especially since in the debate that preceded its adoption the delegates stressed that they were acting under Chapter VI of the Charter. They considered themselves to be dealing with the settlement of a dispute "the continuance of which is likely to endanger the maintenance of international peace and security."[8] There is no doubt that by referring to Chapter VI of the Charter, the speakers conveyed their intention that the resolution was recommendatory in nature.

The contents of the resolution also indicate that it was but a recommendation. The majority of its stipulations constitute a framework, a list of principles, to become operative only after detailed and specific measures would be agreed upon: "It states general principles and envisions 'agreement' on specifics; the parties must put flesh on these bare bones," commented Ambassador Arthur Goldberg, the U.S. Representative.[9] The resolution explicitly entrusted a "Special Representative" with the task of assisting the parties concerned to reach agreement and arrive at a settlement in keeping with its conciliatory spirit.

Had the intention been to impose a "binding decision," agreement between the parties would not have been one of its major preoccupations. In particular, the provision on the establishment of "secure and recognized boundaries" proves that the implementation of the resolution required a prior agreement between the parties. The establishment of secure and recognized boundaries requires a process in which the two states involved respectively on the two sides of the boundary, actually negotiate, come to terms, and agree upon the delimitation and demarcation of their common boundary. Anything less than that would not be in accordance with the requirements of the resolution. In addition, the use of the term "should" in the first paragraph ("which should include the application of both the following principles") underlines the recommendatory character of the resolution.

However, the question arises as to whether the extent of Resolution 242's legal effect was affected by later developments. In this context one must remember that at a certain stage the parties to the conflict expressed their acceptance of the resolution.[10] This acceptance certainly enhanced its legal weight and constituted a commitment to negotiate in good faith. But because the contents of Resolution 242 were only guidelines for a settlement as described above, the acceptance of the document did not commit the parties to a specific outcome.

It has been claimed that Resolution 338 (1973), which was adopted after the October 1973 war, added a binding effect to Resolution 242 (1967).[11] Indeed, there is little doubt that Resolution 338 reinforced 242 in various respects. First, it emphasized that the latter must be implemented "in all of its parts," thus stressing that all of its provisions are of the same validity and effect. Also, while Resolution 242 spoke of an agreed settlement to be reached with the help of the UN Secretary-General's Special Representative, Resolution 338 expressly called for negotiations between the parties.[12] There is no express statement in Resolution 338 that it was intended to be of a binding nature, but rather it reinforced the call to negotiate in accordance with the general guidelines of Resolution 242.

THE ISSUE OF WITHDRAWAL

Two provisions of the resolution are relevant to the issue of withdrawal. The first is in the preamble – the Security Council emphasized the "inadmissibility of the acquisition of territory by war." Does this mean that Israel's occupation of territories in 1967 was illegal? The answer is: no. There is a fundamental difference between occupation and acquisition of territory. The former does not entail any change in the territory's national status, although it does give the occupier certain powers as well as responsibilities and the right to stay in the territory until peace has been concluded. Mere military occupation of the land does not confer any legal title to sovereignty.

Due to the prohibition of the use of force under the UN Charter, the legality of military occupation has been the subject of differing opinions. It is generally recognized that occupation resulting from a lawful use of force (i.e., an act of self-defense) is legitimate. Thus, the 1970 UN General Assembly "Declaration on Principles of International Law concerning Friendly Relations and Cooperation among States,"[13] and its 1974 "Definition of Aggression" resolution,[14] upheld the legality of military occupation provided the force used to establish it was not in contravention of the UN Charter principles. In the words of Prof. Rosalyn Higgins, "[t]here is nothing in either the Charter or general international law which leads one to suppose that military occupation pending a peace treaty is illegal."[15]

The preamble of this Security Council resolution denounces "the acquisition of territory by war," but does not pronounce a verdict on the occupation under the circumstances of 1967.[16] The distinction between the terms "acquisition" and "occupation" in terms of territory, is very significant in this context. "Acquisition" refers to gaining title, ownership, or sovereignty over the land or territory. "Occupation," on the other hand, refers to provisional presence, or holding of the territory pending negotiations on peace or any other agreed-upon determination as to the status, ownership, or sovereignty of the territory. The Security Council did not, in this preambular provision, denounce "occupation" as such. It is revealing to compare the version finally adopted with the formula used in the draft submitted by India, Mali, and Nigeria: there, the relevant passage read that "[o]ccupation or acquisition of territory by military conquest is inadmissible under the Charter of the United Nations."[17] It is, therefore, of some significance that the version of the preamble finally adopted, while reiterating the injunction against the acquisition of territory, offers no comment on military occupation. Consequently, it cannot be argued that the Security Council regarded Israel's presence in these territories as illegal. As an act of self-defense,[18] this military occupation was and continues to be legitimate, until a peace settlement can be reached and permanent borders defined and agreed upon.[19]

Other interpretations of the passage – suggesting, for example, that it was intended to denounce any military occupation – contradict not only its wording but also the established rules of customary international law. Its form, its place in the preamble rather than in the body of the resolution,[20] and a comparison with the subsequent passages all clearly indicate its concern with the implementation of existing norms rather than an attempt to create new ones.

The second provision that is relevant to the issue of withdrawal is to be found in paragraph 1(i): peace should include the application of the principle of "withdrawal of Israel armed forces from territories occupied in the recent conflict." While the Arabs insist on complete Israeli withdrawal from all the territories occupied by Israel in 1967,[21] Israel is of the opinion that the call for withdrawal is applicable in conjunction with the call for the establishment of secure and recognized boundaries by agreement.[22]

The Arab states base their claim on a combination of the abovementioned provision in the preamble about "the inadmissibility of the acquisition of territory by war" and the French version of the sentence which calls for "withdrawal...," namely *"retrait des forces armées israéliennes des territoires occupés lors du récent conflit."* On the other hand, Israel's interpretation is based on the plain meaning of the English text of the withdrawal clause, which is identical with the wording presented by the British delegation. It is also supported by the rejection of proposals to add the words "all" and "the" before "territories."[23] Moreover, in interpreting the withdrawal clause, one must take into consideration the other provisions of the resolution, including the one mentioned above, on the establishment of "secure and recognized boundaries."

It seems that the resolution does not require total withdrawal for a number of reasons:

- As has already been discussed, the phrase in the preamble ("the inadmissibility of the acquisition of territory by war") merely reiterates the principle that military occupation, although lawful if it is the result of an act of self-defense, does not by itself justify annexation and acquisition of title to territory.

- The English version of the withdrawal clause requires only "withdrawal from territories," not from "all" territories, nor from "the" territories. This provision is clear and unambiguous. As Lord Caradon, the Representative of Great Britain, stated in the Security Council on November 22, 1967, "I am sure that it will be recognized by us all that it is only the resolution that will bind us, and we regard its wording as clear."[24] According to Prof. Eugene Rostow, who was at the time Undersecretary of State for Political Affairs in the U.S. Department of State: "For twenty-four years, the Arabs have pretended that the two Resolutions [242 and 338] are ambiguous... Nothing could be further from the truth."[25]

- The French version, which allegedly supports the request for full withdrawal, can perhaps prima facie be considered ambiguous, since the word *"des"* can be either the plural of *"de"* (*article indéfini*) or a contraction of *"de les"* (*article défini*). It seems, however, that the French translation is an idiomatic rendering of the original English text, and possibly the only acceptable rendering into French.[26] Moreover, even Ambassador Bernard, the Representative of France in the Security Council at the time, said that *"des territoires occupés"* indisputably corresponds to the expression "occupied territories."[27]

  If, however, the French version were ambiguous, it should be interpreted in conformity with the English text. Since the two versions are presumed to have the same meaning,[28] one clear and the other ambiguous, the latter should be interpreted in conformity with the former.[29]

Many varied opinions have been expressed on the question of what withdrawal the resolution envisaged. Some consider that the full withdrawal from Sinai in pursuance of the 1979 peace treaty between Egypt and Israel should serve as a precedent that requires full withdrawal from further regions. Others have reached the opposite conclusion – namely, that by carrying out the considerable withdrawal from Sinai (1981) and from the Gaza Strip (in 2005), Israel has already fulfilled any withdrawal requirement. Some have claimed that the lack of a requirement for full withdrawal under the resolution allows Israel to carry out only minor border rectifications, while

Lord Caradon (left), Britain's ambassador to the UN in 1967, who drafted Resolution 242 with Ambassador Arthur Goldberg of the U.S. (AP Photo)

others have coined the slogan "land for peace." None of these attitudes can claim to represent the proper interpretation of Resolution 242. As mentioned, the resolution calls upon the parties to negotiate and reach agreement on withdrawal to agreed boundaries, without indicating the extent and the location of the recommended withdrawal.

RESOLUTION 242 AND THE REFUGEE ISSUE

The problems concerning the refugees have been examined thoroughly in another chapter of this volume, and here I intend to discuss only the meaning of the relevant provision in Resolution 242. In this resolution the Security Council affirmed the necessity "for achieving a just settlement of the refugee problem" (paragraph 2(b)).

From the legal point of view, the refugee problem raises three questions: (1) Who should be considered a Palestinian refugee? (2) Do the Palestinian refugees have a right to return to Israel?[30] And (3) Do they have a right to compensation? Here the discussion will focus mainly on the second question: does Resolution 242 recognize that the Palestinian refugees have a right to return to Israel?

According to the Arab point of view, the answer is yes; according to the Israeli opinion it is no. The Israeli interpretation is based on a plain reading of the text, which speaks of a just settlement, without indicating what that settlement should be. The Arab interpretation, however, claims that Resolution 242 has, by implication, endorsed General Assembly Resolution 194(III) of 1948[31] which, in their opinion, has recognized a right of return for the refugees.

This interpretation is erroneous. If there had been an intention to incorporate GA Resolution 194(III), it should have been said expressly. One cannot read into a resolution something which is not mentioned nor hinted at in it. Moreover, GA Resolution 194(III) does not confer a right of return. Like most General Assembly resolutions, it is a recommendation. It says that "The General Assembly...*Resolves* that the refugees wishing to return to their homes and live at peace with their neighbours should be permitted to do so at the earliest practicable date, and that compensation should be paid for the property of those choosing not to return..." (paragraph 11). This is a very careful recommendation using the word "should" (not shall), and subjecting the recommended return to several conditions.

It follows that the Security Council has not recognized any "right" of return in Resolution 242. Moreover, the relationship between GA Resolution 194(III) and SC Resolution 242 (1967) is not one of incorporation, but rather of substitution – the leading UN provision is now in the Security Council text. The quest for a "just settlement" seems to imply a negotiated and agreed solution.

Interestingly, Resolution 242 has not limited the "just settlement" provision to Palestinian refugees. It may also have envisaged the many Jewish refugees from Arab countries who had to leave all their property behind. Most of them probably do not wish to return to their country of origin, but proper compensation may well be included in the "just settlement" of Resolution 242.

Eugene Rostow, former Dean of Yale Law School and Undersecretary of State for Political Affairs in the Johnson administration

CONCLUDING REMARKS

A careful examination of the wording of the relevant provisions of Resolution 242 (1967) has led to the conclusion that the interpretation favored by the Arab states is misleading. By this resolution the Security Council has laid down several principles that should lead to a peaceful solution of the Arab-Israeli conflict. Among these principles are an Israeli withdrawal from territories occupied in 1967 to new secure and recognized boundaries, to be established by agreement, and the need for a just settlement of the refugee problem, without any reference to a right of return. The solution may include a right to settle in the Palestinian state after its establishment, settlement and integration in other states (Arab and non-Arab), and perhaps the return of a small number to Israel if compelling humanitarian reasons are involved, such as family unification.[32]

Negotiations with Egypt and with Jordan on the basis of Resolution 242 (1967) have already led to two peace treaties (1979 with Egypt, 1994 with Jordan). Let us hope that soon more peace treaties will follow.

NOTES

1 The author wishes to thank Dr. Ofra Friesel for her very helpful remarks.

This article is partly based on a previous paper by the author ("Resolution 242 at Twenty-five") published in 26 Israel Law Review (Is.L.R.) 295 (1992). The following essay is published with the kind permission of the Is.L.R. The author has discussed the subject with a great number of experts, and the list is too long to be fully reproduced. Special thanks are due to Prof. Eugene V. Rostow, Ambassador Joseph Sisco, Prof. William V. O'Brien, Mr. Herbert Hansell, Dr. Shavit Matias, Brig. Gen. Ilan Shiff, Ambassador Dr. Robbie Sabel, Justice Elyakim Rubinstein, and Messrs. Daniel Taub, David Kornbluth, Benjamin Rubin, and Joseph Ben Aharon. Needless to say, the responsibility for the contents is the author's.

2 Adnan Abu Odeh, Nabil Elaraby, Meir Rosenne, Dennis Ross, Eugene Rostow, and Vernon Turner, *UN Security Council Resolution 242: The Building Block of Peacemaking* (Washington, DC: Washington Institute for Near East Policy, 1993).

3 E.g., John McHugo, "Resolution 242: A Reappraisal of the Right-Wing Israeli Interpretation of the Withdrawal Phrase with Reference to the Conflict between Israel and the Palestinians," 51 International and Comparative Law Quarterly (2002) 851-882, reprinted in Victor Kattan, ed., *The Palestine Question in International Law* (London: British Institute of International and Comparative Law, 2008), 357-387.

4 See, e.g., Ruth Lapidoth, supra note 1, at 305-306, 311-316.

5 The French version reads: "retrait des forces armées israéliennes des territoires occupés lors du récent conflit."

6 SCOR, 22nd year, Resolutions and Decisions, 8-9. For the legislative history of the resolution, see Arthur Lall, *The UN and the Middle East Crisis, 1967* (New York: Columbia University Press, 1968).

7 UN Press Release SG/SM/4718 of March 19, 1992, p. 11, and the clarification, DPI of March 20, 1992.

8 Lord Caradon, the Representative of Great Britain, SCOR, 22nd year, 1373rd meeting, November 9, 1967, p. 18, section 164; Ambassador A. Goldberg of the USA, ibid., 1377th meeting, November 15, 1967, p. 6, section 54; the Representative of Denmark, Mr. Borch, at the 1373rd meeting, November 9-10, 1967, p. 24, section 235; the Representative of Canada, Mr. Ignatieff, at the 1373rd meeting, p. 22, section 212, and at the 1377th meeting, p. 9, section 86; the Representative of Nigeria, Mr. Adebe, at the 1373rd meeting, November 9/10, 1967, p. 12, section 107. It is true that in 1971 the International Court of Justice decided that a resolution taken in accordance with Chapter VI can also be a binding decision (Legal Consequences for States of the Continued Presence of South Africa in Namibia (South West Africa) Notwithstanding Security Council Resolution 276 (1970), International Court of Justice, Reports 1971, p. 16, sections 113 and 114). But this was not the prevalent view in 1967, when the discussions on Resolution 242 took place in the Council. See John W. Halderman, *The United Nations and the Rule of Law* (Dobbs Ferry, NY: Oceana, 1967), 65-89. See also Julius Stone, *No Peace-No War in the Middle East* (Sydney: Maitland, 1969), 23-24; Jean Dehaussy, "La crise du Moyen-Orient et l'O.N.U.," 95 Journal de droit international (1968) 853-888; Shabtai Rosenne, "Directions for a Middle East Settlement: Some Underlying Legal Problems," 33 Law and Contemporary Problems (1968) 44-67, at 57; Yehuda Z. Blum, *Secure Boundaries and Middle East Peace in the Light of International Law and Practice* (Jerusalem: Hebrew University, 1971), 63-64, n. 127; Yoram Dinstein, "The Legal Issues of 'Para-War' and Peace in the Middle East," 44 St. John's Law Review (1970) 477; Amos Shapira, "The Security Council Resolution of November 1967: Its Legal Nature and Implications," 4 Is.L.R. (1969) 229-241; Philippe Manin, "Les efforts de l'Organisation des Nations Unies et des Grandes Puissances en vue d'un Règlement de la crise au Moyen-Orient," 15 Annuaire Français de droit international (1969) 154-182, at 158-159; Pierre-Marie Martin, *Le Conflit Israélo-arabe: recherches sur l'emploi de la force en droit international public positif* (Paris: Librairie générale de droit et de jurispru dence, 1973), 232-234.

9 Arthur J. Goldberg, "A Basic Mideast Document: Its Meaning Today," lecture presented at the Annual Meeting of the American Jewish Committee, May 15, 1969.

10 Sydney D. Bailey, *The Making of Resolution 242* (Dordrecht: Martinus Nijhoff, 1985), at 178-179.

11 Eugene V. Rostow, "The Illegality of the Arab Attack on Israel of October 6, 1973," 69 American Journal of International Law (Am.J.Int'l L) (1975) 272-289, at 275. Resolution 338 states:

The Security Council

1. Calls upon all parties to the present fighting to cease all firing and terminate all military activity immediately, no later than 12 hours after the moment of the adoption of this decision, in the positions they now occupy;
2. Calls upon the parties concerned to start immediately after the cease-fire the implementation of Security Council Resolution 242 (1967) in all of its parts;
3. Decides that, immediately and concurrently with the cease-fire, negotiations start between the parties concerned under appropriate auspices aimed at establishing a just and durable peace in the Middle East.

12 The author wishes to express her thanks to Ambassador J. Sisco for having drawn her attention to this fact.

13 General Assembly Resolution 2625 (XXV) of October 24, 1970.

14 General Assembly Resolution 3314 (XXIX) of December 14, 1974.

15 Rosalyn Higgins, "The Place of International Law in the Settlement of Disputes by the Security Council," 64 Am. J. Int'l L. (1970) 1-18, at 8.

16 See Stone, supra note 8, at 33; Rosenne, supra note 8, at 59; Martin, supra note 8, at 258-265; Higgins, supra note 8, at 7-8; Blum, supra note 8, at 80-91.

17 UN Doc. S/8227, of November 7, 1967.

18 See Julius Stone, *The Middle East under Cease-Fire* (Sydney: The Bridge, 1967), 6ff; Quincy Wright, "Legal Aspects of the Middle East Situation," 33 Law and Contemporary Problems (1968) 5-31, at 27; William V. O'Brien, "International Law and the Outbreak of War in the Middle East," 11 Orbis (1967) 692-723, at 722-723; Nathan Feinberg, *The Arab-Israel Conflict in International Law: A Critical Analysis of the Colloquium of Arab Jurists in Algiers* (Jerusalem: Magnes Press, 1970), 114-115; Stephen M. Schwebel, "What Weight to Conquest?," 64 Am. J. Int'l L. (1970) 344-347, at 346; Eugene V. Rostow, "Legal Aspects of the Search for Peace in the Middle East," Proceedings of the American Society of International Law (1970) 80; A. Cocatre-Zilgien, "L'Imbroglio Moyen-oriental et le droit," 73 Revue générale de droit international public (1969) 52-61, at 59; John Norton Moore, "The Arab-Israeli Conflict and the Obligation to Pursue Peaceful Settlement of International Disputes," 19 Kansas Law Review (1971) 403-440, at 425; S. M. Berman, "Recrudescence of the *Bellum justum et pium* Controversy and Israel's Conquest and Integration of Jerusalem," Revue de droit international (1968) 359-374, at 367ff; B. Doell, "Die Rechtslage des Golfes von Akaba" 14 Jahrbuch für Internationales Recht (1969) 225-259, at 258; Martin, supra note 8, at 153-173; Amos Shapira, "The Six-Day War and the Right of Self-Defence," 6 Is.L.R. (1971) 65-80; Allan Gerson, "Trustee-Occupant: The Legal Status of Israel's Presence in the West Bank," 14 Harvard International Law Journal (1973) 1-49, at 14-22; Thomas M. Franck, "Who Killed Article 2(4)," 64 Am. J. Int'l L. (1970) 809-837, at 821; Y. Dinstein, supra note 8, at 466 et seq.; Y. Dinstein, *War, Aggression and Self-Defence*, 4th ed. (Cambridge: Cambridge University Press, 2005), 192; Barry Feinstein, "Self-Defence and Israel in International Law: A Reappraisal," 11 Is.L.R. (1976) 516-562; Edward Miller, "Self-Defence, International Law and the Six Day War," 20 Is.L.R. (1985) 49-73. Cf., however, John L. Hargrove, "Abating the Middle East Crisis through the United Nations (and Vice Versa)," 19 Kansas Law Review (1971) 365-372, at 367; M. Charif Bassiouni, "The 'Middle East': The Misunderstood Conflict," 19 Kansas Law Review (1970) 373-402, at 395; John Quigley, quoted in Eugene V. Rostow, "The Perils of Positivism: A Response to Professor Quigley," 2 Duke J. Comp. & Int'l L. (1992) 229-246, at 229.

19 See, e.g., John N. Moore, "The Arab-Israeli Conflict and the Obligation to Pursue Peaceful Settlement of International Disputes," 19 *Kansas Law Review* (1970) 425; Schwebel, supra note 18, at 344; Rostow, supra note 18, at 276. It should be mentioned, however, that according to various authors, Israel's rights in part of the occupied territories exceed those of a military occupant because of the defectiveness of the title of the authorities who had been in control of those territories prior to the Israel occupation; the principle has been maintained mainly with respect to the West Bank (Judea and Samaria) and the Gaza Strip: see Schwebel, at 345-346; Stone, supra note 18, at 39-40; Elihu Lauterpacht, *Jerusalem and the Holy Places* (London: Anglo-Israel Association, 1968), 46ff; Cocatre-Zilgien, supra note 18, at 60; Yehuda Z. Blum, "The Missing Reversioner: Reflections on the Status of Judea and Samaria," 3 Is.L.R. (1968) 270-301; Martin, supra note 18, at 265-279.

20 Irrespective of the rules that apply to international treaties, it is well known that preambles to Security Council resolutions carry much less weight than the operative part.

21 See, e.g., replies by Jordan (March 23, 1969) and by Lebanon (April 21, 1969) to questions submitted by Ambassador Gunnar Jarring, in the Report by UN Secretary-General U. Thant, UN Doc. S/10070, of January 4, 1971. See also Talcott W. Seelye, "Meaning of '67 Israel Resolution Disputed," *New York Times*, April 1, 1988 (the writer was a U.S. ambassador to Tunisia and Syria).

22 Statement by Ambassador Abba Eban, UN GAOR, 23rd session, 1686th Plenary Meeting, October 8, 1968, pp. 9-13, at 9 (section 92), 11 (section 110).

23 See Lall, supra note 6, at 252-254.

24 SCOR, 22nd year, 1382nd meeting, November 22, 1967, p. 7, section 61. See also Cyrus R. Vance and Joseph J. Sisco, "Resolution 242, Crystal Clear," *New York Times*, March 20, 1988.

25 Rostow, "Perils of Positivism," supra note 18, at 241-242.

26 It seems there was no other way to translate that provision into French: "When the French text appeared, the British and American Governments raised the matter at once with the United Nations Secretariat, and with the French Government, to be told that the French language offered no other solution for the problem.... [N]one of the people involved could think of a more accurate French translation...." See Rostow, "Illegality of the Arab Attack," supra note 11, at 285. See also Shabtai Rosenne, "On Multi-lingual Interpretation," 6 Is.L.R. (1971) 360-365 at 363.

27 SCOR, 1382nd meeting, November 22, 1967, p. 12, section 111.

28 Vienna Convention on the Law of Treaties, 1969, Article 33.

29 Charles Rousseau, *Droit International Public*, vol. 1 (Paris: Pedone, 1970), at 289.

30 On the Arab point of view, see, e.g., John B. Quigley, "Displaced Palestinians and a Right of Return," 34 Harvard International Law Journal (1998) 171-229, reprinted in Victor Kattan, ed., *The Palestine Question in International Law* (London: British Institute of International and Comparative Law, 2008), 41-100. On the Israeli point of view, see, e.g., Yaffa Zilbershats and Nimra Goren-Amittai, *Return of Palestinian Refugees into Area of the State of Israel* (Ruth Gavison, ed.) (Jerusalem, 2010) (Hebrew).

31 GAOR, 3rd session, part I, 1948, Resolutions, pp. 21-24.

32 See, e.g., Ruth Lapidoth, "Are There Viable Solutions to the Palestinian Refugee Problem?," 39 Justice (Jerusalem) (2004) 17-18.

DEFENDING ISRAEL'S LEGAL RIGHTS TO JERUSALEM

Dore Gold

In modern history, nations are measured not by their military strength or economic performance alone, but by their inner conviction about the justice of their cause. Forty-four years ago, at the end of the 1967 Six-Day War, when Israeli paratroopers reached the Western Wall and their commander, Motta Gur, announced "*Har Habyit Beyadainu*" ("the Temple Mount is in our hands"), there was no doubt over the fact that Israel had waged a just war. Overseas, Israel's representatives in the 1960s and 1970s, like Abba Eban and Chaim Herzog, reiterated Israel's rights to Jerusalem before the world community, which may not have always supported them, but at least understood Israel's determination to defend them.

But something has happened since those days. While the arguments they used are still relevant today, they have been forgotten in many quarters. Therefore, Jerusalem is in a paradoxical situation. While Israel has legal rights to retain a united city as its capital, there is a sense that its claim is being challenged more than ever. Indeed, there are multiple arguments being sounded as to why Israel should acquiesce to Jerusalem's re-division.

What makes this particularly troubling is that Jerusalem, in the words of the British historian Sir Martin Gilbert, has always been seen as a "microcosm" of Jewish historical rights.[1]In 70 CE when the Jewish people lost their national sovereignty to the Roman Empire, it was the fall of Jerusalem that marked the end of the Jewish state. Conversely, when the Jewish people restored their majority in Jerusalem in the mid-nineteenth century, they did so before reaching a majority in any other part of their ancestral homeland. Indeed, their movement for the revival of a Jewish state was called "Zionism," exemplifying the centrality of Jerusalem for the overall Jewish national movement.

Jerusalem, in short, has been the focal point of the idea of Jewish national self-determination. Ernst Frankenstein, a British-based authority on international law in the inter-war period, made the case for arguing the legal rights of the Jewish people to restore their homeland by stating that they never relinquished title to their land after the Roman conquests. For that to have happened, the Romans and their Byzantine successors would have had to be in "continuous and undisturbed possession" of the land with no claims being voiced. Yet Jewish resistance movements continued for centuries, most of which were aimed at liberating Jerusalem.[2]

From the standpoint of international law, the fact that the Jewish people never renounced their historic connection to their ancestral homeland provided the basis for their assertion of their historical rights.[3]This came to be understood by those who wrote about the Jewish legal claim to the Land of Israel, as a whole. In the Blackstone Memorial, which was signed by Chief Justice of the U.S. Supreme Court Melville Fuller, university presidents, and members of Congress before it was submitted to President Benjamin Harrison in 1891, Palestine is characterized as "an inalienable possession" of the Jewish people "from which they were expelled by force."[4] In short, they did not voluntarily abandon their land or forget their rights. This was most fervently expressed through centuries of lamentation for Jerusalem's destruction and their constant prayer for its restoration. Jerusalem was the focal point for the historical connection of the Jewish people to the Land of Israel.

That is why it is essential to understand Israel's rights in Jerusalem, as they were known once before. That is also why it is necessary to identify the arguments that have been employed in recent years with the aim of eroding those rights, and the conviction that once underpinned them, in order to protect Jerusalem for future generations. In addition to the historical rights of the Jewish people to Jerusalem that were voiced in the nineteenth century, and were just briefly reviewed, there is a whole new layer of legal rights that Israel acquired in modern times that need to be fully elaborated upon.

MODERN SOURCES OF ISRAEL'S INTERNATIONAL RIGHTS IN JERUSALEM

In 1970, three years after the 1967 Six-Day War, an article appearing in the most prestigious international legal periodical, *The American Journal of International Law*, touched directly on the question of Israel's rights in Jerusalem.[5] It became a critical reference point for Israeli ambassadors speaking at the UN in the immediate decades that followed and also found its way into their speeches. The article was written by an important, but not yet well-known, legal scholar named Stephen Schwebel. In the years that followed, Schwebel's stature would grow immensely with his appointment as the legal advisor of the U.S. Department of State, and then finally when he became the President of the International Court of Justice in The Hague. In retrospect, his legal opinions mattered and were worth considering very carefully.

Schwebel wrote his article, which was entitled "What Weight to Conquest," in response to a statement by then Secretary of State William Rogers that Israel was only entitled to "insubstantial alterations" in the pre-1967 lines. The Nixon administration had also hardened U.S. policy on Jerusalem as reflected in its statements and voting patterns in the UN Security Council. Schwebel strongly disagreed with this approach: he wrote that the pre-war lines were not sacrosanct, **for the 1967 lines were not an international border.** Formally, they were only armistice lines from 1949. As he noted, the armistice agreement itself did not preclude the territorial claims of the parties beyond those lines. Significantly, he explained that when territories are captured in a war, the circumstances surrounding the outbreak of the conflict directly affect the legal rights of the two sides, upon its termination.

Two facts from 1967 stood out that influenced his thinking:

First, Israel had acted in the Six-Day War in the lawful exercise of its right of self-defense. Those familiar with the events that led to its outbreak recall that Egypt was the party responsible for the initiation of hostilities, through a series of steps that included the closure of the Straits of Tiran to Israeli shipping and the proclamation of a blockade on Eilat, an act that Foreign Minister Abba Eban would characterize as the firing of the first shot of the war. Along Israel's eastern front, Jordan's artillery had opened fire, pounding civilian neighborhoods in Jerusalem, despite repeated warnings issued by Israel.

Given this background, Israel had not captured territory as a result of aggression, but rather because it had come under armed attack. In fact, the Soviet Union had tried to have Israel labeled as the aggressor in the UN Security Council on June 14, 1967, and then in the UN General Assembly on July 4, 1967. But Moscow completely failed. At the Security Council it was outvoted 11-4. Meanwhile at the General Assembly, 88 states voted against or abstained on the first vote of a proposed Soviet draft (only 32 states supported it). It was patently clear to the majority of UN members that Israel had waged a defensive war.[6]

A second element in Schwebel's thinking was the fact Jordan's claim to legal title over the territories it had lost to Israel in the Six-Day War was very problematic. The Jordanian invasion of the West Bank – and Jerusalem – nineteen years earlier in 1948 had been unlawful. As a result, Jordan did not gain legal rights in the years that followed, given the legal principle, that Schwebel stressed, according to which **no right can be born of an unlawful act** (*ex injuria jus non oritur*) . It should *not* have come as a surprise that Jordan's claim to sovereignty over the West Bank was not recognized by anyone, except for Pakistan and Britain. Even the British would not recognize the Jordanian claim in Jerusalem itself.

Thus, by comparing Jordan's illegal invasion of the West Bank to Israel's legal exercise of its right of self-defense, Schwebel concluded that "Israel has better title" in the territory of what once was the Palestine Mandate than either of the Arab states with which it had been at war. He specifically stated that Israel had better legal title to "**the whole of Jerusalem**."

Schwebel makes reference to UN Security Council Resolution 242 from November 22, 1967, which over the years would become the main source for all of Israel's peace efforts, from the 1979 Egyptian-Israeli Treaty of Peace to the 1993 Oslo Accords. In its famous withdrawal clause, Resolution 242 did not call for a full withdrawal of Israeli forces from all the territories it captured in the Six-Day War. There was no effort to re-establish the **status quo ante**, which, as noted earlier, was the product of a previous act of aggression by Arab armies in 1948.

As the U.S. ambassador to the UN in 1967, Arthur Goldberg, pointed out in 1980, Resolution 242 did not even mention Jerusalem "and this omission was deliberate." Goldberg made the point, reflecting the policy of the Johnson administration for whom he served, that he never described Jerusalem as "occupied territory," though this changed under President Nixon.[7] What Goldberg wrote about Resolution 242 had added weight, given the fact that he previously had served as a Justice on the U.S. Supreme Court.

Indeed, among the leading jurists in international law and diplomacy, Schwebel was clearly not alone. He was joined by Julius Stone, the great Australian legal scholar, who reached the same conclusions. He added that UN General Assembly Resolution 181 from 1947 (also known as the Partition Plan) did not undermine Israel's subsequent claims in Jerusalem. True, Resolution 181 envisioned that Jerusalem and its environs would become a *corpus separatum*, or a separate international entity. But Resolution 181 was only a recommendation of the General Assembly. It was rejected by the Arab states forcibly, who invaded the nascent State of Israel in 1948.

Ultimately, the UN's *corpus separatum* never came into being in any case. The UN did not protect the Jewish population of Jerusalem from invading Arab armies. Given this history, it was not surprising that Israel's first prime minister, David Ben-Gurion, announced on December 3, 1949, that Revolution 181's references to Jerusalem were "null and void," thereby anticipating Stone's legal analysis years later.[8]

There was also Prof. Elihu Lauterpacht of Cambridge University, who for a time served as legal advisor of Australia and as a judge ad hoc of the International Court of Justice in The Hague. Lauterpacht argued that Israel's reunification of Jerusalem in 1967 was legally valid.[9] He explained that the last state which had sovereignty over Jerusalem was the Ottoman Empire, which ruled it from 1517 to 1917.

After the First World War, the Ottoman Empire formally renounced its sovereignty over Jerusalem as well as all its former territories south of what became modern Turkey in the Treaty of Sevres from 1920. This renunciation was confirmed by the Turkish Republic as well in the Treaty of Lausanne of 1923. According to Lauterpacht, the rights of sovereignty in Jerusalem were vested with the Principal Allied and Associated Powers, which transferred them to the League of Nations.

But with the dissolution of the League of Nations, the British withdrawal from Mandatory Palestine, and the failure of the UN to create a *corpus separatum* or a special international regime for Jerusalem, as had been intended according to the 1947 Partition Plan, Lauterpacht concluded that sovereignty had been put in suspense or in abeyance. In other words, by 1948 there was what he called "a vacancy of sovereignty" in Jerusalem.

It might be asked if the acceptance by the pre-state Jewish Agency of Resolution 181 constituted a conscious renunciation of Jewish claims to Jerusalem back in 1947. However, according to the resolution, the duration of the special international regime for Jerusalem would be "in the first instance for a period of ten years." The resolution envisioned a referendum of the residents of the city at that point in which they would express "their wishes as to possible modifications of the regime of the city."[10] The Jewish leadership interpreted the *corpus separatum* as an interim arrangement that could be replaced. They believed that Jewish residents could opt for citizenship in the Jewish state in the meantime. Moreover, they hoped that the referendum would lead to the *corpus seperatum* being joined to the State of Israel after ten years.[11]

Who then could acquire sovereign rights in Jerusalem given the "vacancy of sovereignty" that Lauterpacht described? Certainly, the UN could not assume a role, given what happened to Resolution 181. Lauterpacht's answer was that Israel filled "the vacancy in sovereignty" in areas where the Israel Defense Forces had to operate in order to save Jerusalem's Jewish population from destruction or ethnic cleansing. The same principle applied again in 1967, when Jordanian forces opened fire on Israeli neighborhoods and the Israel Defense Forces entered the eastern parts of Jerusalem, including its Old City, in self-defense.

A fourth legal authority to contribute to this debate over the legal rights of Israel was Prof. Eugene Rostow, the former dean of Yale Law School and Undersecretary of State for Political Affairs in the Johnson administration. Rostow's point of departure for analyzing the issue of Israel's rights was the Mandate for Palestine, which specifically referred to "the historic connection of the Jewish people with Palestine" providing "the grounds forreconstituting their national home in that country." These rights applied to Jerusalem as well, for the Mandate did not separate Jerusalem from the other territory that was to become part of the Jewish national home.

Rostow contrasts the other League of Nations mandates with the mandate for Palestine. Whereas the mandates for Iraq, Syria, and Lebanon served as trusts for the indigenous populations, the language of the Palestine Mandate was entirely different. It supported the national rights of the Jewish people while protecting only the civil and religious rights of the non-Jewish communities in British Mandatory Palestine.[12] It should be added that the Palestine Mandate was a legal instrument in the form of a binding international treaty between the League of Nations, on the one hand, and Britain as the mandatory power, on the other.

Rostow argued that the mandate was not terminated in 1947. He explained that Jewish legal rights to a national home in this territory, which were embedded in British Mandatory Palestine, survived the dissolution of the League of Nations and were preserved by the United Nations in Article 80 of the UN Charter.[13] Clearly, after considering Rostow's arguments, Israel was well-positioned to assert its rights in Jerusalem and fill "the vacancy of sovereignty" that Lauterpacht had described.

WHY DO ALL THESE LEGAL OPINIONS MATTER?

There will be those who will ask: What is the significance of all these legal opinions by various scholars? Why do they matter? Are they important for establishing Israel's legal claims in Jerusalem? International law is not like domestic law – there is no global government that adopts legislation. So what then determines what is legal and what is illegal? Of course there are treaties and international custom. The Statute of the International Court of Justice in The Hague (ICJ) specifically describes "the teachings of the most highly qualified publicists of the various nations" (Article 38) as one of the four sources of international law upon which international courts are to rely.

In short, what the leading experts of international law wrote after the 1967 Six-Day War matters. When it came to defending Israel's rights to Jerusalem, their writings were extremely clear. Israel had rightful claims to be sovereign in Jerusalem. Of course that does not preclude the UN General Assembly rejecting Israel's argument and denying its legal rights. However, if one compares the relative authority of what the intellectual giants of international law wrote after the Six-Day War to non-binding resolutions of the UN General Assembly, then the writings of Schwebel and Lauterpacht win hands-down.

In the years that followed, Israel's rights to preserving a united Jerusalem became axiomatic. In 1990, both houses of the U.S. Congress adopted Senate Concurrent Resolution 106, which acknowledged that "Jerusalem is and should remain the capital of Israel." It expressed its support for Jerusalem remaining "an undivided city." It acknowledged that since Jerusalem's unification under Israel, religious freedom had been guaranteed. More Congressional resolutions to this effect on Jerusalem were adopted in 1992 and 1995. Israel's legal rights to Jerusalem were not even an issue. Moreover, those rights were not just theoretical. They had strong political backing.

THE EFFORTS TO ERODE ISRAEL'S RIGHTS

However, this discussion about the legality of Israel's claims to a united Jerusalem raises a fundamental question. If Israel's legal case is so strong, why is Israel's back against the wall in the diplomatic struggle over Jerusalem today? What happened? What has eroded Israel's standing on this issue? Was this change caused by skillful Palestinian diplomacy or by a shifting Israeli consensus – or both? The defense of Israel's rights in Jerusalem today requires first and foremost an answer to this question.

What is undeniable is that in the last seventeen years a number of **key misconceptions** about Jerusalem took hold in the highest diplomatic circles in the West as well as in the international media. Some misconceptions were the product of misinformation. Others were the result of deliberate efforts to misrepresent what happened in past negotiations and to mislead the public. Regardless of their source, these misconceptions provided the political ammunition to those who sought to erode and undermine Israel's standing in Jerusalem, forcing it to consider concessions that were unthinkable twenty years ago. Israeli foreign policy had managed to protect Jerusalem for decades, but the diplomatic armor that it had employed began to crack from a determined political assault that followed.

1. DISTORTING ISRAEL'S STANCE: THE GROWING IMPRESSION IN THE 1990s THAT ISRAEL WAS PREPARED TO CONCEDE EASTERN JERUSALEM

When Israel signed the Oslo Agreements in 1993, for the first time since 1967 it agreed to make Jerusalem an issue for future negotiations. That did not mean that Prime Minister Yitzhak Rabin planned to divide Jerusalem. But Palestinian leaders celebrated Israel's acquiescence at the time to putting Jerusalem on the negotiating table.

Nabil Shaath, a Palestinian minister and negotiator, commented at the time: "The Israelis up to this agreement never accepted that the final status of Jerusalem be on the agenda of the permanent status negotiations." Faisal al-Husseini, who became a minister without portfolio for Jerusalem Affairs in the Palestinian Authority, also remarked: "In the Oslo Accords it was established that the status of Jerusalem is open to negotiations on the final arrangement, and the moment you say yes to negotiations, you are ready for a compromise."

Rabin, it should be stated, did not accept this position. To his credit, on October 5, 1995, one month before he was assassinated, he detailed to the Knesset his vision for a permanent status arrangement with the Palestinians, in which he stated: "First and foremost, united Jerusalem, which will include both Ma'ale Adumim and Givat Ze'ev – as the capital of Israel, under Israeli sovereignty, while preserving the rights of the members of the other faiths, Christianity and Islam, to freedom of access and freedom of worship in their holy places, according to their customs and beliefs." In short, Rabin, who had agreed to the Oslo Agreements two years earlier, firmly opposed the re-division of Jerusalem.

In fact, Rabin had a completely different scenario for handling the question of Jerusalem. He secretly negotiated with Jordan what became known as the 1994 Washington Declaration, recognizing the traditional role of the Hashemites as the custodians of the Muslim shrines on the Temple Mount. This Israeli recognition of Jordan's role in the Islamic sites was incorporated into the Israeli-Jordanian Treaty of Peace.

The Jordanian role in Jerusalem envisioned by Rabin had nothing to do with dividing sovereignty, but was supposed to be confined to strictly religious functions. Its practicability was dependent on Jordan's resolve to maintain this role, despite Palestinian encroachments. Yet regardless of the clarity of Rabin's position, there was a growing perception that Israel was preparing itself to make concessions over sovereignty that Rabin never intended.

2. THE MYTHOLOGY OF BACKCHANNEL CONTACTS: BUILDING THE CASE IN THE WEST THAT THERE WAS A WORKABLE FORMULA FOR DIVIDING JERUSALEM

With Jerusalem defined as an issue for future negotiations, there has been an entire intellectual industry that has been busy trying to prove that an Israeli-Palestinian deal on Jerusalem is doable. Take, for instance, what is known as the Beilin-Abu Mazen understandings from October 31, 1995. The idea put forward in those backchannel contacts was that the Palestinians would obtain a capital in the village of Abu Dis, outside of Jerusalem's municipal borders, as defined by Israel, but inside the area that was defined as the county of Jerusalem *(muhafiz)* under Jordan.

These negotiations were hailed worldwide for their creativity in the most important print media outlets from the *New York Times* to *Ha'aretz*. It is interesting to look back and see how the *New York Times* reported them on August 1, 1996; it wrote, "the Palestinians had dropped demands to establish their capital in East Jerusalem." The newspaper reported additionally later on in the article that there would be future negotiations on sovereignty over East Jerusalem, but few noticed this fine print.

In time, Israelis gained the impression that there was a painless formula that could be used for resolving Israeli-Palestinian differences over this extremely difficult subject. Thomas Friedman was also convinced and wrote on September 22, 1997, that a possible final settlement deal on Jerusalem "had been worked out" based on a Palestinian capital in Abu Dis. In his memoirs, Dennis Ross writes that the Beilin-Abu Mazen understandings proved "that even the most existential issues could be resolved."

But was this true? What few knew at the time was that the Palestinian leadership never viewed Abu Dis as an acceptable alternative to its claims to Jerusalem, but rather as a forward position that it would obtain on an interim basis, so that it could increase its hold on its true objective: the Old City of Jerusalem. Moreover, there was the question of the exact status of these understandings. The fact of the matter was that Abu Mazen never signed the 1995 document. Neither Rabin nor Peres approved of its contents. Yasser Arafat called the unsigned Beilin-Abu Mazen exchanges "a basis for further negotiations."

In typical fashion, Arafat managed to pocket the Israeli concessions without undertaking any firm Palestinian commitments himself. More importantly, he managed to pull Israel into a detailed negotiation over Jerusalem, which would set it down the road of more concessions in the future. By May 1999, Abu Mazen appeared on Palestinian Television and disassociated himself completely from the record of his backchannel contacts. He declared: "there is no document, no agreement, and no nothing."[14] Nonetheless, the legacy of these backchannel contacts fired up the imaginations of Israeli and American negotiators years later, who confidently went to Camp David in July 2000 with the expectation that they just might resolve the Israeli-Palestinian conflict, especially the dispute over Jerusalem.

Even after negotiations failed, the myth of bridgeable differences over Jerusalem persisted. After the Camp David summit adjourned in July 2000, Israelis and Palestinians subsequently met in Taba at the end of the year.

At the end of the Taba talks, Israel's foreign minister, Shlomo Ben Ami, was interviewed on Israel Radio and asserted that the parties had "never been so close to reaching an agreement." The Israeli interviewer then asked Muhammad Dahlan, the Gaza security chief, if indeed the parties had never been so close. Dahlan replied in Hebrew slang: "*Kharta barta*" (baloney). Ben Ami's Palestinian counterpart, Abu Ala, was more diplomatic than Dahlan but did not differ with his conclusions: "Now that the ambiguity has been removed, there has never before been a clearer gap in the positions of the two sides."[15]

In fact, in the European Union summaries of the Taba talks, Ambassador Miguel Moratinos revealed that Israel and the Palestinians could not even agree over who had sovereignty over the Western Wall. To this day, the belief persists that a deal over Jerusalem is possible. While this myth is based on misconceptions about the history of Israeli-Palestinian diplomacy, it still feeds misinformed policymakers worldwide.

3. CREATING QUASI-LEGALITY FROM THE PAST DIPLOMATIC RECORD: IS ISRAEL SOMEHOW BOUND TO DIVIDE JERUSALEM BECAUSE IT WAS PROPOSED IN PAST NEGOTIATIONS?

The failed negotiations over Jerusalem, while not producing any signed agreements, nonetheless badly eroded Israel's claims for successive governments. The diplomatic experiment that former Prime Minister Ehud Barak attempted was based on a rule that was supposed to reassure the Israeli side: **"nothing is agreed until everything is agreed."** This approach assumed that if Barak wanted to test the Palestinian side with an idea for dividing Jerusalem, it would be removed from the negotiating table if no overall agreement was reached.

In this spirit, when President Bill Clinton put forward his famous "parameters" for a peace settlement at the White House on December 23, 2000, which contained a proposal for dividing Jerusalem along ethno-religious lines, he stipulated: "These are my ideas. If they are not accepted, they are off the table, they go with me when I leave office." This was not just a theoretical commitment, for Clinton refused to go along with initiatives to take his parameters to the UN Security Council and lock future Israeli governments into the concessions that they would have required, through a new UN Security Council resolution.[16]

At the heart of Clinton's proposal was an idea that sounded simple but would have been disastrous for Jerusalem: "The general principle is that Arab areas are Palestinian and Jewish ones are Israeli. This would apply to the Old City as well." In practice, if Jerusalem was a checkerboard of Jewish and Palestinian squares, Clinton's idea would have put each square under a different sovereignty.

It was no wonder that the Israeli security establishment completely rejected Clinton's plan. At the end of December 2000, Israel's chief of staff, Lt.-Gen. Shaul Mofaz, told the Barak government: "The

Clinton bridging proposal is inconsistent with Israel's security interests and if it will be accepted, it will threaten the security of the state."[17] He specifically warned that the Clinton Plan would turn Jewish neighborhoods in Jerusalem into enclaves within Palestinian sovereign territory that would be hard to defend.

Mofaz was not only speaking for himself, but for the entire general staff of the IDF. These conclusions were not a secret; they appeared in the headlines of a Friday *Yediot Ahronot*. Nonetheless, the people of Israel could be comforted that the State of Israel was not legally bound in any way to the Clinton Parameters, which had been so strongly condemned by the heads of the IDF.

Unfortunately, these formalities turned out to be a total fiction. True, in 2001, the Bush administration informed the Sharon government that the Clinton Parameters were indeed off the table. But many former Clinton officials kept them alive behind the scenes. They began using the refrain that "we all know what the outline of a solution is supposed to look like." That outline included the re-division of Jerusalem. These ideas were not supported by the elected government of Israel, under Prime Minister Ariel Sharon. The Bush administration did not advocate them either. These ideas survived, however, in well-funded research institutes and think tanks inside Washington's capital beltway.

For example, appearing at the Council on Foreign Relations in June 2003, President Clinton's national security advisor, Sandy Berger, typified this approach when he said: "I believe that the contours that we were talking about at Camp David and that later were put out in the Clinton plan in December, and then later [were] even further developed in Taba are ultimately the contours that we will embrace." These ideas also re-surfaced in the 2003 Geneva Initiative, which did not represent the official positions of the Israeli government, but nonetheless kept alive the idea that Jerusalem was to be divided.

The mantra that "we all know what the outline of a solution is supposed to be" turned out to be extremely problematic. What was the underlying assumption behind these statements? How do we all know? How can anyone make this assertion with any degree of certainty? Did Israel sign anything? Did it obligate itself to make concessions on Jerusalem? Instead of asking why Arab-Israeli diplomacy failed during the later 1990s, conducting a reassessment, and coming up with a different approach, former officials dug in deeper into the ideas that had been raised in Camp David and Taba, and tried to enshrine them – including on the issue of Jerusalem. It seemed that there was a shared interest by those who engaged in this activity in binding Israel to the diplomatic record of failed negotiations and to the concessions of previous Israeli governments.

What happened in the course of time was that these proposals seeped back from Washington think tanks and research institutes through the back door to the official level. It was a natural though highly problematic process. There were conferences, seminars, and brown-bag lunches held in private Washington offices where former officials mingled with their successors. The veterans of the diplomacy of the 1990s briefed new politicians coming to Washington, as well. Presidential candidates also sought advice for their future positions, and the record of Camp David and Taba became the new conventional wisdom that was bantered about, without much thought. What emerged was a kind of inevitability that foreign policy experts shared that Jerusalem would have to be divided and Israel's historic rights to a united city were simply forgotten.

Palestinian negotiators contributed to this process. After the U.S. elections in 2008, they presented a summary of their past negotiations with Prime Minister Olmert to the incoming Obama foreign policy team. Secretary of State Condoleezza Rice summarized this material in an 11-page document presented to President Obama. Was this a signed Israeli-Palestinian agreement? No. But it was followed by Palestinian claims that negotiations needed to be resumed where they last broke off, as though a new Israeli government had to accept the concessions of its predecessor, including on the issue of Jerusalem. For example, in a U.S.-Palestinian meeting on September 16, 2009, Saeb Erekat asked: "Why not 'resume' negotiations where parties let off?" David Hale, the deputy to U.S. Middle East envoy George Mitchell, appropriately responded: "We prefer 'relaunch' since there was no agreement – nothing is agreed until everything is agreed."[18]

4. THE JEWISH PEOPLE AS COLONIALIST LATECOMERS TO JERUSALEM

The most ubiquitous argument used against Israel's claims in Jerusalem contends that the Jewish people are an alien presence and at best latecomers to the Holy City. Professor Walid Khalidi, one of the most prominent and articulate Palestinian historians, spoke before a UN committee convened to consider the question of Jerusalem on November 30, 2009. Unfortunately, he started out with this feature of the Palestinian narrative. He placed Israel's control of Jerusalem right in the middle of the struggle between Islam and the West. The effort by Israel to re-unify Jerusalem, he explained, was a "latter-day Western crusade by proxy." Jewish immigration and colonization emanated from Zionism, which he characterized as a "Russian nationalist movement."[19]

Khalidi's narrative left out the simple truth that the Jewish people actually restored their clear-cut majority in Jerusalem not in 1948 or in 1967 but in 1863, according to British consular records.[20] Prussia's consulate was reporting a Jewish plurality already in 1845, when the Jews constituted the largest religious group in Jerusalem. This transformation in Jerusalem occurred well before the arrival of the British Empire in the First World War and the issuing of the Balfour Declaration. It even preceded the actions of Theodor Herzl and the First Zionist Congress. Indeed, in 1914 on the eve of the First World War there were 45,000 Jews in Jerusalem out of a total population of 65,000.[21]

The Jewish majority in Jerusalem reflected the simple fact that the Jewish people had been streaming back to their ancient capital for centuries, despite the dangers to their physical well-being that this entailed and the discriminatory taxes imposed by the Ottoman Empire on its non-Muslim subjects. In the mid-nineteenth century, Baghdad and Damascus were Arab cities, but Jerusalem was already a Jewish city. A careful reading of the Mandate document in fact indicates that the British and the League of Nations were fully cognizant that the Jewish rights they acknowledged were not created with the advent of the First World War. The Mandate itself referred to a pre-existing Jewish claim by specifically basing itself on the "historical connection of the Jewish people with Palestine."

This historical connection is precisely what Palestinian spokesmen have been determined to refute and challenge. In order to reinforce the image of the Palestinian Arabs as the authentic native population of Jerusalem, former PLO Chairman Yasser Arafat added another twist. In his UN speech, Khalidi traces Islamic claims to Jerusalem to the year 638, when the second caliph, Umar bin al-Khattab, came out of the Arabian Peninsula and captured it from the Byzantine Empire.

But Arafat tied Palestinian historical claims to the Jebusites that ruled Jerusalem before King David made it the capital of ancient Israel. Arafat said his ancestors were Canaanite kings. Moreover, he rejected all ancient Jewish connections to Jerusalem by even denying the very existence of the Temple, when he argued over the future of Jerusalem with President Bill Clinton at the Camp David negotiations in July 2000.[22] It is too bad that during his many trips to Rome to meet with the Italian government, Arafat never stopped at the Arch of Titus where he could have seen the menorah and the vessels of the Temple that he claimed did not exist.

This doctrine of Temple denial in the Palestinian narrative has spread like wildfire in recent years. It has been used by Palestinian leaders from Saeb Erakat to Nabil Shaath. PLO Chairman Mahmoud Abbas has also adopted them. When Palestinian Prime Minister Salam Fayyad spoke at the UN General Assembly in November 2008 and devoted his remarks to Jerusalem, it was glaringly noticeable that he spoke about Christian and Muslim links to the city without mentioning a single word about Jewish ties to Jerusalem.

Unfortunately, Western audiences have often bought uncritically into much of this false narrative which was devised to erode Israel's rights. For example, *Time* magazine described the Temple Mount in October 2003 as a place "where Jews *believe* Solomon and Herod built the First and Second Temples (emphasis added)." The Temple was no longer a fact of history but part of an Israeli narrative. It might have existed or maybe it didn't exist. With this doubt embedded, academia began to slip as well. The prestigious University of Chicago Press published a work by Nadia Abu El Haj calling the Temples a "national-historical tale." She subsequently taught at Barnard College.

The irony of this revisionist history is that the Temple is very much part of the history of traditional Islam. The great commentators of the Quran acknowledged the Temple, like al-Jalalayn, who sought to interpret the famous verse about Muhammad's night journey that opens Sura 17, "Glory to him who made His servant go by night from the Sacred Mosque to the Farther Mosque." The Sacred Mosque was in Mecca, but what did the "Farther Mosque" refer to? Their answer was that the Farther Mosque was *Beit al-Maqdis*, which means the Temple, and sounds just like the Hebrew term, *Beit Hamikdash*.[23] That also became the Arabic term for Jerusalem. The Palestinians' use of Temple denial to undermine Israel's claims to Jerusalem not only flew in the face of archaeology and recorded history, it ironically negated their own Islamic tradition.

ISRAELI PUBLIC OPINION AND JERUSALEM

Despite the proliferation of misconceptions about Jerusalem, and the questions that have arisen about Israel's diplomatic stance in past years, the Israeli public, in fact, had not lost faith in

During 1948 synagogues and religious academies come under attack in the Old City of Jerusalem and are shelled by the artillery of the Arab Legion. Here, the Porat Yosef Yeshiva is destroyed. (Phillip John, Getty Images, 1948)

Jerusalem, despite articles that assert the Israeli consensus no longer insists on an undivided city.[24] The efforts to erode public support have not succeeded. According to a poll conducted for the Jerusalem Center for Public Affairs and released on June 6, 2011, by Dahaf Research under the direction of Dr. Mina Tzemach, the Israeli public still backs keeping Jerusalem united. When asked how important is preserving a united Jerusalem in the framework of a peace agreement, 69 percent answered very important, while 16 percent said important. That means **85 percent of the Israeli public still believes a united Jerusalem should be preserved.**

When asked about particular sites in Jerusalem, the results of the poll are very revealing. Responding to different possible concessions in the peace process, 62 percent said that they absolutely would not agree to a solution by which Israel would turn over the Temple Mount to the Palestinians, while Israel keeps the Western Wall. That was one of the scenarios for the Old City in the Clinton Parameters. Approximately 13 percent said they tend to disagree with such a proposal. **Putting these numbers together, 75 percent of Israelis who were asked, opposed giving up the Temple Mount as part of a peace settlement, even if Israel gets to keep the Western Wall.**

Palestinians stand atop the biblical Tomb of Joseph in the West Bank town of Nablus, October 7, 2000. Palestinian gunmen and civilians stormed the Israeli enclave, trashing Hebrew texts and setting fire to the holy site in a show of triumph just hours after Israeli troops evacuated the site. (AP Photo/Lefteris Pitarakis)

THE IMPORTANCE OF PROTECTING JERUSALEM'S HOLY SITES

This data illustrates that the people of Israel are attached to their holy sites in Jerusalem and understand what could happen to them if Israel were to concede them. These positions undoubtedly have been affected by Israel's own experiences. In 1948, after all, the Arab Legion took over the Jewish Quarter and began to systematically destroy or desecrate 55 synagogues and study halls, like the great Porat Yosef Yeshiva. The Old City's Jewish population was ethnically cleansed. The Yohanan Ben Zakai Synagogues became stables for the mules of the Old City's Arab residents. Meanwhile, the Jewish people were denied access to the Western Wall and their other holy sites from 1948 through 1967.

In modern times it is equally clear what would happen to religious sites if the Palestinians obtained control of the Old City. Under the Oslo Agreements, the Palestinian Authority was given responsibility for Jewish holy sites in the territories under its jurisdiction. On October 7, 2000, Joseph's Tomb in Nablus came under attack by a Palestinian mob that included Palestinian civilians and security forces. Hebrew texts were trashed, while the mob tried to dismantle the stones of the tomb with crow bars and pipes. They also cracked the tomb's dome as well. In April 2011, Israelis received another reminder about how the Palestinians fail to fulfill their responsibilities at holy sites, when Palestinian security personnel murdered Ben Yosef Livnat, who had visited Joseph's

Black smoke billows over the Church of the Nativity compound in the West Bank town of Bethlehem on April 11, 2002, after the church was seized by a joint unit of Fatah and Hamas. The clergy were taken hostage and the interior was desecrated. (AP Photo/Peter Dejong)

Tomb with a group of Breslover Chasidim. These events have reinforced Israeli concerns about who will protect the holy sites.

Christian sites have also been attacked under Palestinian rule. On April 2, 2002, a joint Fatah-Hamas force of thirteen terrorists entered the Church of the Nativity in Bethlehem and held the clergy as hostages for thirty-nine days. Generally, over the last decade and a half, holy sites have lost much of their traditional immunity and have come under attack by radical Islamic groups. This trend began when 2,000-year-old Buddhist statues in Afghanistan's Bamiyan Valley were blown up by the Taliban. This act was ultimately supported by Yusuf Qaradawi, the spiritual leader of the Muslim Brotherhood, which is the parent organization of Hamas. These attacks on non-Muslim religious sites have since spread from Pakistan to Iraq and most recently to Egypt, under the banner of radical Islam.

Internationalization is not an answer for Jerusalem either. In 1947, internationalization, in accordance with UN General Assembly Resolution 181, was proposed but was unworkable and ultimately failed. Jerusalem was invaded by three Arab armies. The only force that protected 100,000 Jews in Jerusalem from certain destruction were the forces of Israel. The UN did not lift a finger in 1948 against the threat that was posed to Jerusalem. There is no basis for thinking that an international body, containing members with conflicting interests, would be any more effective in the future than the UN was in 1948.

In short, Israel's own history, as well as more recent events, illustrates what is at stake in Jerusalem. Were Israel to agree to a re-division of Jerusalem, losing control of the Old City, the security of its holy sites would undoubtedly be put in jeopardy. **What Israeli diplomacy must make clear is that only a free and democratic Israel will protect Jerusalem for all faiths.**

Keeping Jerusalem open for all faiths is a historical responsibility of the State of Israel. Yet, Jerusalem has been at the heart of a great internal debate in Israel and the Jewish world more broadly. Many with a more particularistic orientation understand its reunification in 1967 as part of the national renewal of a people who had faced centuries of exile and even attempted genocide just a few decades earlier. It was where the Jews first restored a clear-cut majority back in 1863 at a time when the world began to recall and recognize their historical rights and title. Jerusalem was the meeting point between the nation's ancient history and its modern revival.

Others with a more universalistic view make a priority of integrating the modern State of Israel with the world community by using Jerusalem as a bargaining chip in a peace process presently under the auspices of the EU, Russia, the UN, and the U.S. In fact, the elaborate international ceremonies of world leaders orchestrated around the signing of each peace accord in the 1990s were intended to remind Israelis that their international acceptance, as well as the normalization of their relations with their Arab neighbors, was tied to this very diplomatic process.

The clash between the particularistic instincts inside Israel and its universalistic hopes has been at the heart of the country's political debate for forty years. Jerusalem, however, is where these two national instincts converge, for by protecting Jerusalem under Israeli sovereignty, the State of Israel also serves a universal mission of keeping the holy city truly free and accessible for peoples of all faiths. Particularists will have to understand that there are other religious groups with a stake in the future of the Holy City, while universalists will have to internalize that they have a great national legacy worth protecting for the world and that conceding it would condemn it to total uncertainty at best.

CONCLUSIONS

Prior to the granting of the Mandate for Palestine to Great Britain by the League of Nations, there were many proposals to restore the Jewish people to their ancestral homeland. From Napoleon Bonaparte's proclamation in 1799 to Theodore Roosevelt's writings in 1918, the idea of the historical rights of the Jewish people to their ancient homeland was linked to their rights to Jerusalem. Israel's first president, Chaim Weizmann, quoted in this context the Archbishop of Canterbury during a debate in the late 1930s in the British House of Lords, saying:

It seems to me extremely difficult to justify fulfilling the ideals of Zionism by excluding them from any place in Zion. How is it possible for us not to sympathise in this matter with the Jews? We all remember their age long resolve, lament and longing: "If I forget thee, 0 Jerusalem, let my right hand forget her cunning." They cannot forget Jerusalem.[25]

Thus the return to *Eretz Yisrael* (the Land of Israel) and the restoration of Jerusalem became understood in the West as inseparable aspirations.

Jewish refugees stream out of the Old City of Jerusalem in 1948 escaping the invading Arab Legion.
(Phillip John, Getty Images, 1948)

What struck legal experts writing in this period was the fact that the Jewish people never renounced those rights and indeed acted upon them through prayer, fasting, and pilgrimage. In the diplomacy of modern Israel, that refusal continued in one form or another, especially after the Six-Day War. Significantly, these rights were backed by some of the most important authorities on international law.

In the years of the Arab-Israeli peace process, proposals were raised and considered for the re-division of Jerusalem, but no binding agreements were actually reached and brought to the Knesset for ratification. Israeli opinion remained firm about the rights of the Jewish people to retain their united capital under the sovereignty of Israel. The recognition of those rights in the future by the international community will depend on Israel demonstrating that it alone will protect the Holy City for all faiths. This is a standard which Israel has met in the past and will undoubtedly continue to meet in the future.

NOTES

* This essay is an expanded version of an address given on June 6, 2011, for the Ingeborg Rennert Center for Jerusalem Studies.

1 Martin Gilbert, "Jerusalem: A Microcosm of Jewish Rights," *Israel at 60: Confronting the Rising Challenge to Its Historical and Legal Rights* (Jerusalem: Jerusalem Center for Public Affairs, 2009), p. 22.

2 William Foxwell Albright, et al., *Palestine: A Study of Jewish, Arab and British Policies*, Esco Foundation (New Haven: Yale University Press, 1947), vol. 1, p. 229. Ernst Frankenstein, *Justice for My People: The Jewish Case* (London: Nicholson & Watson, 1943), p. 88.The historical record in fact shows Jewish resistance continued with major armed revolts in 115 against Trajan, 135 against Hadrian, 351 against Gallus, and 614, when the Jews joined the Persians to fight Roman rule. See S. Safarai, "The Era of the Mishnah and Talmud," in H.H. Ben-Sasson (ed.), *A History of the Jewish People* (Cambridge: Harvard University Press, 1976), pp. 330-363.

3 J. Stoyanovsky, *The Mandate for Palestine: A Contribution to the Theory and Practice of International Mandates* (London: Longman, Green and Co., 1928), p. 65.

4 *Ibid.*, p. 241.

5 Stephen M. Schwebel, "What Weight to Conquest?" *American Journal of International Law* (1970):344-347.

6 John Norton Moore (ed.), *The Arab-Israel Conflict Volume IV: The Difficult Search for Peace (1975-1988), Part One* (Princeton: Princeton University Press, 1991), p. 815.

7 Arthur Goldberg, Letter to the Editor, *New York Times*, March 6, 1980.

8 "Letter of March 25, 1999, to the UN Security-General from the PLO Observer Concerning UN General Assembly Resolution 181," United Nations Document A/53/879, S/1999/334, March 24, 1999.

9 Elihu Lauterpacht, *Jerusalem and the Holy Places* (London: Anglo-Israel Association, 1968).

10 "United National General Assembly Resolution 181, November 29, 1947," The Avalon Project at Yale Law School, http://www.yale.edu/lawweb/avalon/un/res181.htm

11 Larry Kleter, "The Sovereignty of Jerusalem in International Law," *Columbia Journal of Transnational Law*, Vol. 20, 1981, p. 350.

12 Eugene V. Rostow, Correspondence, *American Journal of International Law*, July 1990.

13 Eugene V. Rostow, "The Future of Palestine," McNair Paper 24 (Washington: National Defense University, 1993), p. 10.

14 Yael Yehoshua, "Abu Mazen: A Political Profile," Special Report No. 15, MEMRI – The Middle East Media Research Institute, April 29, 2003, http://www.memri.org/report/en/0/0/0/0/0/0/856.htm.

15 "Palestinian Reports on the Taba Negotiations," MEMRI Special Dispatches, No. 184, February 7, 2001, http://www.memri.org/report/en/0/0/0/0/0/0/419.htm.

16 There have been reports that Foreign Minister Shlomo Ben Ami hoped to enshrine the concessions he offered on Jerusalem at the UN Security Council. He admits in his Hebrew memoirs that the U.S. Ambassador to the UN, Richard Holbrooke, warned him that the UN should only be used to endorse an agreement that would be achieved in the future, but it should not *mandate* the solution. See Shlomo Ben Ami, *A Front without a Rearguard: A Voyage to the Boundaries of the Peace Process* (Tel Aviv: Yediot Books, 2004) [in Hebrew], p. 309.

17 *Yediot Ahronot*, December 29, 2000.

18 "Meeting Minutes: Saeb Erekat and David Hale," *Aljazeera Transparency Unit*, http://www.ajtransparency.com/files/4835.pdf.

19 See Walid Khalidi, "Control of Jerusalem," http://www.youtube.com/watch?v=3x8BM0ry1nM&feature=BFa&list=PL001B57CA656A0C49&index=1.
For the classic presentation of the Palestinian legal case on Jerusalem, see Henry Cattan, *Jerusalem* (London: Saqi Books, 2000).

20 For the actual British cable, see Dore Gold, *The Fight for Jerusalem: Radical Islam, the West, and the Future of the Holy City* (Washington: Regnery, 2007), pp. 290-291.

21 Martin Gilbert, "Jerusalem: A Tale of One City," *New Republic*, November 14, 1994.

22 *Ibid.*, pp. 11-13.

23 *Ibid.*, p. 17.

24 James Carroll, "Netanyahu's Extremist Mistake," *Boston Globe*, June 6, 2011.

25 Regarding Napoleon's declaration to restore Jerusalem to the Jewish people, see Albright, et al., Volume 1, Page 2. Teddy Roosevelt's ideas about starting a Zionist state around Jerusalem appear in Michael B. Oren, *Power, Faith and Fantasy: American in the Middle East 1776 to Present* (New York: W. W. Norton, 2007), p. 359. President Weizmann>s address from December 1, 1948, in which he quotes the Archbishop of Canterbury, may be found at http://www.mfa.gov.il/MFA/Foreign+Relations/Israels+Foreign+Relations+since+1947/1947-1974/3+Israel+Claims+Jerusalem-+Address+by+President+We.htm

PALESTINIAN UNILATERALISM AND ISRAEL'S RIGHTS IN ARAB-ISRAELI DIPLOMACY

Dan Diker

INTRODUCTION

The Palestinian leadership's ongoing refusal to negotiate peace with Israel and its stated intention to seek endorsement of statehood at the United Nations along the 1949 armistice lines (1967 "borders") since 2009, represents a watershed in Arab-Israeli diplomacy. This is not the first time the Palestinian leadership made unilateral declarations of statehood. In fact, the current Palestinian leadership based its recent statehood bid on PLO Chairman Yasser Arafat's 1988 unilateral statehood declaration. However, in contrast to Arafat's past pronouncement, this latest Palestinian unilateral declaration to establish "Palestine" on the 1949 armistice lines was undertaken in a far more sophisticated way under more advantageous political circumstances for the Palestinians, and garnered broader support from UN member states and, notably, European powers.

The key elements of this revived Palestinian unilateral strategy require examination and assessment; how did pronouncements by the current Palestinian leadership garner Western support even while the Palestinian move undermines the entire framework of the Western-sanctioned and supported peace process established in Madrid in 1991 and then operationalized during the Oslo peace process? The Palestinian unilateral abrogation of Madrid's principles, which established the foundation for a negotiated solution, and the unilateral nullification of the subsequent framework of the Oslo process violated Israel's most fundamental rights in the peace process, a violation which appears to have been overlooked or ignored by many involved in the international diplomacy that has stuttered and seemingly ground to a halt.

The Palestinian leadership's tactical consideration of whether it ends up seeking formal UN endorsement in September 2011, is a minor matter compared to the major strategic achievement the Palestinians already pocketed. In any future diplomatic process, whether negotiated or unilateral, Palestinian unilateralism will have succeeded in levering up Palestinian legitimacy in the international community while effectively assaulting the legitimacy of Israel's fundamental rights and claims in Arab-Israeli diplomacy.

HOW SEPTEMBER 2011 IS DIFFERENT FROM ALL OTHERS

The Palestinian leadership under Chairman ("Ra'es") Mahmoud Abbas and Prime Minister Salam Fayyad made determined statements regarding their intention to seek UN endorsement of a unilaterally declared Palestinian state in September 2011.[1] The Palestinian statements were treated as far more than mere rhetoric; they triggered scrambling in international diplomatic circles. The Israeli Foreign Ministry formulated and executed a "battle plan" mobilizing its embassies worldwide against UN recognition of a Palestinian state.[2] U.S. President Barack Obama expressed firm U.S. opposition to any Palestinian unilateral move.[3] A majority of U.S. senators supported legislation outright rejecting the Palestinian plan.[4] For its part, Europe has been split over the issue. Italy and Germany have publicly opposed premature UN endorsement of a Palestinian state, while France and the United Kingdom had not decided one way or another just weeks before the expected UN vote. In South America, a swath of countries like Argentina, Bolivia, Brazil, Chile, Costa Rica, Cuba, Ecuador, Guyana, Nicaragua, Paraguay, Peru, Uruguay, and Venezuela recognized the Palestinian state,[5] with Colombia being the only country to declare its opposition to the unilateral declaration of Palestinian statehood.[6] Similar to the UN General Assembly's automatic majority in 1988 that endorsed PLO demands for recognition of Palestinian statehood, another GA endorsement of Palestinian demands for statehood would also likely win majority support.

WHAT HAS CHANGED SINCE THE 1988 PALESTINIAN STATEHOOD DECLARATION?

At first glance, it seems curious that Palestinian pronouncements triggered such frenetic diplomatic scurrying. As noted, the Palestinians first declared the establishment of "Palestine" as far back as November 1988, when Arafat made the unilateral pronouncement in Algiers and nominally accepted UN Security Council Resolutions 242 and 338, thereby accepting Israel's right to exist. Arafat's acceptance of UNSC 242 earned him an invitation to address the UN General Assembly Plenum where 104 countries voted to endorse "The proclamation of the State of Palestine by the Palestinian National Council on November 15, 1988."[7]

Only the United States and Israel voted against recognition. However, it was clear to most observers at the time that the Palestine Liberation Organization had failed to satisfy the international legal criteria required for statehood, including government control over a permanent population, a defined territory, and ability to engage in international relations.[8] Arafat was then in Tunis, where

PLO Chairman Yasser Arafat addresses the Palestine National Council in Algiers, November 12, 1988. (AP Photo)

the PLO was headquartered, and the Palestinians lacked control of permanent territory and were dispersed across the Middle East. However, a 1988 UN vote upgraded the Palestinian presence at the United Nations from "PLO" to "Palestine,"[9] eliciting U.S. threats to withhold all UN dues if the United Nations voted on a resolution construing Palestine as a state.[10]

Since 1988 much changed in international perception, if not reality, which upgraded international support for the has Palestinian unilateral statehood quest. The 1995 Interim has Agreement created a Palestinian Authority with governmental control over a Palestinian population in parts of the West Bank, and established a parliament, courts, stamps, and, according to Abbas, embassies in nearly one hundred countries.[11] Moreover, since 2007, Hamas exercised government control over the Gaza Strip, despite its definition as a terror organization by Europe and the United States. Notwithstanding the favorable international perception of a "Palestine" satisfying the statehood requirements of the 1933 Montevideo Conference, which Abbas himself trumpeted in a May 2011 *New York Times* op-ed,[12] even cursory examination indicates otherwise.[13]

Palestinian governmental and parliamentary elections were to have been held in January 2010. Their absence has rendered Palestinian Chairman Abbas and Prime Minister Fayyad unelected and invalid Palestinian leaders. Despite a nominal unity pact between Hamas and Fatah, Gaza is Hamas's territory and is ruled as a separate mini-state from the Palestinian Authority (Fatah) controlled and governed parts of the disputed West Bank. Hamas control of Gaza resulted in more than twelve thousand rockets fired at Israel since the 2005 Gaza withdrawal, while the West Bank's anti-terror security operations rely heavily on the Israel Defense Forces, despite the presence of about three thousand Palestinian gendarmerie forces.

A CAREFULLY CONSIDERED UNILATERAL STRATEGY TO ESTABLISH "PALESTINE"

The decision of the current Palestinian leadership to pursue a unilateral path to statehood and sidestep direct negotiations with Israel was a carefully weighed strategic option adopted well before the Netanyahu government took power in May 2009, although many believe Netanyahu's "hawkish" government prompted the ensuing declarations on unilateral Palestinian statehood by Abbas and Fayyad in the first six months of 2011.

This is not the case. The Palestinian leadership came to a strategic decision to pursue a unilateral path to statehood following the collapse of the 2008 Annapolis peace process between Abbas and Israeli Prime Minister Ehud Olmert. It was not, as is commonly thought in Western circles, a response to settlement policies of the Netanyahu government.[14] In fact, six months before the end of the Annapolis process, which coincided with Olmert's resignation in November 2008 due to corruption charges, the Palestinian leadership already began to speak of a "Kosovo option" for "Palestine," invoking Kosovo's February 2008 unilateral declaration of independence from Christian Serbia.[15] The United States and two-thirds of the European Union recognized Kosovo within weeks of its unilateral declaration, thus energizing Palestinian leaders.[16]

Palestinian Prime Minister Salam Fayyad, June 28, 2011 (AP Photo/Majdi Mohammed)

The Palestinian unilateral drive for statehood would pick up steam in the months ahead. Just ninety days after the inauguration of Israel's government in May 2009, when Benjamin Netanyahu, Israel's newly elected prime minister, announced a major shift in policy and accepted a Palestinian state with given security provisos, Fayyad announced a major two-year state-building project for the Palestinian-controlled areas of the West Bank, which he said would result in the creation of a "de facto" Palestinian state by September 2011. The Fayyad plan, as it came to be known, elicited great enthusiasm and gained broad financial and political backing from the United Nations, the Quartet, as well as European leaders and the Obama administration.[17]

The plan also paralleled Obama's publicly declared two-year timeline to Middle East peace via direct negotiations.[18] The common understanding in Washington, European capitals, and in the corridors of the United Nations was that in contrast to past Palestinian governments, Fayyad was building Palestinian civil society from the ground up, which was a longstanding U.S. demand that also paralleled the Netanyahu government's insistence on "economic peace" and "bottom-up" institution building in the Palestinian Authority as a prerequisite to any negotiated final status peace agreement.[19] To his credit, Fayyad, a U.S.-trained economist and respected statesman in international circles, broke the violent and failed Palestinian paradigm of belligerency that had characterized past processes with Israel.

However, aware of Israel's suspicions that his plan would serve as a unilateral *fait accompli* in 2011, Fayyad exploited his international reputation as a Western-style state reformer to foster the impression among donor nations and Western observers that the Palestinian state-building plan focused on ground-up state development, with no unilateral declaration attached, which would serve as the prerequisite infrastructure for any future peace agreement with Israel. In a press conference with U.S. lawmakers in Ramallah, Fayyad admitted, "I know some people are concerned that this is unilateral," referring to his development plan. "But it seems to me that it is unilateral in a healthy sense of self-development."[20]

However, the Fayyad plan's endgame was more than mere "self-development." It was a critical step in a sophisticatedly camouflaged unilateral bid for statehood. Attuned ears could detect the language and tone of an ultimatum that would result in a unilateral declaration of statehood or international endorsement of independence if Israel failed to accede to Palestinian demands, specifically that Israel recognize Palestinian sovereignty along the June 4, 1967 lines and cease all Jewish building to their east, including in Jerusalem, although those demands stood in complete contravention to signed agreements between the Palestinian Authority and the state of Israel, which amounts to a basic violation of international law.[21]

Nonetheless, Fayyad stood undeterred. He revealed his intentions to the Arab media shortly after the plan's announcement, saying, "If occupation has not ended by then [2011] and the nations of the world from China to Chile to Africa and to Australia are looking at us, they will say that the Palestinian people have a ready state on the ground. The only problem is the Israeli occupation [Israeli communities and security presence in Judea and Samaria] that should end."[22]

If there remained doubt regarding the overall goal both of Fayyad's plan and of broader Palestinian intentions, the PLO leadership reiterated and amplified declarations in 2011 that "the peace process is over" and that they would publicly declare statehood unilaterally.[23] Abbas publicly declared that he would refer the matter to the UN Security Council and/or the General Assembly where Palestinian Authority supporters would propose a resolution to recognize "Palestine" along the 1967 lines.[24]

SUPPORT FROM EUROPE

European interlocutors and even the European Union itself showed sympathy for Palestinian unilateral aspirations. For example, as early as July 2009, Javier Solana, the European Union's former foreign policy chief, reportedly called on the UN Security Council to recognize a Palestinian state even without a final status agreement between Israel and the Palestinians. He said the United Nations "would accept the Palestinian state as a full member of the UN, and set a calendar for implementation."[25] The Palestinian unilateral gambit also received a boost in early December 2009 when Sweden, in the final thirty days of its rotating EU presidency, proposed that EU foreign ministers back its draft proposal recognizing East Jerusalem as the capital of a future Palestinian state, thus implying EU acceptance of a Palestinian unilateral declaration of statehood.[26]

The EU Foreign Policy Council partly softened its final statement days later. However, the final EU statement still retained the proposal that envisioned Jerusalem as the future capital of two states. Additionally, the statement said that the EU "would not recognize any changes to the pre-1967 borders including with regard to Jerusalem" without the agreement of the parties, thereby enshrining the 1967 lines – a key Palestinian demand – as a previous political border.[27] This was a public expression of EU opposition to the Oslo framework to which the EU was signed as a formal witness signatory, and according to which Jerusalem was left to be negotiated as a final status issue.[28] Remarkably, the EU undermined its own credibility and the value of its own signature as diplomatic interlocutor not only for the Palestinian-Israeli peace process but for any future diplomatic processes that would require European intervention or assistance. The EU's support for the Palestinian position in this case also undermined its central role in the diplomatic Quartet, which established the Road Map that dictated that the peace process be based exclusively on bilateral negotiations.[29]

It should be noted that the intensification and imminence of the Palestinian approach to the United Nations brought the Quartet to elucidate its position. Despite past support for the Palestinian unilateral bid, the Quartet clarified in a statement on February 5, 2011, that "unilateral actions by either party cannot prejudge the outcome of negotiations and will not be recognized by the international community."[30]

However, other international bodies sent conflicting signals. In April 2011, the Palestinian unilateral statehood project received its biggest boost when the International Monetary Fund (IMF) issued a report asserting that if the Palestinian Authority "maintains its performance in institution building and delivery of public services, it is well positioned for the establishment of a state at any point in the near future."[31] It is notable that in the report's first footnote, it is mentioned that the experts who prepared the report were not the professionals from the main office in Brussels. Rather, they were the staff team of the IMF's Ramallah office with whom Fayyad worked very closely since his tenure as a senior IMF official in the West Bank from 1996 to 2001, and with whom close and even intimate cooperation continued until today.[32]

Upon closer inspection, the IMF report emphasizes that the Palestinian Authority's viability would remain heavily dependent on Israeli economic cooperation. The report notes that the PA cannot pay salaries without Israel's monthly transfers of several hundred million shekels.[33] Some Palestinian experts are less optimistic about the PA's economic viability as the Arab donor states paid approximately 30 percent of all contributions to the PA while Saudi Arabia has yet to make good on its pledge. In fact, Palestinian economist Ibrahim Abu Kamesh, writing in the Palestinian paper *Al-Hayat al-Jadida*, warned in June 2011 that "the Arab economic siege on the Palestinian Authority threatens to collapse the PA."[34] It is fair to assess that in the event of a Palestinian unilateral declaration of statehood and international endorsement, Israel would cease economic cooperation with the PA, which would have serious implications for the viability of a stable Palestinian state.

Unfortunately, the IMF report ignored Palestinian anti-Semitic and anti-Israeli indoctrination and incitement of children in schools and on Palestinian television in clear violation of the 1995 Oslo Interim Agreement and the 1991 Madrid Peace Conference principles that girded the Oslo peace process.[35] In short, as Moshe Yaalon, Israel's deputy prime minister and strategic affairs minister noted, there is "the requirement that the Palestinians at all levels of society inculcate in their people a culture of peace."[36] This public culture of violence and incitement is a violation of Israel's basic rights as outlined in the Oslo exchange of letters, as well as the principles of negotiations that were spelled out at Madrid and that will be discussed later in this chapter.

VIOLATING SIGNED AGREEMENTS AND UNDERMINING THE PEACE PROCESS FRAMEWORK

European expressions of support for Palestinian unilateralism are curious in view of the fact that the above-noted Palestinian unilateral action undermines the entire negotiated framework of the Palestinian-Israeli peace process as set forth in the 1993 exchange of letters between the PLO and Israel and detailed even more explicitly in the 1995 Interim Agreement, to which the European Union was a witness signatory along with the United Nations, the United States, Russia, Norway, Egypt, and Jordan,[37] and which still governs relations between the sides until a final permanent status agreement is achieved. As former Israeli Foreign Ministry legal adviser Alan Baker noted, the Palestinian unilateral action would:

- Nullify written assurances made by Arafat to Israeli Prime Minister Yitzhak Rabin in the 1993 Oslo exchange of letters that "all outstanding issues relating to permanent status will be resolved through negotiations."[38]
- Violate article XXXI(7) of the 1995 Palestinian-Israeli Interim Agreement according to which each party undertook not to initiate or take any step that would change the status of the West Bank and the Gaza Strip pending the outcome of the permanent status negotiations. In view of the fact that there has not yet been any outcome of the permanent status negotiations, the Palestinian unilateral action nullifies this commitment and would release Israel from its mutual obligation to avoid taking unilateral action.[39]
- Undermine the very legitimacy and legally sanctioned existence of the Palestinian Authority in view of the fact that the Interim Agreement serves as the legal basis and source of authority of the establishment of the Palestinian Authority itself, including its institutions, parliament, courts, and Office of the Chairman (Ra'es), the Chairman himself and his powers and authorities.[40]

UNITED NATIONS "*ULTRA VIRES*" ITS OWN PRINCIPLES

Palestinian unilateralism also drew encouragement from the United Nations itself, raising serious questions as to whether the UN is not acting *ultra vires* its own Charter principles and its own resolutions.

UN Secretary-General Ban Ki-moon reportedly issued expressions of support for such moves, according to Saeb Erekat in a November 14, 2009 interview with the Palestinian newspaper *Al-Ayyam*.[41] However, UN support for Palestinian unilateral actions including Palestinian declarations of intent to table a resolution of the Security Council and in the event of a U.S. veto to initiate a "Uniting for Peace" resolution in the General Assembly, [42] would amount to the UN engaging in actions that are clearly *ultra vires* the principles of negotiated settlement of disputes as set out both in the UN Charter and in the major Security Council resolutions regarding the Middle East peace process.

In the case of Palestinian unilateralism, and specifically in light of the demand that Israel dismantle its settlements, the United Nations is acting in a biased and even irresponsible manner. First, UN consideration of endorsement of a Palestinian state would be a gross violation of Article 80 of the UN Charter, which protects the League of Nations acceptance of the right of the Jewish people to "close settlement" of the lands of Judea and Samaria (the West Bank) as adopted unanimously by the Council of the League of Nations on July 24, 1922.

That League resolution determines the continued validity of the rights granted to all states or peoples, or already existing international instruments (including those adopted by the League itself). Therefore, the resolution remains valid, and the 650,000 Jews presently resident in the areas of Judea, Samaria, and eastern Jerusalem reside there legitimately.

As noted, the United Nations together with the European Union, the United States, Russia, Egypt, Jordan, and Norway witnessed the signing and acceptance of the 1995 Palestinian-Israeli Interim Agreement. This would render UN support of Palestinian unilateral action a violation of the UN's own credibility as witness signatory.

Palestinian unilateral moves utilizing the forum of the United Nations undermine the very basis of UN Security Council Resolution 242 of November 22, 1967, which served as the agreed-upon legal basis for Arab-Israeli diplomacy since the aftermath of the Six Day War in 1967 and which governed all Arab-Israeli diplomacy since that time including Madrid, Oslo, the 2003 Road Map, and the Annapolis peace process. A former U.S. ambassador to the United Nations, the late Richard Holbrooke, noted that UNSC 242 is considered the most important UN resolution on the Arab-Israel conflict of the past fifty years.[43]

Accordingly, UN support for, affirmation, acceptance, or endorsement of a Palestinian unilateral declaration at the UN undermines its very authority by adopting positions it has no authority to adopt, thereby undermining its own past legal decisions and recommendations and fundamentally threatening its very credibility as the world's primary international legal and diplomatic body.

UPROOTING THE PRINCIPLES OF ARAB-ISRAELI DIPLOMACY AT MADRID

The damage that the Palestinian unilateral race for statehood has done to the Middle East peace process goes well beyond the violations of signed agreements between the sides at Oslo and extends beyond the Palestinian destruction of the Oslo bilateral negotiating framework. It also undermined the broader framework of Arab-Israeli diplomacy that was first established at the 1991 Madrid Peace Conference. Madrid represented a defining moment in Arab-Israeli diplomacy. Its underlying principles of direct, unconditional negotiations between Israel and all of its Arab neighbors, and not just the Palestinians, under the protective umbrella of the principles of mutual compromise, recognition, and a strict code of conduct prohibiting incitement, served as the first substantial building blocks for a comprehensive peace agreement between Israel and the Arab world. The Palestinian unilateral bid for statehood undermined several principles of diplomacy established at Madrid that may prove virtually impossible to recover:

- **Respect for the mutuality of rights and claims of Israel and its neighbors.** Madrid's chief architect, U.S. Secretary of State James Baker, was careful to avoid establishing any preconditions or prejudicing Israel's rights. In a side letter to the United States prior to the conference, Prime Minister Yitzhak Shamir insisted that Jerusalem is not a subject for negotiation.[44] Israel's right to build communities on both sides of the June 4, 1967 "Green Line" and Israeli settlements were not considered an obstacle to advancing either bilateral talks with the Jordanian-Palestinian delegation or multilateral peace talks between Israel and its Arab neighbors.[45]

In contrast, since 2009, the Palestinian Authority, with the backing of the U.S. administration and Europe, made the cessation of Israeli settlement building a precondition for restarting Palestinian-Israeli negotiations, allowing the Palestinians to pursue a unilateral path with greater international support despite Israel's insistence that this precondition was not rooted in any past agreements or principles of past peace processes, which were established at Madrid.

- **The principle of a negotiated solution without imposed boundaries.** Former President George H. W. Bush refused to impose or suggest specific borders, telling the packed plenum at Madrid, "Throughout the Middle East, we seek a stable and enduring settlement. We've not defined what this means. Indeed, I make these points with no map showing where the final borders are to be drawn."[46] In stark contrast, Palestinian leaders Mahmoud Abbas and Salam Fayyad insist that "Palestine" will be born on the 1967 lines unilaterally. Their claims were strengthened by the public declaration of President Barack Obama, who, while opposing Palestinian unilateralism, provided it with a tailwind by reversing forty years of U.S. policy and publicly stating his administration's support for the 1967 lines as a basis for Israel's future borders.[47]

Palestinian President Mahmoud Abbas in Barcelona, Spain, July 20, 2011 (AP Photo/Manu Fernandez)

- **Code of conduct.** Incitement of any kind was prohibited at Madrid and mutual tolerance, cooperation, and respect were encouraged. The Palestinian Authority, and, blatantly and often, its newfound partner in coalition, Hamas, continued to incite Palestinians and Arab citizens of other countries in the region to violence, and engaged in a wholesale political assault against Israel thereby breaching the diplomatic code of conduct of Madrid and the subsequent Oslo Interim Agreement.

Furthermore, the attempt to unilaterally declare statehood most egregiously violates Madrid's provision that all moves leading to a peace agreement be made through direct negotiations with the other party, with respect to its territorial and security rights. As a former director-general of the Israeli Foreign Ministry and a negotiator at Madrid, Eytan Bentsur, noted in his memoir, "The United States called on the sides to refrain from unilateral acts, in word or deed, that could inflame tensions, cause reprisals, or still worse, harm or threaten the process itself."[48] A unilateral declaration of statehood by the Palestinians robs Israel of all its rights and negates the peace process's validity in its entirety. In essence, the Palestinians' rush to unilateral statehood cannibalizes the basis of all past agreements that were built on the Madrid foundation, including the later establishment of the Palestinian Authority as the collective representative of the Palestinians and the concessions already made by Israel during the Oslo Accords and in later agreements.

CONCLUSION

Israel's rights and claims regarding each of the major core issues: borders, settlements, refugees, and Jerusalem, are firmly rooted in the negotiating principles of Madrid which formed the foundation for the bilateral negotiations at Oslo. However, the Palestinian unilateral bid for statehood succeeded to drive a wedge of perception isolating Israel from those fundamental legal rights. Instead, the aggressive Palestinian campaign left Israel seen as possessing no legitimate claims east of the 1949 armistice lines, including its rights in Jerusalem.

In this context, regardless of whether the Palestinians end up withdrawing their intention to submit a resolution proposing a UN endorsement of "Palestine" along the 1949 armistice lines in view of the growing hesitation of some European countries to back it, the Palestinian unilateral bid already achieved a major strategic goal of launching a "diplomatic intifada"[49] against Israel, with the aim of further dislodging Israel from its position as a fair and deserving claimant prepared for a fairly and directly negotiated compromise over the future of the Land of Israel. The Palestinian unilateral bid's simultaneous campaign to undermine Israel's fundamental legitimacy, caused damage to Israel's international standing, especially following the Hamas War in Gaza that resulted in greater support for Palestinian unilateralism by the European Union and sympathies from the United Nations itself, even at the risk of these bodies engaging in the destruction of their own credibility as fair and honest mediators of the Arab-Israeli conflict and other future conflicts in all parts of the world.

NOTES

* The author thanks Julie Feinberg for her assistance in the preparation of this chapter.

1 Mahmoud Abbas, "The Long Overdue Palestinian State," *New York Times*, May 16, 2011, http://www.nytimes.com/2011/05/17/opinion/17abbas.html.

2 Barak Ravid, "Foreign Ministry Cables Outline Battle Plan Against UN Recognition of Palestinian State," *Haaretz*, June 10, 2011.

3 President Obama, speech at the State Department, May 19, 2011, http://www.whitehouse.gov/the-press-office/2011/05/19/remarks-president-middle-east-and-north-africa.

4 "Senators oppose Israel return to 1967 lines," Agence France Presse, http://www.google.com/hostednews/afp/article/ALeqM5jtGYEu1f9NmbJ190wALWuukKQNzA.

5 Jaime Daremblum, "The Palestinians Come to Latin America," *Weekly Standard*, February 21, 2011,
http://www.hudson.org/index.cfm?fuseaction=publication_details&id=7733&pubType=HI_Opeds.

6 Colombian President Juan Manuel Santos told the author on March 31, 2011, that Colombia would not recognize a unilaterally declared Palestinian state.

7 While not recognizing Palestine as a state, 104 countries recognized the 1988 Palestine Liberation Organization's Declaration of Independence. See John Quigly, "The Palestine Declaration to the International Criminal Court: The Statehood Issue," *Rutgers Law Record*, Vol. 35 (Spring 2009), http://www.lawrecord.com/files/35-rutgers-l-rec-1.pdf.] See also Palestinian National Council, Declaration of Independence, November 15, 1988, UN Doc. A/43/827, S/20278, Annex III, November 18, 1988, reprinted in 27 I.L.M. 1668 (1988).

8 Tal Becker, "International Recognition of a Unilaterally Declared Palestinian State: Legal and Policy Dilemmas," Jerusalem Center for Public Affairs, http://www.jcpa.org/art/becker1.htm.

9 This resolution only changes the name of Palestinian representation, not its status: "effective as of 15 December 1988, the designation 'Palestine' should be used in place of the designation 'Palestine Liberation Organization' in the United Nations system, without prejudice to the observer status and functions of the Palestine Liberation Organization within the United Nations system, in conformity with relevant United Nations resolutions and practice;" http://unispal.un.org/UNISPAL.NSF/0/146E6838D505833F852560D600471E25.

10 John Bolton, "How to Block the Palestine Statehood Ploy," *Wall Street Journal*, June 3, 2011.

11 Abbas, "Long Overdue Palestinian State."

12 Ibid.

13 There have been no Palestinian elections since January 2010, indicating that Abbas represents no constituency or public. Hamas, today a possible partner in a national unity government, won the 2006 elections that were unrecognized by Israel, Europe, and the United States. Since 2007, the Fatah-governed West Bank and Hamas-controlled Gaza have remained enemy territories to one another. The Palestinian unity government's control of the West Bank and Gaza is not recognized by the European Union or the United States.

14 Abbas acknowledged to the *Washington Post*'s Jackson Diehl after the failure of Annapolis that Olmert's offer to the Palestinians of 93.5 percent of the West Bank and the recognition of the right of return (which included tens of thousands of Palestinian refugees' return to Israel) was more generous than the offers of either George Bush or Bill Clinton, and yet Abbas said: "The gaps were wide." See Jackson Diehl, "Abbas' Waiting Game," *Washington Post*, May 29, 2009, http://www.washingtonpost.com/wp-dyn/content/article/2009/05/28/AR2009052803614.html.

15 "Palestinians Should Follow Kosovo Example: Negotiator," Agence France Press, February 20, 2008, http://afp.google.com/article/ALeqM5iS_5y-7raxAQIhNgJDtMOIhadGrg. See also Ali Abunimah, "Kosovo and the Question of Palestine," *Electronic Intifada*, February 25, 2008, http://electronicintifada.net/content/kosovo-and-question-palestine/7374.

16 Interviews and meetings between top Palestinian officials and the author, Ramallah, October 2009 to January 2010.

17 Dan Diker and Pinchas Inbari, "Prime Minister Salam Fayyad's Two-Year Path to Statehood: Implications for the Palestinian Authority and Israel," Jerusalem Viewpoints, Vol. 9, No. 11, Jerusalem Center for Public Affairs, October 2, 2009, http://www.jcpa.org/JCPA/Templates/ShowPage.asp?DBID=1&LNGID=1&TMID=111&FID=442&PID=0&IID=3096.

18 Barak Ravid and Akiva Eldar, "Obama Envisions Two Years until Mideast Peace Deal," *Haaretz*, September 1, 2009.

19 Israel's Strategic Affairs Minister and Deputy Prime Minister Moshe Yaalon coined the term "bottom up" in 2008 as a new

approach to Palestinian society-building. See Moshe Yaalon, "A New Strategy for the Palestinian-Israeli Conflict," Jerusalem Issue Briefs, Vol. 8, No. 10, September 2, 2008, http://www.jcpa.org/Templates/ShowPage.asp?DRIT=1&DBID=1&LNGID=1&TMID=111&FID=442&PID=0&IID=2515&TTL=A_New_Strategy_for_the_Israeli-Palestinian_Conflict. Prime Minister Benjamin Netanyahu coined the phrase "economic peace" in 2008 with regard to developing the Palestinian Authority's economy as a key prerequisite for viable and stable Palestinian statehood.

20 Amira Hass, "Palestinian PM: Declaration of statehood just a formality," Page 115, *Haaretz*, November 15, 2009, http://www.haaretz.com/news/palestinian-pm-declaration-of-statehood-just-a-formality-1.4140.

21 Alan Baker, "A Paradox of Peacemaking: How Fayyad's Unilateral Statehood Plan Undermines the Legal Foundations of Israeli Palestinian Diplomacy," Jerusalem Viewpoints, No. 574, Jerusalem Center for Public Affairs, November-December 2009, http://www.jcpa.org/JCPA/Templates/ShowPage.asp?DRIT=2&DBID=1&LNGID=1&TMID=111&FID=443&PID=0&IID=3185&TTL=A_Paradox_of_Peacemaking:_How_Fayyad%27s_Unilateral_Statehood_Plan_Undermines_the_Legal_Foundati.

22 Salam Fayyad, interview with Ali al-Salih, *Al-Sharq al-Awsat*, September 1, 2009.

23 Alan Baker, "The Palestinian UN Gamble: Irresponsible and Ill Advised," Jerusalem Issue Brief, Vol. 10, No. 34, April 3, 2011, http://www.jcpa.org/JCPA/Templates/ShowPage.asp?DBID=1&LNGID=1&TMID=111&FID=442&PID=0&IID=6640; "the current peace process as it has been conducted so far is over" (Palestinian Authority Foreign Minister Riad Malki, March 22, 2011) and "the Palestinian leadership institutions [PLO and Fatah] have decided to submit a request to the UN for recognition of a Palestinian state within the 1967 borders, with its capital in East Jerusalem" (Sa'eb Erekat, AFP, March 20, 2011).

24 Abbas, "Long Overdue Palestinian State." See also Dan Diker, "The Palestinian Unilateral Kosovo Strategy: Implications for the PA and Israel," Jerusalem Viewpoints, No. 575, Jerusalem Center for Public Affairs, January-February 2010, http://www.jcpa.org/JCPA/Templates/ShowPage.asp?DBID=1&TMID=111&LNGID=1&FID=582&PID=0&IID=3271; Baker, "Palestinian UN Gamble."

25 "Solana Wants UN to Establish Palestine," *Jerusalem Post*, July 12, 2009, http://www.jpost.com/servlet/Satellite?pagename=JPost%2FJPArticle%2FShowFull&cid=1246443786047.

26 Barak Ravid, "EU Draft Document on Division of Jerusalem," *Haaretz*, December 2, 2009, http://www.haaretz.com/hasen/spages/1131988.html.

27 Dore Gold, "Europe Seeks to Divide Jerusalem," Jerusalem Issue Brief, Vol. 9, No. 14, Jerusalem Center for Public Affairs, December 10, 2009, http://www.jcpa.org/JCPA/Templates/ShowPage.asp?DBID=1&LNGID=1&TMID=111&FID=442&PID=0&IID=3220.

28 Article xvii of the Oslo Interim Agreement states: "issues that will be negotiated in the permanent status negotiations: Jerusalem, settlements, specified military locations, Palestinian refugees, borders, foreign relations and Israelis," http://www.mideastweb.org/meosint.htm.

29 The Road Map states:

A two state solution to the Israeli-Palestinian conflict will only be achieved through an end to violence and terrorism, when the Palestinian people have a leadership acting decisively against terror and willing and able to build a practicing democracy based on tolerance and liberty, and through Israel's readiness to do what is necessary for a democratic Palestinian state to be established, and a clear, unambiguous acceptance by both parties of the goal of a negotiated settlement as described below.

http://news.bbc.co.uk/2/hi/middle_east/2989783.stm.

30 The Quartet clarified its position in a statement on February 5, 2011, http://www.consilium.europa.eu/uedocs/cms_data/docs/pressdata/EN/foraff/119200.pdf.

31 http://www.imf.org/external/country/WBG/RR/2011/041311.pdf.

32 http://www.imf.org/external/country/WBG/RR/2011/041311.pdf.

33 For example, in 2010 Israel transferred $1.26 billion in clearance revenues to the PA. See also Patrick Clawson and Michael Singh, "Is the Palestinian Authority Ready for Statehood?," Policy Watch, No. 1798, Washington Institute for Near East Policy, April 20, 2011.

34 Ibrahim Abu Kamesh, "The Arab Financial Siege Threatens to Collapse the PA," *Al-Hayat al-Jadida*, June 11, 2011.

35 Alan Baker, "Are the Palestinians Ready for Peace?: Palestinian Incitement as a Violation of International Legal Norms," Jerusalem Issue Brief, Vol. 10, No. 32, Jerusalem Center for Public Affairs, March 22, 2011, http://www.jcpa.org/JCPA/Templates/ShowPage.asp?DRIT=1&DBID=1&LNGID=1&TMID=111&FID=442&PID=0&IID=6515&TTL=Are_the_Palestinians_Ready_for_Peace?_Palest. See also Eytan Bentsur, "The Way to Peace Emerged at Madrid," Jerusalem Viewpoints, No. 472, Jerusalem Center for Public Affairs, http://www.jcpa.org/JCPA/Templates/ShowPage.asp?DBID=1&TMID=111&LNGID=1&FID=582&PID=0&IID=1111 February 15, 2002.

36 Moshe Ya'alon, "Introduction: Restoring a Security-First Peace Policy," in *Israel's Critical Security Needs for a Viable Peace* (Jerusalem: Jerusalem Center for Public Affairs, 2010), p. 16, http://www.defensibleborders.org/security.

37 http://www.mfa.gov.il/MFA/Peace+Process/Guide+to+the+Peace+Process/THE+ISRAELI-PALESTINIAN+INTERIM+AGREEMENT.htm.

38 Baker, "Palestinian UN Gamble."

39 Ibid.

40 Ibid.

41 Alan Baker, "A Paradox of Peacemaking: How Fayyad's Unilateral Statehood Plan Undermines the Legal Foundations of Israeli-Palestinian Diplomacy," Jerusalem Viewpoints, no. 574, November-December 2009, http://www.jcpa.org/JCPA/Templates/ShowPage.asp?DBID=1&LNGID=1&TMID=111&FID=443&PID=0&IID=3185.

42 The "Uniting for Peace" resolution, http://www.un.org/depts/dhl/landmark/pdf/ares377e.pdf.

43 Richard Holbrooke, "60 years of UNSC Resolution 242," Jerusalem Center for Public Affairs, 2007. http://www.jcpa.org/JCPA/Templates/ShowPage.asp?DBID=1&LNGID=1&TMID=84&FID=452&PID=3111.

44 "Israeli Prime Minister Yitzhak Shamir's Letter to Secretary of State Baker, Jerusalem, October 28, 1991," *Journal of Palestine Studies*, Vol. 21, No. 2 (Winter 1992): 124.

45 Former Israeli Foreign Ministry Director-General Eytan Bentsur, one of the Madrid Conference's primary architects, told the author in a conversation on June 9, 2007, that Madrid's conceptual backbone was that both Israel and Arab states were guaranteed the freedom to advance their respective claims in their opening statements without preconditions. See Dan Diker, "Why Israel Must Now Move from Concessions-Based Diplomacy to Rights-Based Diplomacy," Jerusalem Issue Brief, No. 554, Jerusalem Center for Public Affairs, June-July 2007, http://www.jcpa.org.il/JCPAHeb/Templates/ShowPage.asp?DBID=1&LNGID=1&TMID=111&FID=375&PID=0&IID=160.

46 "Speech of President George H. W. Bush at the 1991 Madrid Peace Conference," *Journal of Palestine Studies*, Vol. 21, No. 2 (Winter 1992): 126.

47 President Obama, speech at the State Department, May 19, 2011, http://www.whitehouse.gov/the-press-office/2011/05/19/remarks-president-middle-east-and-north-africa.

48 Eytan Bentsur, *Making Peace: A First-Hand Account of the Arab-Israeli Peace Process* (Westport, CT: Greenwood, 1993), 118.

49 http://www.hudson-ny.org/1899/abbas-intifada.

IS THE GAZA STRIP OCCUPIED BY ISRAEL?[1]

Pnina Sharvit-Baruch

FACTUAL BACKGROUND[2]

Following World War I, the Gaza Strip was part of the British Mandate of Palestine until the dissolution of this Mandate in May 1948. The Gaza Strip was then controlled by Egypt until 1967. Egypt did not purport to annex this area but rather imposed there a military government. In June 1967, the Gaza Strip came under Israel Defense Forces (IDF) control and immediately thereafter a military administration was established in the region.[3]

Following negotiations between the state of Israel and the Palestinian Liberation Organization (PLO), as the representative of the Palestinian people, the Declaration of Principles on Interim Self-Government Arrangements was signed on September 13, 1993 (hereinafter *the DOP*),[4] setting a framework for a phased settlement of the Israeli-Palestinian dispute. Within this framework the parties signed on May 4, 1994, the Agreement on the Gaza Strip and Jericho Area (hereinafter *the Cairo Agreement*).[5] In accordance with this agreement, the IDF withdrew from most of the Gaza Strip, except for the Israeli settlements and main access routes thereto ("lateral roads"), and the military-installations area along the southern border of the Strip with Egypt (known as the Philadelphi Route). Additionally, most of the powers and responsibilities were transferred from the military government to the autonomous governing entity established by virtue of the Cairo Agreement – the Palestinian Authority (PA).[6] On September 28, 1995, the parties signed the Israeli-Palestinian Interim Agreement on the West Bank and Gaza Strip (hereinafter *the Interim Agreement*),[7] which incorporated and superseded the Cairo Agreement.[8]

Based on these agreements, the PA held the powers and responsibilities over all civil affairs and over internal security in the Gaza Strip, except in the abovementioned areas from which Israel did not withdraw (the settlements and the military installations). Israel retained control over external security, the airspace, and the electromagnetic sphere. Israel also controlled all the internal crossings between the Gaza Strip and Israel and the international passage between the Gaza Strip and Egypt located in Rafah. The maritime zone was transferred to PA authority, though under certain conditions and limitations.

Following these agreements, the parties held negotiations aimed at achieving a permanent resolution of the conflict; unfortunately, though, such a resolution has not yet been achieved. Instead violence erupted in the West Bank and the Gaza Strip, including in the form of suicide attacks, and mortar and rocket attacks using steep-trajectory weapons. Such weapons were fired especially from the Gaza Strip toward Israeli settlements in the Strip, at southern communities in Israel situated in proximity to Gaza, at various IDF bases, as well as at the crossing points between Israel and the Strip.[9]

Israel responded forcefully, including some large-scale military operations. Israel, however, did not regain permanent control over the areas under Palestinian control in the Gaza Strip and all operations were limited in scope and in time.

In 2004, against the background of the violent situation on the one hand and lack of progress in the diplomatic process on the other, Israel decided to unilaterally evacuate its troops and citizens from the Gaza Strip – a move which was named the Disengagement Plan.[10] The actual implementation of the Disengagement Plan began on August 17, 2005, and lasted about three weeks. On September 12, 2005, the last of the IDF troops left the Gaza Strip and the IDF commander of the Southern Command signed a proclamation terminating the military government in the area.[11]

The government of Israel and the PA signed on November 15, 2005, the Agreement on Movement and Access (AMA), regarding the movement of people and goods between Israel and the Gaza Strip through the internal crossings. The agreement included in its Annex arrangements for the operation of the Rafah and Kerem Shalom crossing points, through which the movement of people and goods between the Gaza Strip and Egypt, under the supervision of a third party, was supposed to have been enabled.[12]

According to Israeli public statements, the disengagement, namely the evacuation of Israeli citizens and IDF forces from the Gaza Strip, was aimed to reduce friction with the Palestinian population and improve the Palestinian economy and living conditions. The hope was that "the Palestinians will take advantage of the opportunity created by the disengagement in order to break out of the cycle of violence and to reengage in a process of dialogue." It was also intended to "serve to dispel claims regarding Israel's responsibility for the Palestinians in the Gaza Strip."[13]

Unfortunately, despite the aforesaid, the political and security situation in the Gaza Strip continued to deteriorate. In January 2006 the Hamas organization won the elections for the Palestinian Legislative Council, and was invited by Fatah to join a coalition government headed by the latter.[14] In June 2007 Hamas took over the Gaza Strip in a violent campaign, involving the murder and assault

Rocket attacks in Israel from the Gaza Strip lead to Operation Cast Lead. (AP Photo/Hatem Moussa)

of dozens of Fatah officials. Following this coup Hamas gained control over all the government apparatus in the Strip.[15]

In response to attacks from the Gaza Strip toward Israel and in light of the takeover by the hostile Hamas, Israel imposed limitations on the transfer of goods and on the passage of people between Israel and the Strip. Israel also engaged in several counterstrikes and operations, the largest of which was Operation Cast Lead in December 2008.[16]

Based on this factual background the question raised is what is the present status of the Gaza Strip and, more concretely, whether it should be considered as occupied by Israel.

Before turning to the analysis of this question, one preliminary remark is required. It should be noted that already in 1994, following the Israeli withdrawal from most of the Gaza Strip and the transfer of powers and responsibilities of the military government to the PA in accordance with the Cairo Agreement, the question of whether the Gaza Strip should still be considered occupied by Israel arose. Some found that the territories from which the IDF redeployed and for which it handed over authority to the PA were no longer under effective IDF control and as such, no longer under belligerent occupation by Israel.[17] Others contended that Israel continued to control these territories. They relied, inter alia, on the fact that the agreements concluded between Israel and the PLO left the residual authority in Israel's hands, as well as the overall responsibility for security. According to the latter approach, the PA received limited jurisdiction for self-rule in these territories without compromising the existence of the military government there.[18] The government of Israel refrained from making a clear official determination in this regard.

This short chapter will not analyze whether the Cairo Agreement and Interim Agreement changed the status of the Gaza Strip. It will be assumed, for the sake of the argument, that the Gaza Strip remained under Israeli occupation following these agreements and the focus will only be on the question of whether occupation has ended following the disengagement.

DEFINING OCCUPATION

The basic formulation for when a territory is considered to be subject to belligerent occupation is found in Article 42 of the Hague Regulations Respecting the Laws and Customs of War on Land of 1907, which states that:

> Territory is considered occupied when it is actually placed under the authority of the hostile army. The occupation extends only to the territory where such authority has been established and can be exercised.

It is commonly agreed that, at its core, territory will be considered occupied when it is under the "effective control" of the foreign army.[19]

There are different views and understandings of what constitutes "effective control." We will first try to chart the different positions and then briefly analyze their application to the situation in the Gaza Strip.

One rather narrow interpretation was given recently by the International Court of Justice (ICJ), which determined that in order for a belligerent occupation to exist the occupying army must actually exercise its authority in the territory, and thereby supplant the authority of the sovereign government of that area.[20]

This formulation by the ICJ has been subject to criticism as being too narrow,[21] especially since it enables a state which has in fact gained effective control over a certain territory to evade its responsibilities toward the residents of this territory by not actively exercising its powers.

A more flexible approach to the test of "effective control" focuses on the potential ability of the occupying army to maintain its authority over the area and the inability of the sovereign government to exercise its authority.[22]

Focusing on the potential ability does not mean that any military presence in or near the territory is enough to be considered an occupation. In order for effective control to exist, the foreign army must be able to impose its will on the local population whenever it so chooses while the sovereign government is unable to exercise its authority in the territory due to the effective control of the foreign army. This approach is based on the judgment of the International Military Tribunal in Nuremberg[23] and was adopted also in a ruling of the Israeli Supreme Court.[24]

Even according to this more flexible approach, fulfilling "effective control" usually requires the occupier to have forces present on the ground[25] or at least to have the ability to send, within a reasonable time, forces into the area to exercise the authority therein.[26]

Shany concludes his analysis of the relevant authorities on occupation by identifying three cumulative conditions which must be satisfied in order to consider an area occupied: "a) hostile troops are physically located in the area; b) these troops are capable of exercising effective powers of government; and c) the legitimate government is incapable of exercising effective powers of government."[27]

As for the question of when does the occupation end, although the Law of Belligerent Occupation does not provide an explicit answer, the accepted approach is that of a "mirror image" of the conditions for its inception, namely, when the occupying army no longer maintains effective control in the territory and in its place there is a new regime having such control.[28] Occupation can end by way of an agreement or when the occupier is forced out, but also by a unilateral act of the occupying power to depart.[29]

We shall now apply this legal framework to the situation in the Gaza Strip. We shall first examine whether Israel has effective control over the Gaza Strip and then consider whether there is no other legitimate government capable of exercising governmental powers in this area.

DOES ISRAEL HAVE "EFFECTIVE CONTROL" OVER THE GAZA STRIP?

As explained above, in order to determine that the Gaza Strip is under Israeli occupation one must determine that Israel has effective control over this area.

If one applies to the situation in the Gaza Strip the formulation of the ICJ in Congo v. Uganda, namely that occupation means actually exercising authority over the territory, Israel is clearly not an occupier of the Gaza Strip. Israel has fully withdrawn from this area, has officially terminated the military government, and refrains from carrying out governmental authority vis-à-vis the population in this area.

If we focus as a basis for defining occupation on the potential ability to maintain its authority in the area, the result seems the same, since Israel has not retained forces on the ground in the Gaza Strip. As mentioned above, "boots on the ground" seem to be a necessary component of having effective control even for those who apply the "potential control" formula.

Moreover, even if instead of an actual presence it is enough to have the ability to reenter the area and make one's authority felt therein as a condition for "effective control," Israel does not have this capacity either. The cases in which Israel has entered the Gaza Strip since the disengagement were complex, dangerous military operations aimed at stopping attacks from the Gaza Strip against Israel, and during such operations there was no attempt to apply Israeli authority toward the civilian population.

In light of the above, the Supreme Court of Israel, in response to several petitions pertaining to the provision of fuel and electricity to the Gaza Strip in the aftermath of the Disengagement Plan, concluded that:

> In this context we note that since September 2005, Israel no longer has effective control over events in the Gaza Strip. The military government imposed in the territory in the past has been terminated by virtue of a government resolution, and Israeli soldiers are no longer permanently present in the area and do not manage affairs there. In these circumstances, Israel is under no general obligation to provide for the welfare of the residents of the Gaza Strip and to preserve the public order there according to the body of laws pertaining to belligerent occupation in international law. Israel also has no effective capability in its current situation to impose order and to manage civilian life in the Gaza Strip.[30]

This conclusion seems well founded on the factual situation when analyzed in accordance with the prevailing law on occupation.

However, this conclusion has not been accepted by quite a few commentators and NGOs nor by the PLO, who claim that the Gaza Strip should still be considered as occupied by Israel. We will therefore examine the arguments brought in support of this position and try to evaluate their legal validity.

ARGUMENTS THAT THE GAZA STRIP IS OCCUPIED BY ISRAEL

The different arguments made in support of the claim that Israel is still the occupier of the Gaza Strip are based on several factors, which, it is claimed, lead to Israel still remaining in effective control of the area notwithstanding its withdrawal. Different writers have pointed to different factors. The following is an attempt to compile a list of the relevant factors mentioned:[31]

- First, Israel retains control over the external perimeter of the Gaza Strip since it controls the airspace and maritime zone, as well as the land border and the crossing points between Israel and the Gaza Strip. The border with Egypt remains sealed by Egypt.[32] This enables Israel to set policy on matters pertaining to the flow of people and goods to and from the territory.

- Second, Israel retains the right to reenter its forces into the Gaza Strip for security reasons, carries out military incursions in the areas near the border, and has also carried out wider military operations in this area, such as Operation Cast Lead. In addition, Israel enforces "no-go" zones within the Strip (i.e., areas into which Palestinians are prohibited from entering and might be shot at by the IDF upon entry).

- Third, the Gaza Strip remains dependent on Israel in many ways, such as with regard to the supply of water and electricity.
- Fourth, Israel retains, in accordance with the Interim Agreement, overriding powers, such as with regard to external security, final decisions concerning the population registry and other authorities, including the residual authority, namely all powers not explicitly delegated to the PA. The agreements also forbid the PA from engaging in foreign relations.
- Fifth, the West Bank and the Gaza Strip are a single territorial unit and therefore even after the withdrawal from the Gaza Strip, Israel is still an occupier of this unified entity through its control of the West Bank.
- The question is, therefore, if these factors in themselves, or perhaps their cumulative effect, create such Israeli control over the Gaza Strip which might be considered as a sufficient substitute for the physical presence on the ground in a way that creates Israeli "effective control."

We will now analyze each factor separately and then refer to their cumulative effect.

1. Control over the External Perimeter

As for the control over the airspace and the sea, this in itself cannot satisfy the requirement for control over the area.[33] Indeed, IDF activity in Gaza's airspace does not involve the exercise of any governmental authority vis-à-vis Gaza's population and is not carried out by virtue of the security legislation which governed such matters during the era of the military government.[34] Likewise, the activity of IDF naval forces in the maritime space of the Gaza Strip does not establish effective control over the Gaza Strip.[35]

As for the control over the land border between Israel and the Gaza Strip, this cannot serve as an indication of control over the area itself. Israeli control over the Israeli side of the crossing points between Israel and the Gaza Strip is a natural reflection of Israel's sovereignty within Israel, which includes the prerogative to set policy for movement of people and goods from and to its territory, and therefore cannot be regarded as proof of control over the Gaza Strip. This is similar to the control any state has over its border crossings.

As for the border between the Gaza Strip and Egypt and the Rafah crossing point located therein, these are not under Israeli control, but rather are under Palestinian and Egyptian control. Until recently, the border with Egypt had been kept relatively closed due to the Egyptian policy.[36] This meant that once the Egyptians changed their policy, the Gaza Strip would have an open external border without any Israeli control. This has indeed happened. Following the dramatic developments in Egypt, the new Egyptian authorities have reopened the Rafah crossing. This was coordinated directly between Egypt and Hamas without any Israeli involvement.[37] Therefore today there is no doubt that Israel does not in fact possess control over the external borders of the Strip. The opening of the Rafah crossing also means that Israel does not control the flow of people and goods to and from the Gaza Strip.

2. Military Incursions into the Area

As for the contention that Israel continues to occupy the Gaza Strip due to the fact that it retained the right to reenter the area, in light of its continued performance of military incursions into this area, and since it established "no-go" zones on the Gazan side of its border, let us examine each of these claims.

As Bell and Shefi correctly point out, Israel never stated that it retains the *right* to reenter the Gaza Strip at will.[38] Israel does, however, consider itself in the midst of an ongoing armed conflict with the Hamas government and in this context has the right to engage in military operations, which sometimes take place in the Gaza Strip. However, this right is not derived from a sense of continued control of this area. The situation resembles that of Lebanon, from where Israel withdrew its forces in 2000, but has since retained the right to fight back against attempted attacks, even if that means reentering the country as it did in the Second Lebanon War of 2006.[39]

As for the instances in which Israel did enter the area and carry out military incursions therein, these have been military operations against forces of Hamas and other armed groups operating in this area aimed at stopping attacks from the Gaza Strip against the territory of Israel. These operations have not intended nor succeeded in "making the authority of Israel felt" within the Gaza Strip, to use the words of the U.S. Army Field Manual.[40] The fact that notwithstanding these incursions, Israel continues to be under constant attacks from the Gaza Strip is a further indication of the lack of any practical effective control.[41]

The "no-go" zones refer to vacant areas near the border with Israel where Palestinians are warned not to approach.[42] It is doubtful whether this amounts to effective control, but even if it does then, at best, one might say that these areas remain occupied, but this cannot suffice to conclude that the whole of Gaza is under occupation.

3. The Dependency of the Gaza Strip on Israel

The next factor to be analyzed is the contention that the Gaza Strip is dependent on Israel in economic and other aspects in a way that entails effective control. Firstly, with the opening of the Rafah crossing mentioned above, the Gaza Strip is much less dependent on Israel than it was until recently. Moreover, having an effect on the population of an area cannot be considered in itself as rising to the level of exercising effective powers of government over this population. Many states are strongly affected by their neighbors and yet are not considered occupied by them.[43]

This dependency does, however, in practice, affect the relationship between Israel and the Gaza Strip. Hence in its judgment in the fuel and electricity case of January 2008 the Supreme Court, based on the position presented by the Israeli authorities, found that while Israel is not bound by the laws of belligerent occupation, it still has certain obligations toward the Gaza population:

> In the prevailing circumstances, the main obligations of the State of Israel relating to the residents of the Gaza Strip derive from the state of armed conflict that exists between it

> and the Hamas organization that controls the Gaza Strip; these obligations also derive from the degree of control exercised by the State of Israel over the border crossings between it and the Gaza Strip, as well as from the relationship that was created between Israel and the territory of the Gaza Strip after the years of Israeli military rule in the territory, as a result of which the Gaza Strip is currently almost completely dependent upon the supply of electricity from Israel.[44]

Dinstein finds this as another proof of the continued existence of occupation, since the laws of armed conflict do not contain any duty by a belligerent party to supply electricity and fuel to the enemy.[45] While I accept that the scope of the duty a belligerent has toward the civilian population of the enemy is much more limited than that of an occupier, I believe that the fact that both the Israeli government and the court did impose an obligation to safeguard the basic humanitarian needs of the civilian population in the Gaza Strip does not necessarily prove that the area is still occupied by Israel and subject to the entire law of occupation. Instead this is evidence of the complex situation in the Gaza Strip and of the sui generis nature of this area, as will be discussed below.

4. Authorities Retained by Israel in the Agreements

As for the factor based on the stipulations of the Interim Agreement, which provide Israel with authorities regarding the Gaza Strip, including the residual authority, and which impose restrictions on the Palestinian powers of government, this seems to be also of limited significance.[46] The facts on the ground, especially in the Gaza Strip, are dramatically different from those envisioned in the Interim Agreement. Therefore it is questionable to what extent the provisions of this agreement relating to the Gaza Strip still apply.[47] Moreover, since occupation is a factual situation and not a legal creation, the analysis must rely on the reality of the situation and not on legal obligations, even if they are assumed to still be valid.

The same goes with regard to the limitation on having foreign relations. The PA has disregarded this obligation altogether. Hamas also carries out foreign relations with those willing to engage with it, such as the Arab countries.[48] Israel has no ability to influence the foreign relations of the Palestinians and therefore this element is actually only further proof of the lack of control on its part.

As for the population registry, Hamas maintains its own population registry. Israel maintains a Palestinian registry that is used in order to make decisions at the crossing points. It is not clear how this can signify effective control.[49]

5. Continued Control over the West Bank

As for the contention that since Israel still controls the West Bank, the Gaza Strip is also still occupied, this has no legal basis whatsoever. The fact that the West Bank and the Gaza Strip are considered one unit politically does not change the reality that they are separate geographical units. The fact that the Gaza Strip is in fact controlled by a separate government run by Hamas, which does not regard itself as subject to the authority of the PA government in the West Bank, further underlines the fact that these areas are administered independently.[50] In any event even if they are regarded as one unified unit, the fact that the one part is still controlled by Israel does not create de facto control over the other. As already explained, the existence of an occupation is a factual determination based on the factual situation. Moreover, since occupation law recognizes the occupation of part of a state while other parts remain unoccupied, there is no reason not to accept that part of the Palestinian entity is considered occupied while another part is not.[51]

CUMULATIVE EFFECT OF ALL THE FACTORS

The above analysis shows that none of the factors mentioned is sufficient in itself to regard Israel as having "effective control" over the Gaza Strip. Does their cumulative effect change this result? The underlying question is whether Israel has in fact sufficient control over the Gaza Strip to deem it an occupier despite its physical absence from this area.

Our analysis shows that Israel does not really possess full control over the external perimeter and that it has no military ability to influence the situation in the Gaza Strip and make its authority felt therein. This means that it has no effective control over the area. None of the other factors mentioned, namely the economic dependency of the Gaza Strip on Israel, the provisions of the Interim Agreement, nor the continued occupation of the West Bank by Israel, change this analysis, since they are not relevant in concluding whether a factual situation of having effective control exists or not.

In light of the above, the reasonable conclusion is that, notwithstanding all these factors, Israel cannot be regarded as the occupier of the Gaza Strip.[52]

Furthermore, as explained above, an additional cumulative condition for determining the existence of occupation is that the legitimate government is incapable of exercising such powers. We shall now turn to analyze this aspect.

IS THERE A LEGITIMATE GOVERNMENT CAPABLE OF EXERCISING AUTHORITY IN THE GAZA STRIP?

As mentioned above, the Gaza Strip is controlled by the Hamas government. The question is whether this government can be considered a legitimate one capable of exercising governmental powers in this area in a way that entails that Israel cannot be viewed as possessing effective control.

According to Article 47 of the Fourth Geneva Convention, agreements with the authorities of the occupied territory do not release the occupier from its obligations under the laws of occupation. Accordingly, transfer of authority to local authorities or the appointment of an administration in the occupied territory does not end the applicability of the laws of occupation. On the other hand, if there is a central government that can exercise its authority in the relinquished territory and is not subject to the occupier, this would seem to fall outside the scope of Article 47.[53]

The first question is, therefore, whether the Hamas government can be regarded as an independent government of the territory.

In the present case, with the IDF withdrawal and the termination of the military government, the PA – which had control over most of the Gaza Strip at the time of the Disengagement Plan – acted to impose its authority on the areas evacuated by the IDF.[54] Hamas took over, and very effectively exercises powers of government. This is neither a local government nor a subsidiary government appointed by Israel to carry out its duties.

The second question is whether Hamas can be viewed as a legitimate government.

Admittedly the legality of the Hamas government has been questioned, but it must be regarded as the de facto replacement of the PA government. The PA government was viewed by the international community (and by Israel) as the legitimate government in the West Bank and the Gaza Strip at the time of the disengagement. Consequently, if the latter is accepted as a genuine independent government which is not subject to Israel, so must the Hamas government be regarded, notwithstanding its brutal takeover and political unacceptability.

Admittedly, the PA and the Hamas government are not a replacement of the previous government that was in control of the territory on the eve of the belligerent occupation. However, in the unique case of the Gaza Strip (and the West Bank), which never belonged to another sovereign country, and in light of the widely recognized Palestinian right of self-determination (acknowledged also by Egypt and Jordan, the former occupiers of these areas), a Palestinian government seems to be the equivalent of the former sovereign government the laws of occupation refer to.[55]

In viewing the impact the existence of an effective Hamas government in the Gaza Strip has on the definition of the Israeli status in this area, it is interesting to compare the situation with that in the Congo as described in the ICJ case of Congo v. Uganda.[56] There part of the territory of the Congo was transferred to the control of two of the rebel movements in the Lusaka Agreement. Judge Kooijmans, who viewed Uganda as occupier of these parts of the Congo since it possessed there effective control, determined that "After Lusaka, territorial authority could no longer be seen as vested exclusively in the central Government but as being shared with 'armed opposition' movements which had been recognized as part of the national authority."[57] And consequently:

> Only in those places where it remained in full and effective control, like Ituri district, did Uganda retain its status as occupying Power… Even if it retained its military grip on the airports and other strategic locations, it can, as a result of the arrangements made in the Lusaka Agreement, no longer be said to have substituted itself for or replaced the authority of the territorial government since under the terms of the Agreement that authority was also exercised by the rebel movements.[58]

In other words, according to Judge Kooijmans, occupation ceased where the effective control of Uganda stopped being "full." This was so even though the area was transferred to the control of rebel movements, and not to the Congolese government.

To sum up this point, there is a government in the Gaza Strip that is capable of exercising governmental powers, which took over from the legitimate government and is its substitute. Consequently, the second condition for deeming the Gaza Strip as occupied by Israel, namely that there is no other functioning government, is also not fulfilled.

CONCLUSION

In conclusion, our analysis shows that there is no valid legal basis to regard Israel as the occupying power of the Gaza Strip. This stems from the fact that Israel has no effective control over this area and that the Hamas government is capable of exercising effective powers of government therein. Consequently, the laws of occupation do not apply there as such.[59]

On the other hand, admittedly there is a unique relationship between Israel and the Gaza Strip, based on the continuing links between them and the special circumstances of the situation, which leads to certain duties and responsibilities on the part of Israel. These do not stem from a defined body of legal norms, such as occupation law, but from a *sui generis* situation requiring suitable and flexible definitions.[60] The extent of these duties and responsibilities is influenced by the changing factual circumstances. Therefore, for example, the recent opening of the Rafah crossing calls for a further review in this regard. We, as lawyers, might feel more comfortable to have defined categories with clear-cut answers, but reality does not always grant us that privilege.[61]

NOTES

1 The opinions and conclusions expressed in this article are those of the author and do not necessarily reflect the views of the IDF or the government of Israel. I would like to thank Nimrod Karin for his valuable comments.

2 See a good overview in the Report of the Public Commission to Examine the Maritime Incident of 31 May 2010 (the Turkel Commission) – Part one (hereinafter – Turkel Report – Part one), pp. 26 – 32 (paras. 14 – 19).See also the analysis in HCJ 1661/05, The Gaza Coast Regional Council et al v. the Knesset et al, *P.D.* 59(2) 481, paras. 1-3, 10 (2005) (hereinafter The Gaza Coast Case).

3 Several Israeli settlements were also established in the Gaza Strip. In 2003 the number of settlers was estimated at around eight thousand people – The Gaza Coast Case, ibid., para. 12 and references therein.

4 Declaration of Principles regarding Interim Agreements of Self-Governance with PLO (signed in 1994) [hereinafter DOP], available at www.knesset.gov.il/process/docs/oslo.htm.

5 Agreement regarding Gaza Strip and Jericho Region (signed in 1994) [hereinafter Cairo Agreement], available at www.knesset.gov.il/process/docs/cairo_agreement.htm.

6 The Cairo Agreement provisions and division of authorities were incorporated into the domestic law of the area through the Proclamation concerning the Implementation of the Gaza Strip and Jericho Area Agreement (Gaza Strip Area) (No. 4), 5754-1994.

7 Israeli-Palestinian Interim Agreement regarding the West Bank and the Gaza Strip (signed in 1995) [hereinafter The Interim Agreement], available at www.knesset.gov.il/process/docs/heskemb1.htm.

8 Article 31(2) to the Interim Agreement. The Interim Agreement provisions and the updated division of authorities set out therein were incorporated into the domestic law of the area through the Proclamation concerning the Implementation of the Interim Agreement (Gaza Strip Area) (No. 5), 5756-1995.

9 In 2001, four Qassam rockets were fired from the Gaza Strip area (the first of these was fired at the end of October); in 2002 the number increased to thirty-five rockets; in 2003 – 135 rockets; in 2004 – 281 rockets. In each of these years, a total of 245, 257, 265, and 876 mortar shells were fired, respectively. Since mortars have a shorter range (up to 3 km) they were mainly directed at Israeli settlements then located in the Gaza Strip, and at IDF forces; while the rockets were fired at the communities of southern Israel located in proximity to the Strip. These figures are taken from a study conducted by the Meir Amit Intelligence and Terrorism Information Center headed by Dr. Reuven Erlich, entitled "The Rocket Threat from the Gaza Strip 2000-2007" (Hebrew), available at http://terrorism-info.org.il/malam_multimedia/Hebrew/heb_n/pdf/rocket_threat.pdf).

10 "Israel will evacuate the Gaza Strip including all existing Israeli towns and villages, and will redeploy outside the Strip... Upon completion of this process, there shall be no permanent presence of Israeli security forces on the ground in the areas to be evacuated" (Section 2(a)(3.1) of Government Resolution No. 1996, dated June 6, 2004). Initially the plan was to leave an Israeli presence in the area of the border between the Gaza Strip and Egypt, but ultimately the GOI decided to withdraw completely, as stated in Government Resolution No. 4235 of 11.9.2005 ("...the IDF will withdraw its forces from the territory of the Gaza Strip, including from the area of the border between the Gaza Strip and Egypt ('Philadelphi Route')."

11 "As of the end of this day, the military government in the Gaza Strip area is terminated" (Section 1 of the Proclamation concerning the Termination of the Military Government (No. 6) (Gaza Strip Area), 5765-2005).

12 The agreement is available at http://www.mfa.gov.il/MFA/Peace+Process/Reference+Documents/Agreed+documents+on+movement+and+access+from+and+to+Gaza+15-Nov-2005.htm.

13 Israel Ministry of Foreign Affairs, "The Disengagement Plan – General Outline," April 18, 2004, available at http://www.mfa.gov.il/MFA/Peace+Process/Reference+Documents/Disengagement+Plan+-+General+Outline.htm.

14 Hamas is an extreme organization which calls for an Islamic-law state in the whole of the territory of Mandatory Palestine, does not recognize the right of Israel to exist, and rejects reaching peaceful agreements with Israel – Turkel Report – Part one, 29, para. 18.

15 Ibid., 29-30, para. 18. See also "Timeline: Hamas-Fatah Power Struggle," *Haaretz*, May 20, 2009, available at http://www.haaretz.com/news/timeline-hamas-fatah-power-struggle-1.276388. Recently there have been attempts to reach a reconciliation between Hamas and Fatah, but many issues have yet to be settled between them – Joel Greenberg, "Palestinian factions Fatah and Hamas formally sign unity accord," *Washington Post*, May 4, 2011, available at http://www.washingtonpost.com/world/palestinian-factions-formally-sign-unity-accord/2011/05/04/AFD89MmF_story.html?hpid=z6.

16 Turkel Report – Part one, 29-31, paras. 18-19.

17 E. Benvenisti, Responsibility for the protection of human rights under the Israeli-Palestinian Agreements, 28 Israel LR (1994) 297, 312; G. R. Watson, *The Oslo Accord: International Law and the Israeli-Palestinian Peace Agreements* (New York: Oxford University Press, 2000), 176.

18 Y. Dinstein, The International Law of Belligerent Occupation 274-275 (2009). P. Malanczuk, "Some Basic aspects of the agreements between Israel and the PLO from the perspective of international law" 7 Eur. JIL (1996) 481, 497.

19 Dinstein, 43.

20 *Armed Activities on the Territory of the Congo* (DRC v. Uganda), 2005 ICJ Rep. 168, 173. Thus the court concluded that: "In the present case the Court will need to satisfy itself that the Ugandan armed forces in the DRC were not only stationed in particular locations but also that they had substituted their own authority for that of the Congolese Government."

21 See, e.g., the separate legal opinion of Judge *Kooijmans* who criticizes the minimalist approach that has been adopted by the majority, paras.44-45, 49. See also Y. Shany, Faraway, so close: The legal status of Gaza after Israel's Disengagement,8 Y. B. Int'l. Hum. Law 369 (2005), 378.

22 This approach was adopted, for example, by the U.S. Army Field Manual (Department of the Army, Field Manual No. 27-10: The Law of the Land Warfare, 18 July 1956 (revised 15 July 1976) paras. 355-356) and in the UK Ministry of Defence, The Manual of the Law of Armed Conflict (2004), paras. 11.2, 11.3.

23 See The Hostages Trial (Trial of Wilhelm List and others), United States Military Tribunal, Nuremberg (Case no. 47), reprinted in VIII Law Reports of Trials of War Criminals (Selected and prepared by the United Nations War Crimes Commission, 1949) 34, 55-56.

24 See HCJ 102/82 Tzemel v. Minister of Defense, 37(3) PD 365, 373-376 (excerpt in English in Israel Yearbook on HR 360 (1983)) ("a military force can raid or invade an area in order to pass through it on its way to a destination that it set for itself, while leaving the area behind it without effective control. *But if the force took control over some area in a practical and effective manner, the temporary nature of the stay in the area or the intention to impose a non-permanent military control do not derogate from the fact that the factual conditions have been met for applying the laws of war that deal with the collateral implications of belligerent occupation.* This and more, the application of the third chapter of the Hague Convention and the application of the corresponding articles in the Fourth Geneva Convention are not contingent on the fact that a special organizational system be established in the form of a military rule. *The duties and authorities of the military force, which are derived from its effective occupation of some area, are established and created by the very fact that there is military control over the area, namely, even if the military force exercises control only by means of its regular combat units, without creating and dedicating a special military framework for military rule purposes* (emphasis added)). See also HCJ 201/09 Physicians for Human Rights v. The Prime Minister, Takdin Elyon 2009(1) 565, 571, para 14. ("The applicability of the laws of occupation of international humanitarian law is conditioned on the potential for exercising government authorities in the area following the invasion of military forces, and not necessarily on the actual exercise of those authorities de-facto.")

25 H. P. Gasser, "Protection of the civilian population," The Handbook of Humanitarian Law in Armed Conflicts 237, 274 (2nd. ed., D. Fleck ed., 2008); see also the first of the three cumulative conditions detailed by Yuval Shany in order to consider an area occupied, which are based on several judicial decisions from international and national courts and on several military manuals: "a) hostile troops are physically located in the area;..." Shany, 376, 380.

26 This is the formulation in the U.S. Army Field Manual – "It is sufficient that the occupying force can, within a reasonable time, send detachments of troops to make its authority felt within the occupied district." And of the UK Manual, para. 11.3.2. See also Dinstein, 44.

27 Shany, 376. See also Benvenisti, who states that: "The law of occupation is applicable to regions in which foreign forces are present, and in which they can maintain control over the life of the local population and exercise the authority of the legitimate power. The test for effective control is not the military strength of the foreign army which is situated outside the borders that surround the foreign area. What matters is the extent of that power's effective control over civilian life within the occupied area; their ability, in the words of Article 43 of the Hague Regulations, to 'restore and ensure public order and civil life.'" Benvenisti, 308-309.

28 Thus, Greenspan states that: "Once an occupation has started, it must be maintained effectively if it is to be regarded as valid. If the occupant evacuated the territory, is driven out, or ceases to maintain effective control for any reason, and the legitimate government is able to resume its authority and functions, occupation ceases." M. Greenspan, The Modern Law of Land Warfare 223 (1959). See also L. C. Green, The Contemporary Law of Armed Conflict 258 (2nd ed., 2000) ("But if the [Occupying Power] evacuates or retreats from the territory and the legitimate government is able to reassert its authority, the occupation ceases."); UK Manual, 11.7; Shany, 378; Yutaka Arai-Takahashi, The law of occupation 16 (2009).

29 Dinstein, 272-273.

30 HCJ 9132/07, Al-Bassiouni v. The Prime Minister, *Takdin Elyon* 2008(1) 1213, 1217 (hereinafter: The Al-Bassiouni Case), *available in English at* http://elyon1.court.gov.il/verdictssearch/EnglishVerdictsSearch.aspx.

31 The list is based on a compilation of arguments from the following sources: PLO Negotiation Affairs Department, "The Israel Disengagement Plan: Gaza still occupied," available at http://domino.un.org/unispal.nsf/0145a8233e14d2b585256cbf005af141/f7c5f26122c733598525707b006097a9?OpenDocument; Dinstein, 276-280; J. Dugard, *Report of the Special Rapporteur*

on the Situation of Human Rights in the Palestinian Territories Occupied since 1967, U.N. Doc. A/HRC/4/17 (2007), available at http://unispal.un.org/UNISPAL.NSF/0/B59FE224D4A4587D8525728B00697DAA; Amnesty International, *Occupied Palestinian Territories: The Conflict in Gaza: A Briefing on Applicable Law, Investigations, and Accountability*, available athttp://www.amnesty.org/en/library/asset/MDE15/007/2009/en/4dd8f595-e64c-11dd-9917-ed717fa5078d/mde150072009en.pdf (2009); Human Rights Watch, *Israel: "Disengagement" Will Not End Gaza Occupation*, available athttp://www.hrw.org/en/news/2004/10/28/israel-disengagement-will-not-end-gaza-occupation (2007); Gisha, *Disengaged Occupiers: The Legal Status of Gaza*, available athttp://www.gisha.org/UserFiles/File/Report%20for%20the%20website.pdf (2007); B'Tselem, *Israel's Obligations According to International Law*, available athttp://www.btselem.org/english/gaza_strip/israels_obligations.asp. For a detailed critical analysis of the different positions, see Bell and Shefi, "The mythical post-2005 Israeli occupation of the Gaza Strip" 16 Israel Affairs 268 (2010), who analyze each set of arguments separately in pp. 276-288. See also the analysis of Shany, 379-383.

32 The factual situation has changed in this regard and the Rafah crossing has recently been opened, as will be explained below. The reference here is to the arguments made by those claiming that Israel is the occupier of Gaza, and at the time these arguments were made the crossing was still closed.

33 See Schmitt's analysis regarding the no-fly zone imposed on the northern and southern parts of Iraq by the United States, the UK, and France following the First Gulf War: "...the concept of aerial occupation is not a legal one. In traditional humanitarian law, occupation is a term of art for physical control by one belligerent over land territory of another (or of a State occupied against its will, but without resistance). When an occupation occurs, rights and duties arise as between the occupying power and individuals located in the occupied area. An aerial occupation, by contrast, is simply a *de facto*, vice *de jure*, status in which limits are placed on a States' use of its own airspace," M. N. Schmitt, *Clipped Wings: Effective and Legal No-fly Zone Rules of Engagement*, 20 Loy. L.A. Int'l & Comp. L.J. 727, 729, fn. 6 (1998). Dinstein states categorically that "Belligerent occupation cannot rest solely on either naval power or air power, however formidable that may be." Dinstein, 44.

34 See Shany, 380.

35 See Bell and Shefi, 282-283.

36 The term "relatively" is used since the Rafah Crossing has been opened several times, some of them in a forcible manner. In addition there is an expansive system of underground tunnels connecting the Gaza Strip and the Egyptian side, which serves the flow of goods, arms, funds, and operatives.

37 See, e.g., the report of Hansen Join, Agene France-Presser, "Egypt to throw open Rafah border crossing with Gaza: FM," The dailynewsegypt, April 29, 2011, available at http://www.thedailynewsegypt.com/egypt/egypt-to-throw-open-rafah-border-crossing-with-gaza-fm.html. According to this report the Egyptian foreign minister, Nabil al-Araby, said on April 29, 2011, that Egypt will permanently open the Rafah border crossing to ease the blockade on Gaza.

38 Bell and Shefi, 277.

39 Sampson points out that reserving the right to reenter a territory because of security considerations is a common reservation made by a withdrawing occupying power. This was done by the Allied forces when they left West Germany after signing the treaty ending the occupation in 1955 – E. Samson, "Is Gaza occupied? Redefining the legal status of Gaza" 83 Mideast Security and Policy Studies at 31 (2010), available at http://www.biu.ac.il/Besa/MSPS83.pdf.

40 In para. 356.

41 Shany, 382. Curiously, Dinstein, at 279, finds that these incursions are enough to find that Israel has made its "authority felt" in the area, although it is quite clear from his analysis elsewhere (pp. 43-44) that the meaning of this term is actual authority in a manner supplanting the authority of the displaced sovereign. Dinstein also states (on p. 45) that occupation ends when the occupying power "loses its grip" over an occupied territory, in whole or in part. Israel clearly has no "grip" over the Gaza Strip nor the ability to "make its authority felt" therein, otherwise it would arguably have been more successful in stopping attacks against it stemming from this area.

42 Bell and Shefi, 283

43 See also Shany, 380.

44 The Al-Bassiouni Case, para. 12.

45 Dinstein, 279.

46 See Shany, 381.

47 See analysis in the Turkel Report – Part one, 27 fn. 36. See also Y. Shany, "Binary law meets complex reality: The occupation of Gaza debate" 41 Isr. L. R. 68, 79 (2008).

48 See, e.g., News Agencies, "Hamas appoints foreign minister for first time in cabinet reshuffle," *Haaretz*, March 10, 2011, available at http://www.haaretz.com/news/diplomacy-defense/hamas-appoints-foreign-minister-for-first-time-in-cabinet-reshuffle-1.348342. See also Bell and Shefi, 277.

49 Bell and Shefi, 283.

50 Hence, for example, even within the current attempts at reconciliation there is no agreement to subordinate the armed forces of Hamas in the Gaza Strip to the commanders of the PA forces in the West Bank – see, e.g., J. Greenberg, "Palestinian factions Fatah and Hamas formally sign unity accord," *Washington Post*, May 4, 2011, available at http://www.washingtonpost.com/world/palestinian-factions-formally-sign-unity-accord/2011/05/04/AFD89MmF_story.html?hpid=z6.

51 Shany, 380-381. Dinstein bases his conclusion that the Gaza Strip is still occupied also on the unity between the Gaza Strip and the West Bank (p. 277), but in another part of his book (p. 45) explains that the territory subject to effective control of the occupying power may grow or shrink in size according to the circumstances and that occupation ends in the areas where the occupier loses its grip. In other words, this is a factual question that has nothing to do with the political unity of the occupied territory. The Congo-Uganda Case, supra note 19, is again a good example of partial occupation over certain parts of a country, which changes in scope according to the factual situation.

52 See also the analysis of Shany, 380, 382.

53 *See* M. Sassoli, *Legislation and Maintenance of Public Order and Civil Life by Occupying Power*, 16 Eur. J. Int'l L. 661, 682 (2005) ("This raises the question of when the devolution of governmental authority to a national government is effective enough to end the applicability of IHL on belligerent occupation altogether... The decisive factor is, therefore, who effectively exercises governmental authority."); Malanczuk, supra note 17, at 498.

54 On August 20, 2005, the chairman of the PA, Mahmoud Abbas (Abu Mazen) issued an edict transferring all territories vacated by Israel to the PA. The edict stipulates that the PA "will assert its immediate control over the areas from which Israeli forces will withdraw" and "will lay its hands on a temporary basis on all assets, movable or immovable, until their status will be determined by the law." A committee of ministers was formed by the PA government in order to coordinate and oversee the preparations for assuming responsibility for these areas (see http://www.terrorism-info.org.il/malam_multimedia/html/final/sp/heb_n/d2laung_05.htm).

55 Compare Dinstein, 52.

56 Supra note 19.

57 Para. 53 of his opinion.

58 Para. 54.

59 Bell and Shefi (at 286) exemplify that even those claiming that occupation still exists do not expect nor desire Israel to implement all the rules of occupation, since this would require it to reenter the Gaza Strip and interfere in its internal affairs. See also the analysis of N. Rostow, Gaza, Iraq, Lebanon: Three Occupations under International Law, 37 Isr. Yearbook Hum. Rts. 205, 218-221 (2008).

60 This short chapter will not enter into an analysis of the legal consequences of this situation. These were the subject matter of The Al-Bassiouni Case.

61 Compare the conclusion of Shany – Binary Law, 83-86. See also Samson, 37-38.

THE VIOLATION OF ISRAEL'S RIGHT TO SOVEREIGN EQUALITY IN THE UNITED NATIONS

Alan Baker

INTRODUCTION

It is assumed, and even goes without saying, that as a nation-state within the framework of international diplomacy, Israel enjoys the most elementary and basic right of all states: to be regarded and accepted, and to conduct itself vis-à-vis other states **on the basis of full equality**.

The concept of statehood implies that an entity exercises the requisite components of orderly governance of its population, responsibility for its actions, capability to enter into and implement its obligations vis-à-vis other entities, and those other qualities that render it a viable member of international society.

As such, statehood inherently implies commonality with a wider framework of parallel sovereign entities that carry the same or similar capabilities and qualities, so as to function as an international community. Thus, implicit in the concept of statehood is the characteristic of interrelationships with like entities on an equal basis, without which statehood as such would be purely introvert and relate only to the inner framework of relationships between the government and the population.

While theoretically such assumptions may be both correct and logical, in practice they are not applied to Israel in several contexts within the international community.

The intergovernmental framework in which this situation is typified is the United Nations, which practices a blatant and open policy of discrimination against Israel that is clearly *ultra vires* the very Charter that guides the UN's functioning.

Similarly, but to a lesser degree, the International Red Cross movement has, for over sixty years since the establishment of the state of Israel, avoided acceptance of Israel as a fully-fledged member of the movement, despite the operation by Israel of a well-organized medical and humanitarian assistance organ, under the emblem of the Red Shield of David.

SOVEREIGN EQUALITY IN INTERNATIONAL LAW

The very concept of sovereign equality is rooted in the emergence of the state as an entity that interrelates with other states. It emerged with the 1648 Peace of Westphalia, which put an end to a series of conflicts between Europe's Catholic and Protestant monarchs in the early seventeenth century. This document legitimized the right of sovereigns to govern their people free from outside interference.

During the initial drafting of the Charter of the United Nations, the expert in jurisprudence Hans Kelsen, in an article in the 1944 *Yale Law Journal*, makes reference to the Moscow Declaration of October 1943 in which the governments of the United States, the United Kingdom, the Soviet Union, and China jointly declared that they recognized "the necessity of establishing at the earliest practicable date a general international organization, based on the principle of sovereign equality of all peace-loving States and open to membership by all such States, large and small for the maintenance of international peace and security."[1] Kelsen goes on to analyze the connection between the two concepts as follows:

> The term "sovereign equality" used in the Four Power Declaration probably means sovereignty *and* equality; two generally recognized characteristics of States as subjects of international law; for to speak of "sovereign equality" is justified only insofar as both qualities are considered to be connected with each other. Frequently the equality of states is explained as a consequence of or as implied by their sovereignty.

Being subjects of international law, member states in the international community are, by definition, equal to each other. Sir Robert Jennings, former president of the International Court of Justice, notes that:

> This equality is not equality of power, territory or economy: States are, by their nature, unequal as regards their territorial, financial, military and other characteristics. Rather, this equality is as members of the international community, whatever the differences between States. Thus sovereign equality refers to the legal equality of States, as opposed to the political equality, and is often described as "juridical equality," i.e., equality before the law; in the case of States, international law.[2]

Sovereign equality is a fundamental component of the 1945 UN Charter. The principle of equality is set down in the introductory paragraph, which states: "We the peoples of the United Nations determined...to reaffirm faith...in the equal rights...of nations large and small."[3]

The principle itself is incorporated in Article 2, according to which:

> The Organization and its Members, in pursuit of the Purposes stated in Article 1, shall act in accordance with the following Principles:
>
> 1. The Organization is based on the principle of the sovereign equality of all its Members.[4]

This principle was given added clarification and weight by the UN General Assembly in the 1970 "Declaration on Principles of International Law concerning Friendly Relations and Co-operation among States in accordance with the Charter of the United Nations,"[5] a document intended to clarify the provisions of the UN Charter for implementation purposes. In its twelfth preambular paragraph the declaration reaffirmed:

> Reaffirming, in accordance with the Charter, the basic importance of sovereign equality and stressing that the purposes of the United Nations can be implemented only if States enjoy sovereign equality and comply fully with the requirements of this principle in their international relations,

In detailing the principle of sovereign equality, the declaration stated as follows:

All States enjoy sovereign equality. They have equal rights and duties and are equal members of the international community, notwithstanding differences of an economic, social, political or other nature.

In particular, sovereign equality includes the following elements:
(a) States are judicially equal;
(b) Each State enjoys the rights inherent in full sovereignty;
(c) Each State has the duty to respect the personality of other States;
(d) The territorial integrity and political independence of the State are inviolable;
(e) Each State has the right freely to choose and develop its political, social, economic and cultural systems;
(f) Each State has the duty to comply fully and in good faith with its international obligations and to live in peace with other States.

SOVEREIGN EQUALITY AND ISRAEL'S RIGHTS

But theory and practice pull apart. Most theorists acknowledge the fact that sovereign equality is not a principle that actually characterizes the *modus operandi* of the UN.

> ...the view that States are fundamentally equal appears to be mostly theoretical; they are not truly equal under the UN Charter system.[6]

This is especially evident in Israel's case where the assumptions inherent in sovereign equality – judicial equality, equality of voting, equality in participation in all UN activities and processes, and equality in membership in all fora – break down and leave Israel isolated and discriminated-against.

THE REGIONAL GROUP SYSTEM

The root-cause of Israel's isolation in the United Nations is the regional group system, ostensibly intended as a means of instituting a system of "equitable geographical representation" within the organization, which, while not formally dictated by the terms of the UN Charter, nevertheless has become an essential component in the working structure of the organization.[7]

The abovementioned Sir Robert Jennings refers to the regional group system as follows:[8]

> The regional group system has become the central mechanism for the representation and participation of UN Members in the UN system. Membership of a regional group is the only way full participation in the work of the UN system can be ensured.

On the issue of selection of candidates for positions in UN organs or bodies, he goes on to state:[9]

> In those UN bodies where regional group voting has been formalized...membership of a regional group is the only way a state can have its candidate put forward for a position...
>
> In summary, a state that is not a regional group member can never be elected to a UN body which formally or informally has adopted the regional group system for distribution of elected places...
>
> Even where the distribution of elected places has not been established according to a fixed formula, if distribution of elected places is to take place according to "equitable geographical distribution," this is to be interpreted by members as meaning that elected places should be distributed according to the regional group system. In such a case, regional groups consult amongst themselves over the distribution of positions and then consult [internally]...to agree upon which of their members are to be "nominated"...[10]

The geographical groups ostensibly encompassing all UN member states are the Western European and Others Group (WEOG), the Asian Group, the African Group, the Eastern European Group, and the Latin America and Caribbean Group (GRULAC).This system places the entire process of elections to organs and committees throughout the UN system, as well as consultations on virtually all issues on the agenda, under the exclusive jurisdiction of the regional groups.

Since Israel is excluded from its geographical regional group – the Asian Group (by vote of the Arab and Muslim members of that group) – and is not accepted as a full member in the Western European and Others Group, and does not enjoy any other special or *ex-officio* position in the United Nations, Israel is, to all intents and purposes, denied its Charter-guaranteed equality.

CONSEQUENCES OF ISRAEL'S EXCLUSION

In such a situation Israel can never put up its candidacy for membership of the Security Council, the Economic and Social Council, or the other major UN organs such as the International Court of Justice, it is denied any chance of having its jurists chosen as candidates for the major juridical institutions, tribunals, and courts within the UN system, and it cannot participate in consultations between states, organized within the regional group system, to determine positions and voting on issues, resolutions, and other matters.

A particularly sad and frustrating, yet typical example of this boycott of Israel's candidates is the case of the late Prof. Shabtai Rosenne, generally considered to have been the world's greatest expert on the International Court of Justice, the laws of international treaties, and the law of the sea. Prof. Rosenne was nominated at different periods to be a judge on the International Court of Justice, and later to be a judge on the International Tribunal on the Law of the Sea. However, due to the fact that Rosenne, an Israeli, was not supported by any regional group, his election failed.

This case of clear discrimination against Israel was, for several years, raised annually by both Prof. Rosenne and Ambassador Alan Baker, respectively, Israel's representatives to the Sixth (Legal) Committee of the General Assembly, under the agenda item entitled "Report of the Special Committee on the Charter of the United Nations and on Strengthening of the Role of the Organization." Referring to a working paper that had been discussed in the Special Committee, on the improvement of cooperation between the United Nations and regional organizations, Israel's representative (Alan Baker) stated the following on October 20, 1992:

> 89. Before determining viable regional procedures for dealing with crises through regional organizations, the Special Committee might wish to consider such questions as universality and equality within regional organizations, given that those principles are basic components of the United Nations Charter and would have to be more or less applicable with respect to the regional organizations concerned. The United Nations is a universal intergovernmental organization, and an equal opportunity must be given to all Members to participate fully in its activities. Regional organizations that could potentially function in cooperation with the United Nations pursuant to the principle

enunciated in Article 52 of the Charter, according to which their activities should be "consistent with the Purposes and Principles of the United Nations," must also seek to involve all the States in the geographical Region in question. Regional activities directed towards the settlement of local disputes, the establishment of regional security mechanisms or the establishment of information networks could only be pursued when all the countries of a region were regarded as fully accepted and equal parties to them. His delegation trusted that the element of universality and equality within regional organizations would be considered in revised versions of the working paper and in their consideration by the Special Committee with a view to placing the elements of the working paper within the framework envisaged in Chapter VIII of the Charter.

> 91. The principles of the sovereign equality of States and the universality of the United Nations had not yet been fully implemented within the United Nations system as a whole. Israel, which had been confined to membership of a regional group composed of a single State, had repeatedly deplored the imbalance in the organs of the General Assembly and other bodies of the United Nations system. Elections were inevitably a function of political considerations, and regional groupings were *clearly* identified. In the context of giving reality to the Secretary-General's observations in his report, "An agenda for peace," regarding "democracy within the family of the United Nations" and the need for "the fullest consultation, participation and engagement of all States, large and small, in the work of the Organization" (A/47/277-S/24111, para. 82), it would perhaps be advisable for the Special Committee to consider giving substance to the principles of the sovereign equality of States and the universality of the United Nations by examining alternative systems of representation in organs and bodies which would better ensure the realization of those principles.[11]

Some years later, in a speech on March 25, 1998, addressing Israel's exclusion from the regional group system, the UN Secretary-General admitted:

> one way to write that new chapter [in Israeli-UN relations] would be to rectify an anomaly: Israel's position as the only Member State that is not a Member of one of the regional groups, which means it has no chance of being elected to serve on main organs such as the Security Council or Economic and Social Council. We must uphold the principle of equality among all UN member states.

He reiterated this view a year later, on May 12, 1999, stating:

> Israel could do much more for the United Nations were it not for a significant obstacle: its status as the only Member State that is not a member of a regional group, which is the basis of participation in many United Nations bodies and activities.[12]

In his detailed legal opinion regarding the "Exclusion of Israel from the United Nations Regional Group System" dated November 4, 1999, Sir Robert Jennings analyzed in detail the nature of the

Reprinted from The New York Times, September 23, 1998

Countries eligible to sit on the United Nations Security Council:

Afghanistan
Albania
Algeria
Andorra
Angola
Antigua and Barbuda
Argentina
Armenia
Australia
Austria
Azerbaijan
Bahamas
Bahrain
Bangladesh
Barbados
Belarus
Belgium
Belize
Benin
Bhutan
Bolivia
Bosnia and Herzegovina
Botswana
Brazil
Brunei Darussalam
Bulgaria
Burkina Faso
Burundi
Cambodia
Cameroon
Canada
Cape-Verde
Central African Republic
Chad
Chile
China
Colombia
Comoro Islands
Congo
Costa Rica
Côte d'Ivoire
Croatia
Cuba
Cyprus
Czech Republic
Democratic People's Republic of Korea
Democratic Republic of the Congo
Denmark
Djibouti
Dominica
Dominican Republic
Ecuador
Egypt
El Salvador
Equatorial Guinea
Eritrea
Estonia
Ethiopia
Fiji
Finland
France
Gabon
Gambia
Georgia
Germany
Ghana
Greece
Grenada
Guatemala
Guinea
Guinea-Bissau
Guyana
Haiti
Honduras
Hungary
Iceland
India
Indonesia
Iran
Iraq
Ireland
Italy
Jamaica
Japan
Jordan
Kazakhstan
Kenya
Kuwait
Kyrgyzstan
Laos
Latvia
Lebanon
Lesotho
Liberia
Libya
Liechtenstein
Lithuania
Luxembourg
Madagascar
Malawi
Malaysia
Maldives
Mali
Malta
Marshall Islands
Mauritania
Mauritius
Mexico
Micronesia
Moldova
Monaco
Mongolia
Morocco
Mozambique
Myanmar
Namibia
Nepal
Netherlands
New Zealand
Nicaragua
Niger
Nigeria
Norway
Oman
Pakistan
Palau
Panama
Papua New Guinea
Paraguay
Peru
Philippines
Poland
Portugal
Qatar
Republic of Korea
Romania
Russian Federation
Rwanda
St. Kitts and Nevis
St. Lucia
St. Vincent and the Grenadines
Samoa
San Marino
São Tomé and Principe
Saudi Arabia
Senegal
Seychelles
Sierra Leone
Singapore
Slovakia
Slovenia
Solomon Islands
Somalia
South Africa
Spain
Sri Lanka
Sudan
Suriname
Swaziland
Sweden
Syria
Tajikistan
Tanzania
Thailand
The Former Yugoslav Republic of Macedonia
Togo
Trinidad and Tobago
Tunisia
Turkey
Turkmenistan
Uganda
Ukraine
United Arab Emirates
United Kingdom
United States
Uruguay
Uzbekistan
Vanuatu
Venezuela
Viet Nam
Yemen
Yugoslavia
Zambia
Zimbabwe

Countries not eligible to sit on the United Nations Security Council:

Israel

Believe it or not, Israel is the only one of the 185 member countries ineligible to serve on the United Nations Security Council, the key deliberative group of the world body. Even Iraq is eligible. So is Iran. And so, too, are Cuba, Libya, North Korea, Sudan and Syria.

Why is it that these seven nations, all cited by the U.S. State Department as sponsors of terrorism, are eligible to serve rotating terms on the Security Council, yet Israel, a democratic nation and member of the UN since 1950, is not?

To be eligible for election, a country must belong to a regional group. Every UN member state—from the smallest to the largest—is included in one of the five regional groups. By geography, Israel should be part of the Asian bloc but such countries as Iraq and Saudi Arabia have prevented its entry for decades.

But only Israel among all UN members is denied the right to belong to any regional group. As a temporary measure, Israel has sought acceptance in the West European and Others Group (WEOG), which includes not only the democracies of Western Europe but also the United States and other Western countries.

The UN Secretary General, Kofi Annan, on March 25, 1998, called for an end to this injustice to Israel and "the normalization of Israel's status within the United Nations..." Moreover, several countries, including the U.S., Australia, Canada and Norway, have expressed support for Israel's admission to WEOG, but the 15-member European Union refuses to act.

Thus, without membership in a regional group, Israel can never be elected to serve a term on the Security Council or, for that matter, to the other most important bodies of the UN system, such as the Economic and Social Council, the World Court, and the Commission on Human Rights.

What should you do? Make yourself heard! You can make a difference.

Mail the coupons below to the current European Union leaders, or e-mail them from our web site. For more information, please contact us.

The American Jewish Committee

Full-page advertisement of the American Jewish Committee in the New York Times illustrating the fact that only Israel was not eligible to sit on the UN Security Council in 1998 (New York Times)

breach of the UN Charter by the UN itself in enabling the continued and ongoing exclusion of Israel from the enjoyment of its right to sovereign equality:

> Exclusion of one member from an essential part of the workings of an international organization in which all other members are entitled to participate is a crude breach of the rule on non-discrimination. Discriminatory exclusion of a UN member from the regional group system therefore places the United Nations in breach of Article 2.1[13]

> The actual situation for the State of Israel...is that its rights as a Member of the United Nations to participate in the work of the United Nations are largely nullified by its exclusion from membership of a regional group. In practical terms it is simply denied participation in any (indeed most) of the activities, functions, and offices in which all other Members do participate and are able by generally accepted means to exercise influence and power, to nominate for appointments including appointments or elections to UN agencies and organs. This hobbled and undignified position in which the State of Israel uniquely finds itself is without doubt morally shocking; but it is also manifestly unlawful and constitutes a breach of both the letter and the spirit of the Charter of the United Nations.[14]
>
> Israel's continuing exclusion from the regional group system is both unlawful and strikes at the roots of the principles on which the United Nations exists. The remedy for the illegality is clear: Israel's admission to full participation in one of the regional groups. I venture to suggest that Israel's exclusion should no longer be tolerated; and that it is now an issue of primary importance for the Organization itself to see that it be remedied. So long as it continues, the Organization is itself in breach of its own Charter.[15]

Despite these very serious and ominous words from a former president of the UN's main judicial organ – the International Court of Justice – himself a world-renowned international lawyer, nothing was done by the UN to remedy this breach of the UN Charter by the organization itself.

Had there been established a monitoring or supervisory body above the UN, empowered to review actions by the organization in light of the Charter requirements and to declare UN actions and resolutions *ultra vires* the Charter, there is no doubt that the discrimination against Israel in denying its sovereign equality would have been remedied long ago.

LATER DEVELOPMENTS

Efforts have been made over the years to improve Israel's situation, even by means of a compromise step of seeking admission to another geographical group. A limited element of success was achieved in May 2000, when Israel became a "temporary" member of the Western European and Others Group (WEOG) in New York. WEOG is unique in that geography is not the sole defining factor, and WEOG members include states from North America, Western Europe, the Pacific region, and Asia. Israel's "temporary" membership was limited chiefly to participation in consultations rather than nominating candidates for election to main UN bodies (although election to the lower bodies was envisaged), and it was conditioned on a formal commitment by Israel to continue to seek acceptance into its own geographic group – the Asian Group.

As such it remains highly unlikely that Israel will ever be elected to such major UN organs as the Security Council, ECOSOC, or the International Court of Justice. Furthermore, the positive yet limited implications of Israel's temporary admission into WEOG in New York notwithstanding, Israel remains excluded from the regional group system outside New York. As such, Israel can

Ambassador Richard Holbrooke, U.S. Permanent Representative to the UN in 1999, sought to obtain for Israel the right of sovereign equality in the UN system, including the right to be elected to the UN Security Council. (AP Photo/Thierry Charlier)

neither participate in Western group consultations and meetings in the UN bodies outside New York, nor can it nominate candidates to UN positions in UN bodies where elections for those bodies are not organized by the New York regional group system.

A slight improvement occurred recently, in January 2010, when a group of non-EU democracies within the UN Human Rights Council (Japan, the United States, Canada, Australia, and New Zealand, collectively called JUSCANZ) admitted Israel into membership of their group, in light of Israel's being considered by them a "likeminded" state.[16]

IS THERE A REMEDY FOR THE EXCLUSION OF ISRAEL?

In light of this situation that has existed since the very commencement of Israel's membership of the United Nations, and despite best efforts by Israel's representatives and others, the blatant discrimination against one member state, in clear contravention of the UN Charter, has not changed. The question remains how, if at all, this situation might be remedied.

Since the regional group system was never formalized or articulated within the UN Charter, but rather developed informally outside the Charter's confines, so theoretically, any change in the system could be achieved without the need for amending the Charter, a Herculean task that would be virtually impossible to achieve.

Such a change could be achieved, as hoped-for by Israel over the years, within the Special Committee on the Charter of the United Nations and on the Strengthening of the Role of the Organization, whose mandate clearly could cover the need to correct inconsistencies between the Charter principles and the performance of the organization. Logically, it would require replacing the discriminative and defective regional group system with a simpler system of an all-embracing roster of the member states, which would be called upon to serve on the various UN bodies in turn. However, such an option would require an extensive consensus among members of the Special Committee and the Sixth (Legal) Committee, which would be called upon to confirm any such recommendation by the Special Committee.

Another possibility might be to establish an ad hoc committee to review the implementation of sovereign equality, and recommend practical changes in UN procedures with a view to assuring full observance of the Charter principles. Such recommendations would then be adopted by resolution or decision of the General Assembly.

Shabtai Rosenne (center) together with Abba Eban (left) and Reuven Shiloah, 1949 (Israel National Photo Collection/ Pinn Hans)

Finally, the reference above to the lack, in the UN context, of any superior monitoring body, an ombudsman, or some type of "Council of Wise Persons," composed of former Secretaries-General, senior ICJ and other judges, and prominent experts, who would review UN actions and resolutions and determine their validity and compliance with the Charter principles, is particularly relevant in the present situation. Some consideration might be given to establishing such a body, which could restore to the organization an element of credibility and realism that seems to be missing.

As stressed by Jennings in his 1999 opinion over eleven years ago, this situation must be remedied, and Israel given its right to full equality. But this can only be achieved if likeminded member states of the United Nations act in a concerted manner to bring about the necessary change.

NOTES

1. *The Principle of Sovereign Equality of States as a Basis for International Organization* at 207. 53 Yale Law Journal, March 1944.
2 Sir Robert Jennings, *Opinion Regarding the Exclusion of Israel from the United Nations Regional Group System*, November 1999, at 19. For a detailed analysis of the concept of sovereign equality in international law see Brierly, *The Law of Nations*, 4th ed. (1949) at 117; Dickenson, *The Equality of States in International Law* (1920) at 334-5; H. Kelsen, *General Theory of Law and the State* (1945) at 253-4; Oppenheim's *International Law*, 9th ed. (1992) at 340; H. Weinschel, *The Doctrine of Equality of States and its Recent Modifications*, 45(3) AJIL (1951) at 438.
3. UN Charter Preamble, 6 June 1945.
4 Charter of the United Nations, 1945.
5 UNGA Resolution 2625 (XXV), 24 October 1970.
6 Snigdha Nahar, *Sovereign Equality in International Law*, http://www.globalpolitician.com/print.asp?id=4351.
7 For a full analysis of the UN regional group system see Hudson Institute, New York, "Inter-governmental groups and alliances operating within the UN system" http://www.eyeontheun.org/view.asp?p=55&l=11.
8 Sir Robert Jennings, *Opinion Regarding the Exclusion of Israel from the United Nations Regional Group System*, 4 November 1999, para. 2.1.
9 Id. para. 2.2.
10 Id. para 2.3.
11 Statement by Alan Baker A/C.6/47/SR.17 paras. 89, 92, at pp. 22-3.
12 Id. para 5.5.
13 Jennings, id. para. 3.16.
14 I d. para.4 of the summary by Jennings of his opinion.
15 Id. para.13 of the summary by Jennings of his opinion.
16 http://www.israel-un.org/israel-and-the-un/israel-at-the-un and http://www.ajc.org/site/apps/nlnet/content2.aspx?c=i jITI2PHKoG&b=849241&ct=7872849.Israel's admission to this group came about despite protracted opposition by New Zealand.

COUNTERING CHALLENGES TO ISRAEL'S LEGITIMACY

Alan M. Dershowitz

Of all the nations on the face of the earth, Israel has the most lawful origin. It was conceived in law, born through law, and has survived lawfully. It is not among the nations, such as the United States, born in bloodshed through revolution. Nor has it, like other nations, been expanded through aggressive warfare. It was not settled by outsiders, as were Australia, New Zealand, Canada, the United States, and other countries. It did not, like those countries, rid itself of virtually the entire native population, since Jews were its aboriginal people and approximately a million Arabs now constitute a fifth of its population.

Yet despite its origins in resolutions of the League of Nations, the United Nations, and its own declaration of statehood, recognized by most of the world, Israel is the only country in the world today whose legitimacy is rejected by its enemies and questioned by others. Other countries are criticized, as is Israel, for their policies, their actions, and their omissions. But only with respect to Israel does criticism quickly transform into demonization, delegitimization, and calls for its destruction.

Four unfounded charges represent some of the most recurrent efforts to delegitimize the Jewish state, namely:

1. Israel is an illegitimate "colonial" state.
2. Israel secured its statehood unlawfully.
3. Israel is an apartheid state.
4. Israel and a Palestinian entity must become one state.

These charges must be vigorously refuted wherever and whenever they arise. My responses are based on fact, morality, and law.

1. THE CHARGE THAT ISRAEL IS AN ILLEGITIMATE "COLONIAL" STATE

To believe that Israel is a colonial state is to be naïve. Unlike colonial settlers who served the expansionist, commercial, and military goals of imperial nations such as Great Britain and France, Jewish refugees who settled the Land of Israel were escaping countries that had oppressed them for centuries. These refugees came from places such as Czarist Russia, where they were discriminated against and persecuted – even killed – because of their faith. They retained no connection with their "home" countries, a necessary element of colonization. Moreover, they did not simply establish new "colonies," but reestablished and joined with native Jewish communities in a place that the Jewish people have called home – and lived in – for more than three thousand years.

Historians believe the Hebrews arrived in present-day Israel sometime in the second millennium BCE. According to Martin Gilbert, "For more than one thousand six hundred years the Jews formed the main settled population of Palestine."[1] During much of this time, the land was ruled by independent Hebrew kingdoms under King David and his successors. When the Romans finally seized control by suppressing revolts in 70 and 135 CE, they named the land "Palestine" in an explicit attempt to de-Judaize it. Despite continued efforts to rid "Palestine" of Jews throughout the years, however, thousands managed to remain and to immigrate. Among the Jews who lived in Palestine in the seventh century, for instance, were refugees from Muhammad's bloody massacre of two Arabian Jewish tribes.

After the Crusades, Jews reestablished centers of Jewish learning and commerce in the Land of Israel. From this time on, Palestine was never without a significant and well-documented Jewish presence. When the Ottomans occupied Palestine in 1516, approximately ten thousand Jews lived in the Safed region alone. Many more Jews lived in Jerusalem, Hebron, Acre, and in other locations. Jerusalem, in fact, has had a Jewish majority since the first population figures were gathered in the nineteenth century, and, according to the British consul there, the Muslims of Jerusalem "scarcely exceed[ed] one quarter of the whole population."[2]

More than merely a population center, Palestine remained a center of Jewish piety and mysticism throughout the ages. European Jews contributed to the Jewish religious institutions in Palestine and prayed for a return to Zion and Jerusalem. Jews outside the Land of Israel referred to themselves as living in the "Diaspora" and never abandoned their claim to return to the land from which so many of their ancestors had been forcibly driven.

Life in Palestine was difficult for Jews well before widespread immigration. During the Egyptian occupation of Palestine in the 1830s, indigenous Jews were persecuted mercilessly by Muslim zealots for no other reason than religious bigotry. Even so, a return to Zion was the natural choice for oppressed European Jews. In Palestine these Jews could realize, in their own words, their "civil and political rights," while assisting their Sephardic cousins in mounting a defense against religiously inspired violence. When these new immigrants arrived – or in their words, returned – the land that they lived upon and cultivated was not taken from its rightful owners by force or confiscated by colonial law. It was purchased, primarily from absentee landlords and real estate speculators, at fair or often exorbitant prices.

As Martin Buber observed in 1939, "Our settlers do not come here as the colonists from the Occident, to have natives do their work for them; they themselves set their shoulders to the plow and they spend their strength and their blood to make the land fruitful."[3] The hardworking settlers whom Buber describes were not the tools of the hated czar of Russia or the anti-Semitic regimes of Poland or Lithuania. They sought not to enrich their European homelands but to leave them permanently. They chose to settle a materially worthless piece of real estate in a backwater of the world whose significance to the Jews was religious, historical, and familial. This type of benign immigration simply cannot, in good faith, be called "colonialism." To make such a false charge is to ignore history, blink reality, impose a double standard, and promote bigotry.

2. THE CHARGE THAT ISRAEL SECURED ITS STATEHOOD UNLAWFULLY

Another frequent criticism of Israel is that it secured its statehood unlawfully. The criticism is patently false; Israel has the most lawful origin of any country in the world.

Explaining the origins of Israel's statehood requires an extended historical narrative. Even before World War I, there was a de facto Jewish national home in Palestine consisting of 80,000-90,000 Jews. The Jewish refugees in Palestine had established this homeland without the assistance of any colonial or imperialist power. They had relied on their own hard work in building an infrastructure and cultivating land they had legally purchased. These Jews had the right to determine their own futures consistent with the Wilsonian principle of self-determination. The claim to self-determination was bolstered by the enthusiastic support for a Jewish homeland by other states. The 1917 Balfour Declaration announced that the British government favored "the establishment in Palestine of a national home for the Jewish people."[4] The French, Italians, and Americans agreed. In 1922, the League of Nations Mandate for Palestine proclaimed that "The mandatory [Britain] shall be responsible for placing the country under such...conditions as will secure the establishment of the Jewish national home."[5]

The Jews earned the Balfour Declaration through sweat and blood. The Jewish Legion fought alongside the British army to defeat the Ottoman army during World War I; it was the Palestinian Arabs who had sided with the imperialist, colonialist Turkish Empire against those who favored self-determination. Despite picking the wrong side – which they did again in World War II – the Arabs got 80 percent of Palestine, Transjordan, set aside as an exclusively Arab state, with no Jewish settlement permitted.

Yet Arab opposition to a Jewish home in any part of Palestine, even where Jews were a majority, became increasingly violent. Innocent Jews were brutally murdered and raped. The Grand Mufti of Jerusalem, Haj Amin al-Husseini, preached "Itbah al-Yahud" ("Kill the Jews") and "Nashrab dam al-Yahud" ("We will drink the blood of the Jews"). He told his flock that it would violate Islamic law for even a single inch of Palestine to be controlled by Jews. It was he who sought a truly apartheid Palestine. Of course, this meant that agreeing to mutual self-determination would be impossible.

The Peel Commission of 1937 investigated the "causes of the disturbances" in Palestine and concluded that "one side [the Palestinian Arabs] put itself, not for the first time, in the wrong by resorting to force, whereas the other side patiently kept the law."[6] The commission realized that it would be unfair to force Jews to take minority status in an all-Muslim state.[7] By 1937, after all, Tel Aviv had 150,000 Jews and Jerusalem had 76,000. Half of Haifa's population of 100,000 was Jewish. Jews had their own newspapers, schools, universities, and governance system. The Peel Commission proposed a Jewish home in areas where there was a clear Jewish majority, divided into two noncontiguous sections. The Jews accepted the Peel Commission's suggestion of a two-state solution; the Palestinian Arabs categorically rejected it. Despite the Peel Commission's acknowledgments that "Jews enter Palestine as of right and not on sufferance" and that "Jewish immigration is not merely sanctioned but required by international agreements,"[8] the British issued the White Paper of 1939, limiting Jewish immigration to seventy-five thousand over the next five years. This was, of course, almost precisely the time during which six million European Jews were murdered.[9]

The end of World War II presented the world community with a new set of problems. At the time of the UN partition plan, a quarter-million Jewish refugees were living in deplorable prison camps in the very country that had murdered their parents, children, and siblings. They could not return to Poland because the Poles continued to murder Jews even after the Nazis had been defeated. Nor could they be expected to remain in Germany, where the refugee camps were temporarily located. In addition, there were growing problems in Arab countries with significant Jewish populations. Some of these Arab countries practiced a discriminatory system under which *dhimmis* – a religious category that includes Jews and Christians – were deemed inferior and subject to special unequal rules.

Thus in 1947 the United Nations attempted to solve the problem once and for all by proposing a final partition of Palestine. The Palestinians were offered nearly the same deal they had rejected in 1937 (with the exception of the barren Negev). This was despite the fact of Palestinian and widespread Arab support for the Nazis and despite Winston Churchill's warning that Nazi support meant the Arabs were "owed...nothing in a postwar settlement." The United Nations found, however, "[T]he claims to Palestine of the Arabs and Jews, both possessing validity, are irreconcilable... It is a fact that both of these peoples have their historic roots in Palestine... Only by means of partition can these conflicting national aspirations find substantial expression and qualify both peoples to take their places as independent nations in the international community and in the United Nations." The General Assembly adopted Resolution 181 on November 27, 1941, calling for "Independent Arab and Jewish States and the Special International Regime for the City of Jerusalem."[10]

Israel accepted the partition plan's offer of a majority-Jewish, noncontiguous state. The Palestinians again rejected partition. When the British Mandate expired, the Jews declared independence and promised to "guarantee freedom of religion, conscience, language, education and culture... safeguard the Holy Places of all religions...[and] be faithful to the principles of the Charter of the

United Nations."[11] Just as soon, Egypt, Jordan, Syria, Iraq, and Lebanon, with help from Saudi Arabia, Yemen, and Libya, attacked the newborn state, including its civilian population centers. Israel won the war and was recognized by numerous countries, including both the United States and the Soviet Union. In the course of defeating Arab armies, it also captured more land than allocated to it by UN partition. Much of this land had significant Jewish populations and settlements; its capture was necessary to assure the safety of Jewish residents. The Egyptians and Jordanians also captured land, but for no other reason than to increase their own territory and control Palestinian residents. The Jordanians, occupying the West Bank, and the Egyptians, occupying the Gaza Strip, denied Palestinians the right of self-determination in those lands. Yet this occupation was neither subject to UN condemnation nor widely protested by the Palestinians. Regardless, Israel was accepted as a member state of the United Nations on May 11, 1949.[12]

Israel's statehood was secured lawfully by, among other instruments and acts, the Balfour Declaration of 1917, subsequent declarations to the same effect by other countries, the 1922 League of Nations Mandate, the 1937 Peel Commission Report, the 1947 United Nations partition resolution, Israel's Declaration of Independence, subsequent recognition of the state of Israel by numerous world powers, and Israel's acceptance into the United Nations. I challenge anyone to show me another country that has its origins so steeped in international law.

3. THE CHARGE THAT ISRAEL IS AN APARTHEID STATE

Apartheid, an evil system of racial subjugation, has zero relevance to the Israeli-Palestinian conflict; the concept's use in this context is simply inflammatory provocation. Yet the apartheid charge is leveled again and again by Desmond Tutu, John Dugard, Jimmy Carter, and numerous radical groups that host the annual Israel Apartheid Week on college campuses.[13] The apartheid charge is not a constructive call for change in Israeli policies; it is meant to strike at the very foundations of Israel's legitimacy as a nation. It associates the Jewish state with a system declared a "crime against humanity." It implies –and many of those who make the accusation declare openly – that Israel is illegitimate, racist, and deserving of destruction. Just as the apartheid system in South Africa had to be dismantled entirely, the analogy posits, "apartheid Israel" must be utterly destroyed. It suggests that academic boycotts and divestment campaigns, the tools used against apartheid South Africa, are appropriate for use against Israel.

Institutionalized racism is the sine qua non of apartheid, and without it the word has no accepted meaning. The Rome Statute of the International Criminal Court, for instance, defines apartheid as "inhuman acts…committed in the context of an institutionalized regime of systematic oppression and domination by one racial group over any other racial group or groups and committed with the intention of maintaining that regime." Those who accuse Israel of this type of racism exhibit a fundamental misunderstanding of the nature of the Jewish state. The Jews of Israel themselves comprise *multiple* racial and ethnic groups. Jewish Israelis comprise Europeans, Africans, Ethiopians, Georgians, Persians, and other groups. Race, therefore, cannot form the basis for alleged institutionalized discrimination in Israel because the alleged discriminators (Jewish Israelis) are multiracial themselves.

The analogy still fails even if we extend the apartheid concept to religion. Israeli Jews themselves are not a single religious group. Some actively practice Judaism, many do not. But Israel, unlike neighboring Arab nations, does not use religious coercion; neither is there segregation or discrimination against minorities who are not Jewish. In fact, Israel has consistently maintained and defended sites that are holy to Christians and Muslims, as well as Jewish sites, while Jordan destroyed synagogues – including an ancient Jewish site that was the Jewish equivalent of the Dome of the Rock – and other Jewish institutions as soon as it unlawfully conquered the Jewish Quarter of Jerusalem in 1948.[14]

Apartheid means pervasive racial segregation laws, media censorship, banning of political parties, torture and murder of human rights activists in detention, indoctrination of children with racial ideology, removal of voting rights, and use of the death penalty for political crimes. But in Israel, Muslim and Christian citizens (of which there are more than a million) have the right to vote and regularly elect members of the Knesset, some of whom even oppose Israel's right to exist. There is an Arab member of the Supreme Court, and have been Arab members of the cabinet. Numerous Israeli Arabs hold important positions in businesses, universities, and the cultural life of the nation. There is complete freedom of dissent in Israel and it is practiced vigorously by Muslims, Christians, and Jews alike. And Israel is a vibrant democracy.

That Israel is not an "apartheid state" does not mean that there is not some *de facto* discrimination against its Arab citizens. Most Arabs cannot serve in the army, but few would choose to fight against fellow Arabs even if given that option. In the past, Arabs could not buy homes in certain Jewish areas, just as Jews cannot buy homes in Arab villages. The Israeli Supreme Court, however, ruled that the government may not allocate land based on religion or ethnicity and may not prevent Arab citizens from living wherever they choose.[15] It is fair to say that Israel is making considerable progress in eliminating the vestiges of anti-Arab discrimination that were largely a product of the refusal of the Arab world to accept a Jewish state. It is also fair to say that despite some lingering inequalities, there is far less discrimination in Israel than in any Middle Eastern, Arab, or Muslim nation.

What is true of Israel proper, including Israeli Arab areas, is not true of the occupied territories. Israel ended its occupation of Gaza several years ago, only to be attacked by Hamas rockets. Israel maintains its occupation of the West Bank only because the Palestinians walked away from a generous offer of statehood on 97 percent of the West Bank, with its capital in Jerusalem and with a $35 billion compensation package for refugees. Had they accepted that offer by President Bill Clinton and Prime Minister Ehud Barak – or a later, even more generous offer by former Prime Minister Ehud Olmert[16] – there would be a Palestinian state in the West Bank. There would be no separation barrier. There would be no roads restricted to Israeli citizens (Jews, Muslims, and Christians).[17] And there would be no "illegal" civilian settlements. Many Israelis and others have opposed, and continue to oppose civilian settlements in the West Bank. But to call an occupation, which continues because of the refusal of the Palestinians to accept the two-state solution, "apartheid" is to misuse that word.[18] As those of us who fought in the actual struggle against apartheid well understand, there is no comparison between what happened in South Africa and what is now taking place on the West Bank.

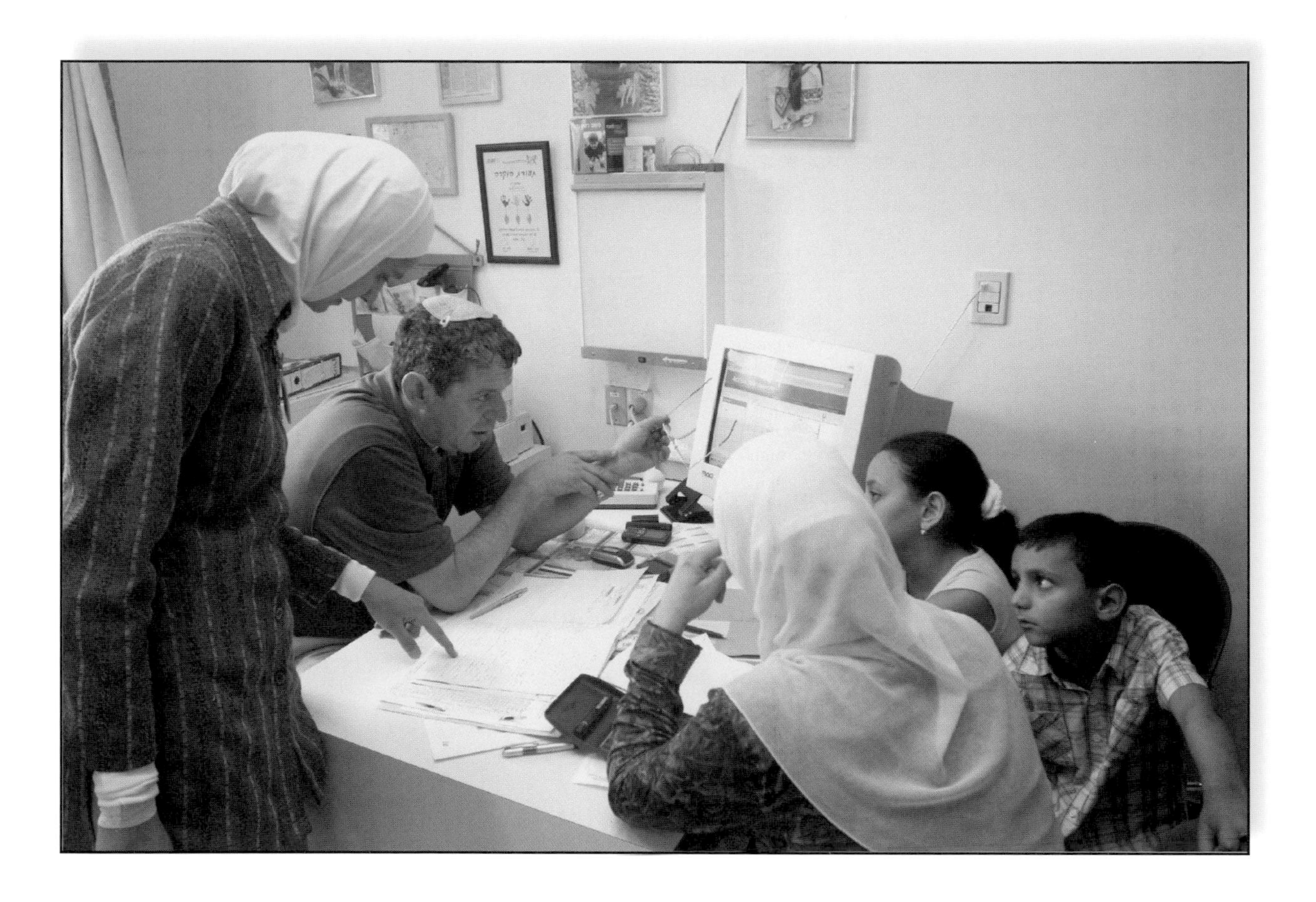

Left to right: Dr. Maha Atwan and Dr. David Zangen with the mother of an Arab child suffering from diabetes, at the Pediatric Endocrinology Department at Hadassah Mount Scopus Hospital in Jerusalem, May 17, 2007. In apartheid South Africa, there were separate hospitals for blacks and whites. (Ariel Jerozolimski)

4. THE CHARGE THAT ISRAEL AND A PALESTINIAN ENTITY MUST BECOME ONE STATE

Because the two-state solution requires recognition of Israel's right to continue to exist as a Jewish democracy, those who oppose Israel's existence have been trying to sell the "one-state" or "binational" solution. I first challenged this ploy – and that is all it is – in a debate with Noam Chomsky in 1973. Chomsky's proposal at that time was consistent with the PLO party line. He wanted to abolish the state of Israel and to substitute a "secular, binational state," based on the model of binational "brotherhood" that then prevailed in Lebanon. Chomsky repeatedly pointed to Lebanon, where Christians and Muslims "lived side by side," sharing power in peace and harmony. This was just two years before Lebanon imploded in fratricidal disaster. Chomsky also used to point to the former Yugoslavia as a model of a one-state solution.[19] This was before it too blew up into five separate states.

I believe now about the one-state solution what I believed then: "Why do not considerations of self-determination and community control favor two separate states: one Jewish and one Arab? Isn't it better for people of common backgrounds to control their own life, culture, and destiny (if they choose), than to bring together in an artificial way people who have shown no ability to live united in peace?"

The consequences of a one-state solution are all too clear. Forcibly integrating Israel proper and the occupied territories into a single political entity would be the surest way to destroy Israel's secular, democratic character. There would be an immediate struggle for demographic superiority. Every death would be seen as a victory by the other side and every birth a defeat. Within decades, the different birthrates would ensure that Palestinians would outnumber Jews, and the binational state would become another Islamic state – Greater Palestine. Israel would thus be destroyed politically, diplomatically, and demographically, rather than by armed struggle – but it would be destroyed nonetheless. The one-state solution is thus an attempt to accomplish by law and demography what Hamas seeks to achieve by terrorism: the extinction of Israel. The practical consequences of such a state would be to leave millions of Jews geographically isolated, politically powerless, and physically defenseless. The one-state solution is rejectionism, pure and simple.

An Arab majority would bode ominously for a Jewish minority. Jewish life within Arab nations, as well as within the British Mandate of Palestine, has been marked by discriminatory laws against *dhimmis* (Jews and Christians), expulsions, and pogroms.[20] Considering the close proximity and history of hostilities between Israeli Jews and Palestinians, it is more than likely that Jews would fare even worse in a Greater Palestine than they have elsewhere in the Arab world. There would be, as Benny Morris puts it, "old scores" to settle.[21] And the wide economic gap between Jews and Palestinians would certainly not "make for peaceful co-existence."[22] It is for good reason that I have likened the proposed one-state solution in the Middle East to Hitler's one-state solution for Europe. Only this time, the Jews would be geographically concentrated and easier to identify.

Five hundred thousand Hindus and Muslims died in the process of partitioning the Indian subcontinent. No one today recommends that those two ethnicities be reintegrated into a binational state so as to resolve the Kashmir dispute. Likewise, Israelis and Palestinians are already, for the most part, geographically distinct. It would be absurd to suggest that they both forgo their separate aspirations to self-determination as a testing ground for failed multicultural fantasies.

What is certain, though, is that neither Israeli Jews nor Palestinians want to be subsumed in a Greater Palestine. A binational state would not only imperil its Jewish population, but would eradicate the one state in the Middle East that affords its Muslim citizens more expansive civil liberties and political prerogatives than any other. Israeli Arabs are better off – as measured by longevity, health care, legal rights, even religious liberty – than other Arabs in the Middle East.

Israel is the nation-state of the Jews and not a Jewish state in the sense that the Vatican is a Catholic state or in the sense that Saudi Arabia is a Muslim state. Israel is a secular state, comprised largely of Jews, and a place of asylum for Jews all over the world. If one people deserve to have a state of their own it is the Jewish people. Israel is not – and it should not become – a theocracy or a state in which freedom of religion is lacking.

In a world with numerous Muslim states, there is surely room for one Jewish state. The one-state solution will fail, but it is also important that it be taken off the table immediately, because its very advocacy – at best a tactical ploy, and at worst a deliberate attempt to sabotage any real prospect for peace – poses a serious barrier to the only peace that has any realistic chance for success: peace based on the two-state solution.

NOTES

1 Martin Gilbert, *The Routledge Atlas of the Arab-Israeli Conflict*, 7th ed. (London: Routledge Taylor Francis Group, 2002), 1.

2 James Finn to Earl of Clarendon, January 1, 1858.

3 Buber to Gandhi, quoted in Arthur Hertzberg, *The Zionist Idea* (Philadelphia: Jewish Publication Society, 1997), 464.

4 Quoted in Benny Morris, *Righteous Victims* (New York: Vintage Books, 2001), 75.

5 League of Nations, Palestine Mandate, July 24, 1922, http://avalon.law.yale.edu/20th_century/palmanda.asp#art1.

6 *Palestine Royal Commission Report (Peel Report)* (London: His Majesty's Stationery Office, 1937), 2.

7 Ibid., 61.

8 Ibid., 147.

9 The Palestinian leadership was not blameless for the Holocaust. The Grand Mufti, who Edward Said noted "represented the Palestinian Arab national consensus," formed an alliance with the Nazis and spent the war years with Hitler in Berlin. The Nazis and the Italian Fascists supported the violence against Jews in Palestine, sending the Mufti millions of dollars. Al-Husseini was apparently planning to return to Palestine in the event of a German victory to construct a death camp near Nablus, modeled after Auschwitz. For more on the connection between the Nazis and the Palestinian leadership, see Alan Dershowitz, *The Case for Israel* (Hoboken, NJ: Wiley, 2003), 54-57. See also Alan Dershowitz, introduction to David G. Dalin and John F. Rothman, *Icon of Evil: Hitler's Mufti and the Rise of Radical Islam* (New Brunswick, NJ: Transaction, 2009), ix–xviii.

10 UN General Assembly, Resolution 181, "Future Government of Palestine," November 29, 1947, http://daccess-dds-ny.un.org/doc/RESOLUTION/GEN/NR0/038/88/IMG/NR003888.pdf?OpenElement.

11 Declaration of the Establishment of the State of Israel, May 14, 1948, http://www.mfa.gov.il/MFA/Peace+Process/Guide+to+the+Peace+Process/Declaration+of+Establishment+of+State+of+Israel.htm.

12 Thomas J. Hamilton, "Israel Wins a Seat in U.N. by 37-12 Vote," *New York Times*, May 12, 1949.

13 See, e.g., Desmond Tutu, "An International Campaign: Build Moral Pressure to End the Occupation," *International Herald Tribune*, June 14, 2002, www.iht.com/articles/2002/06/14/edtutu_ed3_.php; Desmond Tutu, "Apartheid in the Holy Land," *Guardian*, April 29, 2002, www.guardian.co.uk/world/2002/apr/29/comment; John Dugard, "Apartheid: Israelis Adopt What South Africa Dropped," *Atlanta Journal-Constitution*, November 29, 2006; Jimmy Carter, *Palestine: Peace Not Apartheid* (New York: Simon & Schuster, 2006).

14 See, e.g., Sam Pope Brewer, "11-Day Fight Over; 350 Israeli Combatants Are Captured – Hurva Synagogue Razed," *New York Times*, May 29, 1948.

15 *Quadan v. Israel Lands Administration*, HCJ (Israeli Supreme Court) 6698/95, March 8, 2000.

16 See Alan Dershowitz, "Whose Fault Is the Ongoing Occupation of the West Bank?," *Jerusalem Post*, December 5, 2010, http://www.jpost.com/Home/Article.aspx?id=198096.

17 Despite repeated false claims to the contrary, there are absolutely no "for Jews only" roads in the territories or in Israel, as there are "for Muslims only" roads in Saudi Arabia.

18 See Carter, *Palestine*.

19 "One thinks at once of Yugoslavia, where in the course of a successful social revolution, the old conflict-provoking ethnic ties (Serb, Croat, and so forth) give some evidence of being less 'irrational' and less binding, with more individuals thereby willing to think of themselves quite simply as individuals operating within a broad Yugoslav context." Noam Chomsky, *Middle East Illusions* (Lanham, MD: Rowman & Littlefield, 2003), 62, quoting George Zaninovich, *Development of Socialist Yugoslavia* (Baltimore: Johns Hopkins University Press, 1968), 105.

20 Dershowitz, *Case for Israel*, 42-43 (recounting the Hebron massacre of 1929) and 88-89 (describing in detail Jewish treatment in Arab countries following Israeli independence, culminating in the creation of 850,000 Jewish refugees); Michael Oren, *Six Days of War: June 1967 and the Making of the Modern Middle East* (Oxford, UK: Oxford University Press, 2002), 3-4 (on the 1936-1939 Arab pogrom against Jews in Palestine, Baghdad, Cairo, Tunis, and Casablanca), 306-307 (cataloging the pogroms and expulsions of Jews in Arab countries following the Six Day War).

21 Benny Morris, "Politics by Other Means," *New Republic*, March 22, 2004.

22 Ibid.

APPENDICES

THE BALFOUR DECLARATION

November 2, 1917

Foreign Office
November 2nd, 1917

Dear Lord Rothschild,
I have much pleasure in conveying to you, on behalf of His Majesty's Government, the following declaration of sympathy with Jewish Zionist aspirations which has been submitted to, and approved by, the Cabinet.
"His Majesty's Government view with favour the establishment in Palestine of a national home for the Jewish people, and will use their best endeavours to facilitate the achievement of this object, it being clearly understood that nothing shall be done which may prejudice the civil and religious rights of existing non-Jewish communities in Palestine, or the rights and political status enjoyed by Jews in any other country."
I should be grateful if you would bring this declaration to the knowledge of the Zionist Federation.

Yours sincerely,
Arthur James Balfour

THE PALESTINE MANDATE

December, 1922

The Council of the League of Nations:
Whereas the Principal Allied Powers have agreed, for the purpose of giving effect to the provisions of Article 22 of the Covenant of the League of Nations, to entrust to a Mandatory selected by the said Powers the administration of the territory of Palestine, which formerly belonged to the Turkish Empire, within such boundaries as may be fixed by them; and
Whereas the Principal Allied Powers have also agreed that the Mandatory should be responsible for putting into effect the declaration originally made on November 2nd, 1917, by the Government of His Britannic Majesty, and adopted by the said Powers, in favor of the establishment in Palestine of a national home for the Jewish people, it being clearly understood that nothing should be done which might prejudice the civil and religious rights of existing non-Jewish communities in Palestine, or the rights and political status enjoyed by Jews in any other country; and
Whereas recognition has thereby been given to the historical connection of the Jewish people with Palestine and to the grounds for reconstituting their national home in that country; and
Whereas the Principal Allied Powers have selected His Britannic Majesty as the Mandatory for Palestine; and
Whereas the mandate in respect of Palestine has been formulated in the following terms and submitted to the Council of the League for approval; and
Whereas His Britannic Majesty has accepted the mandate in respect of Palestine and undertaken to exercise it on behalf of the League of Nations in conformity with the following provisions; and
Whereas by the afore-mentioned Article 22 (paragraph 8), it is provided that the degree of authority, control or administration to be exercised by the Mandatory, not having been previously agreed upon by the Members of the League, shall be explicitly defined by the Council of the League Of Nations;
confirming the said Mandate, defines its terms as follows:

ARTICLE 1.

The Mandatory shall have full powers of legislation and of administration, save as they may be limited by the terms of this mandate.

ART. 2.

The Mandatory shall be responsible for placing the country under such political, administrative and economic conditions as will secure the establishment of the Jewish national home, as laid down in the preamble, and the development of self-governing institutions, and also for safeguarding the civil and religious rights of all the inhabitants of Palestine, irrespective of race and religion.

ART. 3.

The Mandatory shall, so far as circumstances permit, encourage local autonomy.

ART. 4.

An appropriate Jewish agency shall be recognised as a public body for the purpose of advising and co-operating with the Administration of Palestine in such economic, social and other matters as may affect the establishment of the Jewish national home and the interests of the Jewish population in Palestine, and, subject always to the control of the Administration to assist and take part in the development of the country.

The Zionist organization, so long as its organization and constitution are in the opinion of the Mandatory appropriate, shall be recognised as such agency. It shall take steps in consultation with His Britannic Majesty's Government to secure the co-operation of all Jews who are willing to assist in the establishment of the Jewish national home.

ART. 5.

The Mandatory shall be responsible for seeing that no Palestine territory shall be ceded or leased to, or in any way placed under the control of the Government of any foreign Power.

ART. 6.

The Administration of Palestine, while ensuring that the rights and position of other sections of the population are not prejudiced, shall facilitate Jewish immigration under suitable conditions and shall encourage, in co-operation with the Jewish agency referred to in Article 4, close settlement by Jews on the land, including State lands and waste lands not required for public purposes.

ART. 7.

The Administration of Palestine shall be responsible for enacting a nationality law. There shall be included in this law provisions framed so as to facilitate the acquisition of Palestinian citizenship by Jews who take up their permanent residence in Palestine.

ART. 8.

The privileges and immunities of foreigners, including the benefits of consular jurisdiction and protection as formerly enjoyed by Capitulation or usage in the Ottoman Empire, shall not be applicable in Palestine.

Unless the Powers whose nationals enjoyed the afore-mentioned privileges and immunities on August 1st, 1914, shall have previously renounced the right to their re-establishment, or shall have agreed to their non-application for a specified period, these privileges and immunities shall, at the expiration of the mandate, be immediately reestablished in their entirety or with such modifications as may have been agreed upon between the Powers concerned.

ART. 9.

The Mandatory shall be responsible for seeing that the judicial system established in Palestine shall assure to foreigners, as well as to natives, a complete guarantee of their rights.

Respect for the personal status of the various peoples and communities and for their religious interests shall be fully guaranteed. In particular, the control and administration of Wakfs shall be exercised in accordance with religious law and the dispositions of the founders.

ART. 10.

Pending the making of special extradition agreements relating to Palestine, the extradition treaties in force between the Mandatory and other foreign Powers shall apply to Palestine.

ART. 11.

The Administration of Palestine shall take all necessary measures to safeguard the interests of the community in connection with the development of the country, and, subject to any international obligations accepted by the Mandatory, shall have full power to provide for public ownership or control of any of the natural resources of the country or of the public works, services and utilities established or to be established therein. It shall introduce a land system appropriate to the needs of the country, having regard, among other things, to the desirability of promoting the close settlement and intensive cultivation of the land.

The Administration may arrange with the Jewish agency mentioned in Article 4 to construct or operate, upon fair and equitable terms, any public works, services and utilities, and to develop any of the natural resources of the country, in so far as these matters are not directly undertaken by the Administration. Any such arrangements shall provide that no profits distributed by such agency, directly or indirectly, shall exceed a reasonable rate of interest on the capital, and any further profits shall be utilised by it for the benefit of the country in a manner approved by the Administration.

ART. 12.

The Mandatory shall be entrusted with the control of the foreign relations of Palestine and the right to issue exequaturs to consuls appointed by foreign Powers. He shall also be entitled to afford diplomatic and consular protection to citizens of Palestine when outside its territorial limits.

ART. 13.

All responsibility in connection with the Holy Places and religious buildings or sites in Palestine, including that of preserving existing rights and of securing free access to the Holy Places, religious buildings and sites and the free exercise of worship, while ensuring the requirements of public order and decorum, is assumed by the Mandatory, who shall be responsible solely to the League of Nations in all matters connected herewith, provided that nothing in this article shall prevent the Mandatory from entering into such arrangements as he may deem reasonable with the Administration for the purpose of carrying the provisions of this article into effect; and provided also that nothing in this mandate shall be construed as conferring upon the Mandatory authority to interfere with the fabric or the management of purely Moslem sacred shrines, the immunities of which are guaranteed.

ART. 14.

A special commission shall be appointed by the Mandatory to study, define and determine the rights and claims in connection with the Holy Places and the rights and claims relating to the different religious communities in Palestine. The method of nomination, the composition and the functions of this Commission shall be submitted to the Council of the League for its approval, and the Commission shall not be appointed or enter upon its functions without the approval of the Council.

ART. 15.

The Mandatory shall see that complete freedom of conscience and the free exercise of all forms of worship, subject only to the maintenance of public order and morals, are ensured to all. No discrimination of any kind shall be made between the inhabitants of Palestine on the ground of race, religion or language. No person shall be excluded from Palestine on the sole ground of his religious belief.
The right of each community to maintain its own schools for the education of its own members in its own language, while conforming to such educational requirements of a general nature as the Administration may impose, shall not be denied or impaired.

ART. 16.

The Mandatory shall be responsible for exercising such supervision over religious or eleemosynary bodies of all faiths in Palestine as may be required for the maintenance of public order and good government. Subject to such supervision, no measures shall be taken in Palestine to obstruct or interfere with the enterprise of such bodies or to discriminate against any representative or member of them on the ground of his religion or nationality.

ART. 17.

The Administration of Palestine may organist on a voluntary basis the forces necessary for the preservation of peace and order, and also for the defence of the country, subject, however, to the supervision of the Mandatory, but shall not use them for purposes other than those above specified save with the consent of the Mandatory. Except for such purposes, no military, naval or air forces shall be raised or maintained by the Administration of Palestine.
Nothing in this article shall preclude the Administration of Palestine from contributing to the cost of the maintenance of the forces of the Mandatory in Palestine.
The Mandatory shall be entitled at all times to use the roads, railways and ports of Palestine for the movement of armed forces and the carriage of fuel and supplies.

ART. 18.

The Mandatory shall see that there is no discrimination in Palestine against the nationals of any State Member of the League of Nations (including companies incorporated under its laws) as compared with those of the Mandatory or of any foreign State in matters concerning taxation, commerce or navigation, the exercise of industries or professions, or in the treatment of merchant vessels or civil aircraft. Similarly, there shall be no discrimination in Palestine against goods originating in or destined for any of the said States, and there shall be freedom of transit under equitable conditions across the mandated area.
Subject as aforesaid and to the other provisions of this mandate, the Administration of Palestine may, on the advice of the Mandatory, impose such taxes and customs duties as it may consider necessary, and take such steps as it may think best to promote the development of the natural resources of the country and to safeguard the interests of the population. It may also, on the advice of the Mandatory, conclude a special customs agreement with any State the territory of which in 1914 was wholly included in Asiatic Turkey or Arabia.

ART. 19.

The Mandatory shall adhere on behalf of the Administration of Palestine to any general international conventions already existing, or which may be concluded hereafter with the approval of the League of Nations, respecting the slave traffic, the traffic in arms and ammunition, or the traffic in drugs, or relating to commercial equality, freedom of transit and navigation, aerial navigation and postal, telegraphic and wireless communication or literary, artistic or industrial property.

ART. 20.

The Mandatory shall co-operate on behalf of the Administration of Palestine, so far as religious, social and other conditions may permit, in the execution of any common policy adopted by the League of Nations for preventing and combating disease, including diseases of plants and animals.

ART. 21.

The Mandatory shall secure the enactment within twelve months from this date, and shall ensure the execution of a Law of Antiquities based on the following rules. This law shall ensure equality of treatment in the matter of excavations and archaeological research to the nationals of all States Members of the League of Nations.

(1) "Antiquity" means any construction or any product of human activity earlier than the year 1700 A. D.

(2) The law for the protection of antiquities shall proceed by encouragement rather than by threat.

Any person who, having discovered an antiquity without being furnished with the authorization referred to in paragraph 5, reports the same to an official of the competent Department, shall be rewarded according to the value of the discovery.

(3) No antiquity may be disposed of except to the competent Department, unless this Department renounces the acquisition of any such antiquity.

No antiquity may leave the country without an export licence from the said Department.

(4) Any person who maliciously or negligently destroys or damages an antiquity shall be liable to a penalty to be fixed.

(5) No clearing of ground or digging with the object of finding antiquities shall be permitted, under penalty of fine, except to persons authorised by the competent Department.

(6) Equitable terms shall be fixed for expropriation, temporary or permanent, of lands which might be of historical or archaeological interest.

(7) Authorization to excavate shall only be granted to persons who show sufficient guarantees of archaeological experience. The Administration of Palestine shall not, in granting these authorizations, act in such a way as to exclude scholars of any nation without good grounds.

(8) The proceeds of excavations may be divided between the excavator and the competent Department in a proportion fixed by that Department. If division seems impossible for scientific reasons, the excavator shall receive a fair indemnity in lieu of a part of the find.

ART. 22.

English, Arabic and Hebrew shall be the official languages of Palestine. Any statement or inscription in Arabic on stamps or money in Palestine shall be repeated in Hebrew and any statement or inscription in Hebrew shall be repeated in Arabic.

ART. 23.

The Administration of Palestine shall recognise the holy days of the respective communities in Palestine as legal days of rest for the members of such communities.

ART. 24.

The Mandatory shall make to the Council of the League of Nations an annual report to the satisfaction of the Council as to the measures taken during the year to carry out the provisions of the mandate. Copies of all laws and regulations promulgated or issued during the year shall be communicated with the report.

ART. 25.

In the territories lying between the Jordan and the eastern boundary of Palestine as ultimately determined, the Mandatory shall be entitled, with the consent of the Council of the League of Nations, to postpone or withhold application of such provisions of this mandate as he may consider inapplicable to the existing local conditions, and to make such provision for the administration of the territories as he may consider suitable to those conditions, provided that no action shall be taken which is inconsistent with the provisions of Articles 15, 16 and 18.

ART. 26.

The Mandatory agrees that, if any dispute whatever should arise between the Mandatory and another member of the League of Nations relating to the interpretation or the application of the provisions of the mandate, such dispute, if it cannot be settled by negotiation, shall be submitted to the Permanent Court of International Justice provided for by Article 14 of the Covenant of the League of Nations.

ART. 27.

The consent of the Council of the League of Nations is required for any modification of the terms of this mandate.

ART. 28.

In the event of the termination of the mandate hereby conferred upon the Mandatory, the Council of the League of Nations shall make such arrangements as may be deemed necessary for safeguarding in perpetuity, under guarantee of the League, the rights secured by Articles 13 and 14, and shall use its influence for securing, under the guarantee of the League, that the Government of Palestine will fully honour the financial obligations legitimately incurred by the Administration of Palestine during the period of the mandate, including the rights of public servants to pensions or gratuities.
The present instrument shall be deposited in original in the archives of the League of Nations and certified copies shall be forwarded by the Secretary-General of the League of Nations to all members of the League.
Done at London the twenty-fourth day of July, one thousand nine hundred and twenty-two.

UN GENERAL ASSEMBLY RESOLUTION 181

29 Nov 1947

The General Assembly,
Having met in special session at the request of the mandatory Power to constitute and instruct a Special Committee to prepare for the consideration of the question of the future Government of Palestine at the second regular session;
Having constituted a Special Committee and instructed it to investigate all questions and issues relevant to the problem of Palestine, and to prepare proposals for the solution of the problem, and
Having received and examined the report of the Special Committee (document A/364)(1) including a number of unanimous recommendations and a plan of partition with economic union approved by the majority of the Special Committee,
Considers that the present situation in Palestine is one which is likely to impair the general welfare and friendly relations among nations;
Takes note of the declaration by the mandatory Power that it plans to complete its evacuation of Palestine by l August 1948;
Recommends to the United Kingdom, as the mandatory Power for Palestine, and to all other Members of the United Nations the adoption and implementation, with regard to the future Government of Palestine, of the Plan of Partition with Economic Union set out below;
Requests that

a. The Security Council take the necessary measures as provided for in the plan for its implementation;

b. The Security Council consider, if circumstances during the transitional period require such consideration, whether the situation in Palestine constitutes a threat to the peace. If it decides that such a threat exists, and in order to maintain international peace and security, the Security Council should supplement the authorization of the General Assembly by taking measures, under Articles 39 and 41 of the Charter, to empower the United Nations Commission, as provided in this resolution, to exercise in Palestine the functions which are assigned to it by this resolution;

c. The Security Council determine as a threat to the peace, breach of the peace or act of aggression, in accordance with Article 39 of the Charter, any attempt to alter by force the settlement envisaged by this resolution;

d. The Trusteeship Council be informed of the responsibilities envisaged for it in this plan;

Calls upon the inhabitants of Palestine to take such steps as may be necessary on their part to put this plan into effect;
Appeals to all Governments and all peoples to refrain from taking any action which might hamper or delay the carrying out of these recommendations, and
Authorizes the Secretary-General to reimburse travel and subsistence expenses of the members of the Commission referred to in Part 1, Section B, Paragraph I below, on such basis and in such

form as he may determine most appropriate in the circumstances, and to provide the Commission with the necessary staff to assist in carrying out the functions assigned to the Commission by the General Assembly.*

The General Assembly,
Authorizes the Secretary-General to draw from the Working Capital Fund a sum not to exceed 2,000,000 dollars for the purposes set forth in the last paragraph of the resolution on the future government of Palestine.

PLAN OF PARTITION WITH ECONOMIC UNION

PART I. - FUTURE CONSTITUTION AND GOVERNMENT OF PALESTINE

A. TERMINATION OF MANDATE, PARTITION AND INDEPENDENCE

1. The Mandate for Palestine shall terminate as soon as possible but in any case not later than 1 August 1948.

2. The armed forces of the mandatory Power shall be progressively withdrawn from Palestine, the withdrawal to be completed as soon as possible but in any case not later than 1 August 1948.

   The mandatory Power shall advise the Commission, as far in advance as possible, of its intention to terminate the mandate and to evacuate each area. The mandatory Power shall use its best endeavours to ensure that an area situated in the territory of the Jewish State, including a seaport and hinterland adequate to provide facilities for a substantial immigration, shall be evacuated at the earliest possible date and in any event not later than 1 February 1948.

3. Independent Arab and Jewish States and the Special International Regime for the City of Jerusalem, set forth in Part III of this Plan, shall come into existence in Palestine two months after the evacuation of the armed forces of the mandatory Power has been completed but in any case not later than 1 October 1948. The boundaries of the Arab State, the Jewish State, and the City of Jerusalem shall be as described in Parts II and III below.

4. The period between the adoption by the General Assembly of its recommendation on the question of Palestine and the establishment of the independence of the Arab and Jewish States shall be a transitional period.

B. STEPS PREPARATORY TO INDEPENDENCE

1. A Commission shall be set up consisting of one representative of each of five Member States. The Members represented on the Commission shall be elected by the General Assembly on as broad a basis, geographically and otherwise, as possible.

2. The administration of Palestine shall, as the mandatory Power withdraws its armed forces, be progressively turned over to the Commission, which shall act in conformity with the

recommendations of the General Assembly, under the guidance of the Security Council. The mandatory Power shall to the fullest possible extent coordinate its plans for withdrawal with the plans of the Commission to take over and administer areas which have been evacuated.

In the discharge of this administrative responsibility the Commission shall have authority to issue necessary regulations and take other measures as required.

The mandatory Power shall not take any action to prevent, obstruct or delay the implementation by the Commission of the measures recommended by the General Assembly.

3. On its arrival in Palestine the Commission shall proceed to carry out measures for the establishment of the frontiers of the Arab and Jewish States and the City of Jerusalem in accordance with the general lines of the recommendations of the General Assembly on the partition of Palestine. Nevertheless, the boundaries as described in Part II of this Plan are to be modified in such a way that village areas as a rule will not be divided by state boundaries unless pressing reasons make that necessary.

4. The Commission, after consultation with the democratic parties and other public organizations of the Arab and Jewish States, shall select and establish in each State as rapidly as possible a Provisional Council of Government. The activities of both the Arab and Jewish Provisional Councils of Government shall be carried out under the general direction of the Commission.

   If by 1 April 1948 a Provisional Council of Government cannot be selected for either of the States, or, if selected, cannot carry out its functions, the Commission shall communicate that fact to the Security Council for such action with respect to that State as the Security Council may deem proper, and to the Secretary-General for communication to the Members of the United Nations.

5. Subject to the provisions of these recommendations, during the transitional period the Provisional Councils of Government, acting under the Commission, shall have full authority in the areas under their control including authority over matters of immigration and land regulation.

6. The Provisional Council of Government of each State, acting under the Commission, shall progressively receive from the Commission full responsibility for the administration of that State in the period between the termination of the Mandate and the establishment of the State's independence.

7. The Commission shall instruct the Provisional Councils of Government of both the Arab and Jewish States, after their formation, to proceed to the establishment of administrative organs of government, central and local.

8. The Provisional Council of Government of each State shall, within the shortest time possible, recruit an armed militia from the residents of that State, sufficient in number to maintain internal order and to prevent frontier clashes.

This armed militia in each State shall, for operational purposes, be under the command of Jewish or Arab officers resident in that State, but general political and military control, including the choice of the militia's High Command, shall be exercised by the Commission.

9. The Provisional Council of Government of each State shall, not later than two months after the withdrawal of the armed forces of the mandatory Power, hold elections to the Constituent Assembly which shall be conducted on democratic lines.

The election regulations in each State shall be drawn up by the Provisional Council of Government and approved by the Commission. Qualified voters for each State for this election shall be persons over eighteen years of age who are (a) Palestinian citizens residing in that State; and (b) Arabs and Jews residing in the State, although not Palestinian citizens, who, before voting, have signed a notice of intention to become citizens of such State.

Arabs and Jews residing in the City of Jerusalem who have signed a notice of intention to become citizens, the Arabs of the Arab State and the Jews of the Jewish State, shall be entitled to vote in the Arab and Jewish States respectively.

Women may vote and be elected to the Constituent Assemblies.

During the transitional period no Jew shall be permitted to establish residence in the area of the proposed Arab State, and no Arab shall be permitted to establish residence in the area of the proposed Jewish State, except by special leave of the Commission.

10. The Constituent Assembly of each State shall draft a democratic constitution for its State and choose a provisional government to succeed the Provisional Council of Government appointed by the Commission. The Constitutions of the States shall embody Chapters 1 and 2 of the Declaration provided for in section C below and include, inter alia, provisions for:

    a. Establishing in each State a legislative body elected by universal suffrage and by secret ballot on the basis of proportional representation, and an executive body responsible to the legislature;

    b. Settling all international disputes in which the State may be involved by peaceful means in such a manner that international peace and security, and justice, are not endangered;

    c. Accepting the obligation of the State to refrain in its international relations from the threat or use of force against the territorial integrity or political independence of any State, or in any other manner inconsistent with the purpose of the United Nations;

    d. Guaranteeing to all persons equal and non-discriminatory rights in civil, political, economic and religious matters and the enjoyment of human rights and fundamental freedoms, including freedom of religion, language, speech and publication, education, assembly and association;

e. Preserving freedom of transit and visit for all residents and citizens of the other State in Palestine and the City of Jerusalem, subject to considerations of national security, provided that each State shall control residence within its borders.

11. The Commission shall appoint a preparatory economic commission of three members to make whatever arrangements are possible for economic co-operation, with a view to establishing, as soon as practicable, the Economic Union and the Joint Economic Board, as provided in section D below.

12. During the period between the adoption of the recommendations on the question of Palestine by the General Assembly and the termination of the Mandate, the mandatory Power in Palestine shall maintain full responsibility for administration in areas from which it has not withdrawn its armed forces. The Commission shall assist the mandatory Power in the carrying out of these functions. Similarly the mandatory Power shall co-operate with the Commission in the execution of its functions.

13. With a view to ensuring that there shall be continuity in the functioning of administrative services and that, on the withdrawal of the armed forces of the mandatory Power, the whole administration shall be in the charge of the Provisional Councils and the Joint Economic Board, respectively, acting under the Commission, there shall be a progressive transfer, from the mandatory Power to the Commission, of responsibility for all the functions of government, including that of maintaining law and order in the areas from which the forces of the mandatory Power have been withdrawn.

14. The Commission shall be guided in its activities by the recommendations of the General Assembly and by such instructions as the Security Council may consider necessary to issue.

    The measures taken by the Commission, within the recommendations of the General Assembly, shall become immediately effective unless the Commission has previously received contrary instructions from the Security Council.

    The Commission shall render periodic monthly progress reports, or more frequently if desirable, to the Security Council.

15. The Commission shall make its final report to the next regular session of the General Assembly and to the Security Council simultaneously.

C. DECLARATION

A declaration shall be made to the United Nations by the Provisional Government of each proposed State before independence. It shall contain, inter alia, the following clauses:

General Provision

The stipulations contained in the Declaration are recognized as fundamental laws of the State and no law, regulation or official action shall conflict or interfere with these stipulations, nor shall any law, regulation or official action prevail over them.

Chapter 1: Holy Places, Religious Buildings and Sites

1. Existing rights in respect of Holy Places and religious buildings or sites shall not be denied or impaired.

2. In so far as Holy Places are concerned, the liberty of access, visit, and transit shall be guaranteed, in conformity with existing rights, to all residents and citizen of the other State and of the City of Jerusalem, as well as to aliens, without distinction as to nationality, subject to requirements of national security, public order and decorum.

   Similarly, freedom of worship shall be guaranteed in conformity with existing rights, subject to the maintenance of public order and decorum.

3. Holy Places and religious buildings or sites shall be preserved. No act shall be permitted which may in an way impair their sacred character. If at any time it appears to the Government that any particular Holy Place, religious, building or site is in need of urgent repair, the Government may call upon the community or communities concerned to carry out such repair. The Government may carry it out itself at the expense of the community or community concerned if no action is taken within a reasonable time.

4. No taxation shall be levied in respect of any Holy Place, religious building or site which was exempt from taxation on the date of the creation of the State.

   No change in the incidence of such taxation shall be made which would either discriminate between the owners or occupiers of Holy Places, religious buildings or sites, or would place such owners or occupiers in a position less favourable in relation to the general incidence of taxation than existed at the time of the adoption of the Assembly's recommendations.

5. The Governor of the City of Jerusalem shall have the right to determine whether the provisions of the Constitution of the State in relation to Holy Places, religious buildings and sites within the borders of the State and the religious rights appertaining thereto, are being properly applied and respected, and to make decisions on the basis of existing rights in cases of disputes which may arise between the different religious communities or the rites of a religious community with respect to such places, buildings and sites. He shall receive full co-operation and such privileges and immunities as are necessary for the exercise of his functions in the State.

Chapter 2: Religious and Minority Rights

1. Freedom of conscience and the free exercise of all forms of worship, subject only to the maintenance of public order and morals, shall be ensured to all.

2. No discrimination of any kind shall be made between the inhabitants on the ground of race, religion, language or sex.

3. All persons within the jurisdiction of the State shall be entitled to equal protection of the laws.

4. The family law and personal status of the various minorities and their religious interests, including endowments, shall be respected.

5. Except as may be required for the maintenance of public order and good government, no measure shall be taken to obstruct or interfere with the enterprise of religious or charitable bodies of all faiths or to discriminate against any representative or member of these bodies on the ground of his religion or nationality.

6. The State shall ensure adequate primary and secondary education for the Arab and Jewish minority, respectively, in its own language and its cultural traditions.
The right of each community to maintain its own schools for the education of its own members in its own language, while conforming to such educational requirements of a general nature as the State may impose, shall not be denied or impaired. Foreign educational establishments shall continue their activity on the basis of their existing rights.

7. No restriction shall be imposed on the free use by any citizen of the State of any language in private intercourse, in commerce, in religion, in the Press or in publications of any kind, or at public meetings.(3)

8. No expropriation of land owned by an Arab in the Jewish State (by a Jew in the Arab State)(4) shall be allowed except for public purposes. In all cases of expropriation full compensation as fixed by the Supreme Court shall be said previous to dispossession.

Chapter 3: Citizenship, International Conventions and Financial Obligations

1. Citizenship

Palestinian citizens residing in Palestine outside the City of Jerusalem, as well as Arabs and Jews who, not holding Palestinian citizenship, reside in Palestine outside the City of Jerusalem shall, upon the recognition of independence, become citizens of the State in which they are resident and enjoy full civil and political rights. Persons over the age of eighteen years may opt, within one year from the date of recognition of independence of the State in which they reside, for citizenship of the other State, providing that no Arab residing in the area of the proposed Arab State shall have the right to opt for citizenship in the proposed Jewish State and no Jew residing in the proposed Jewish State shall have the right to opt for citizenship in the proposed Arab State. The exercise of this right of option will be taken to include the wives and children under eighteen years of age of persons so opting.

Arabs residing in the area of the proposed Jewish State and Jews residing in the area of the proposed Arab State who have signed a notice of intention to opt for citizenship of the other State shall be eligible to vote in the elections to the Constituent Assembly of that State, but not in the elections to the Constituent Assembly of the State in which they reside.

2. International conventions

a. The State shall be bound by all the international agreements and conventions, both general and special, to which Palestine has become a party. Subject to any right of denunciation provided for therein, such agreements and conventions shall be respected by the State throughout the period for which they were concluded.

b. Any dispute about the applicability and continued validity of international conventions or treaties signed or adhered to by the mandatory Power on behalf of Palestine shall be referred to the International Court of Justice in accordance with the provisions of the Statute of the Court.

3. Financial obligations

a. The State shall respect and fulfil all financial obligations of whatever nature assumed on behalf of Palestine by the mandatory Power during the exercise of the Mandate and recognized by the State. This provision includes the right of public servants to pensions, compensation or gratuities.

b. These obligations shall be fulfilled through participation in the Joint Economic Board in respect of those obligations applicable to Palestine as a whole, and individually in respect of those applicable to, and fairly apportionable between, the States.

c. A Court of Claims, affiliated with the Joint Economic Board, and composed of one member appointed by the United Nations, one representative of the United Kingdom and one representative of the State concerned, should be established. Any dispute between the United Kingdom and the State respecting claims not recognized by the latter should be referred to that Court.

d. Commercial concessions granted in respect of any part of Palestine prior to the adoption of the resolution by the General Assembly shall continue to be valid according to their terms, unless modified by agreement between the concession-holders and the State.

Chapter 4: Miscellaneous Provisions

1. The provisions of chapters 1 and 2 of the declaration shall be under the guarantee of the United Nations, and no modifications shall be made in them without the assent of the General Assembly of the United Nations. Any Member of the United Nations shall have the right to bring to the attention of the General Assembly any infraction or danger of infraction of any of these stipulations, and the General Assembly may thereupon make such recommendations as it may deem proper in the circumstances.

2. Any dispute relating to the application or interpretation of this declaration shall be referred, at the request of either party, to the International Court of Justice, unless the parties agree to another mode of settlement.

D. ECONOMIC UNION AND TRANSIT

1. The Provisional Council of Government of each State shall enter into an undertaking with respect to Economic Union and Transit. This undertaking shall be drafted by the Commission provided for in section B, paragraph 1, utilizing to the greatest possible extent the advice and cooperation of representative organizations and bodies from each of the proposed States. It shall contain provisions to establish the Economic Union of Palestine and provide for other matters of common interest. If by 1 April 1948 the Provisional Councils of Government have not entered into the undertaking, the undertaking shall be put into force by the Commission.

The Economic Union of Palestine

2. The objectives of the Economic Union of Palestine shall be:

    a. A customs union;

    b. A joint currency system providing for a single foreign exchange rate;

    c. Operation in the common interest on a non-discriminatory basis of railways inter-State highways; postal, telephone and telegraphic services and ports and airports involved in international trade and commerce;

    d. Joint economic development, especially in respect of irrigation, land reclamation and soil conservation;

    e. Access for both States and for the City of Jerusalem on a non-discriminatory basis to water and power facilities.

3. There shall be established a Joint Economic Board, which shall consist of three representatives of each of the two States and three foreign members appointed by the Economic and Social Council of the United Nations. The foreign members shall be appointed in the first instance for a term of three years; they shall serve as individuals and not as representatives of States.

4. The functions of the Joint Economic Board shall be to implement either directly or by delegation the measures necessary to realize the objectives of the Economic Union. It shall have all powers of organization and administration necessary to fulfil its functions.

5. The States shall bind themselves to put into effect the decisions of the Joint Economic Board. The Board's decisions shall be taken by a majority vote.

6. In the event of failure of a State to take the necessary action the Board may, by a vote of six members, decide to withhold an appropriate portion of the part of the customs revenue to which the State in question is entitled under the Economic Union. Should the State persist in its failure to cooperate, the Board may decide by a simple majority vote upon such further sanctions, including disposition of funds which it has withheld, as it may deem appropriate.

7. In relation to economic development, the functions of the Board shall be planning, investigation and encouragement of joint development projects, but it shall not undertake such projects except with the assent of both States and the City of Jerusalem, in the event that Jerusalem is directly involved in the development project.

8. In regard to the joint currency system, the currencies circulating in the two States and the City of Jerusalem shall be issued under the authority of the Joint Economic Board, which shall be the sole issuing authority and which shall determine the reserves to be held against such currencies.

9. So far as is consistent with paragraph 2(b) above, each State may operate its own central bank, control its own fiscal and credit policy, its foreign exchange receipts and expenditures, the grant of import licences, and may conduct international financial operations on its own faith and credit. During the first two years after the termination of the Mandate, the Joint Economic Board shall have the authority to take such measures as may be necessary to ensure that - to the extent that the total foreign exchange revenues of the two States from the export of goods and services permit, and provided that each State takes appropriate measures to conserve its own foreign exchange resources - each State shall have available, in any twelve months' period, foreign exchange sufficient to assure the supply of quantities of imported goods and services for consumption in its territory equivalent to the quantities of such goods and services consumed in that territory in the twelve months' period ending 31 December 1947.

10. All economic authority not specifically vested in the Joint Economic Board is reserved to each State.

11. There shall be a common customs tariff with complete freedom of trade between the States, and between the States and the City of Jerusalem.

12. The tariff schedules shall be drawn up by a Tariff Commission, consisting of representatives of each of the States in equal numbers, and shall be submitted to the Joint Economic Board for approval by a majority vote. In case of disagreement in the Tariff Commission, the Joint Economic Board shall arbitrate the points of difference. In the event that the Tariff Commission fails to draw up any schedule by a date to be fixed, the Joint Economic Board shall determine the tariff schedule.

13. The following items shall be a first charge on the customs and other common revenue of the Joint Economic Board:

a. The expenses of the customs service and of the operation of the joint services;

b. The administrative expenses of the Joint Economic Board;

c. The financial obligations of the Administration of Palestine, consisting of:

   i. The service of the outstanding public debt;

   ii. The cost of superannuation benefits, now being paid or falling due in the future, in accordance with the rules and to the extent established by paragraph 3 of chapter 3 above.

14. After these obligations have been met in full, the surplus revenue from the customs and other common services shall be divided in the following manner: not less than 5 per cent and not more than 10 per cent to the City of Jerusalem; the residue shall be allocated to each State by the Joint Economic Board equitably, with the objective of maintaining a sufficient and suitable level of government and social services in each State, except that the share of either State shall not exceed the amount of that State's contribution to the revenues of the Economic Union by more than approximately four million pounds in any year. The amount granted may be adjusted by the Board according to the price level in relation to the prices prevailing at the time of the establishment of the Union. After five years, the principles of the distribution of the joint revenue may be revised by the Joint Economic Board on a basis of equity.

15. All international conventions and treaties affecting customs tariff rates, and those communications services under the jurisdiction of the Joint Economic Board, shall be entered into by both States. In these matters, the two States shall be bound to act in accordance with the majority of the Joint Economic Board.

16. The Joint Economic Board shall endeavour to secure for Palestine's exports fair and equal access to world markets.

17. All enterprises operated by the Joint Economic Board shall pay fair wages on a uniform basis.

Freedom of Transit and Visit

18. The undertaking shall contain provisions preserving freedom of transit and visit for all residents or citizens of both States and of the City of Jerusalem, subject to security considerations; provided that each State and the City shall control residence within its borders.

Termination, Modification and Interpretation of the Undertaking

19. The undertaking and any treaty issuing therefrom shall remain in force for a period of ten years. It shall continue in force until notice of termination, to take effect two years thereafter, is given by either of the parties.

20. During the initial ten-year period, the undertaking and any treaty issuing therefrom may not be modified except by consent of both parties and with the approval of the General Assembly.

21. Any dispute relating to the application or the interpretation of the undertaking and any treaty issuing therefrom shall be referred, at the request of either party, to the International Court Of Justice, unless the parties agree to another mode of settlement.

E. ASSETS

1. The movable assets of the Administration of Palestine shall be allocated to the Arab and Jewish States and the City of Jerusalem on an equitable basis. Allocations should be made by the United Nations Commission referred to iii section B, paragraph 1, above. Immovable assets shall become the property of the government of the territory in which they are situated.

2. During the period between the appointment of the United Nations Commission and the termination of the Mandate, the mandatory Power shall, except in respect of ordinary operations, consult with the Commission on any measure which it may contemplate involving the liquidation, disposal or encumbering of the assets of the Palestine Government, such as the accumulated treasury surplus, the proceeds of Government bond issues, State lands or any other asset.

F. ADMISSION TO MEMBERSHIP IN THE UNITED NATIONS

When the independence of either the Arab or the Jewish State as envisaged in this plan has become effective and the declaration and undertaking, as envisaged in this plan, have been signed by either of them, sympathetic consideration should be given to its application for admission to membership in the United Nations in accordance with article 4 of the Charter of the United Nations.

PART II. - BOUNDARIES

A. THE ARAB STATE

The area of the Arab State in Western Galilee is bounded on the west by the Mediterranean and on the north by the frontier of the Lebanon from Ras en Naqura to a point north of Saliha. From there the boundary proceeds southwards, leaving the built-up area of Saliha in the Arab State, to join the southernmost point of this village. There it follows the western boundary line of the villages of 'Alma, Rihaniya and Teitaba, thence following the northern boundary line of Meirun village to join the Acre-Safad Sub-District boundary line. It follows this line to a point west of Es Sammu'i village and joins it again at the northernmost point of Farradiya. Thence it follows the sub-district boundary line to the Acre-Safad main road. From here it follows the western boundary of Kafr-I'nan village until it reaches the Tiberias-Acre Sub-District boundary line, passing to the west of the junction of the Acre-Safad and Lubiya-Kafr-I'nan roads. From the south-west corner of Kafr-I'nan village the boundary line follows the western boundary of the Tiberias Sub-District to a point close to the boundary line between the villages of Maghar and 'Eilabun, thence bulging out to the west to include as much of the eastern part of the plain of Battuf as is necessary for the reservoir proposed by the Jewish Agency for the irrigation of lands to the south and east.

The boundary rejoins the Tiberias Sub-District boundary at a point on the Nazareth-Tiberias road south-east of the built-up area of Tur'an; thence it runs southwards, at first following the sub-district boundary and then passing between the Kadoorie Agricultural School and Mount Tabor, to a point due south at the base of Mount Tabor. From here it runs due west, parallel to the horizontal grid line 230, to the north-east corner of the village lands of Tel Adashim. It then runs to the northwest corner of these lands, whence it turns south and west so as to include in the Arab State the sources of the Nazareth water supply in Yafa village. On reaching Ginneiger it follows the eastern, northern and western boundaries of the lands of this village to their south-west comer, whence it proceeds in a straight line to a point on the Haifa-Afula railway on the boundary between the villages of Sarid and El-Mujeidil. This is the point of intersection. The south-western boundary of the area of the Arab State in Galilee takes a line from this point, passing northwards along the eastern boundaries of Sarid and Gevat to the north-eastern corner of Nahalal, proceeding thence across the land of Kefar ha Horesh to a central point on the southern boundary of the village of 'Ilut, thence westwards along that village boundary to the eastern boundary of Beit Lahm, thence northwards and north-eastwards along its western boundary to the north-eastern corner of Waldheim and thence north-westwards across the village lands of Shafa 'Amr to the southeastern corner of Ramat Yohanan. From here it runs due north-north-east to a point on the Shafa 'Amr-Haifa road, west of its junction with the road of I'billin. From there it proceeds north-east to a point on the southern boundary of I'billin situated to the west of the I'billin-Birwa road. Thence along that boundary to its westernmost point, whence it turns to the north, follows across the village land of Tamra to the north-westernmost corner and along the western boundary of Julis until it reaches the Acre-Safad road. It then runs westwards along the southern side of the Safad-Acre road to the Galilee-Haifa District boundary, from which point it follows that boundary to the sea.

The boundary of the hill country of Samaria and Judea starts on the Jordan River at the Wadi Malih south-east of Beisan and runs due west to meet the Beisan-Jericho road and then follows the western side of that road in a north-westerly direction to the junction of the boundaries of the Sub-Districts of Beisan, Nablus, and Jenin. From that point it follows the Nablus-Jenin sub-District boundary westwards for a distance of about three kilometres and then turns north-westwards, passing to the east of the built-up areas of the villages of Jalbun and Faqqu'a, to the boundary of the Sub-Districts of Jenin and Beisan at a point northeast of Nuris. Thence it proceeds first northwestwards to a point due north of the built-up area of Zie'in and then westwards to the Afula-Jenin railway, thence north-westwards along the District boundary line to the point of intersection on the Hejaz railway. From here the boundary runs southwestwards, including the built-up area and some of the land of the village of Kh. Lid in the Arab State to cross the Haifa-Jenin road at a point on the district boundary between Haifa and Samaria west of El- Mansi. It follows this boundary to the southernmost point of the village of El-Buteimat. From here it follows the northern and eastern boundaries of the village of Ar'ara rejoining the Haifa-Samaria district boundary at Wadi 'Ara, and thence proceeding south-south-westwards in an approximately straight line joining up with the western boundary of Qaqun to a point east of the railway line on the eastern boundary of Qaqun village. From here it runs along the railway line some distance to the east of it to a point just east of the Tulkarm railway station. Thence the boundary follows a line half-way between the railway and the Tulkarm-Qalqiliya-Jaljuliya and Ras El-Ein road to a point just east of Ras El-Ein station, whence it proceeds along the railway some distance to the east of it to the point on the railway line south of the junction of the Haifa-Lydda and Beit Nabala lines, whence it proceeds along the southern border of Lydda airport to its south-west corner, thence in a south-westerly direction to a point just west of the built-up area of Sarafand El 'Amar, whence it turns south, passing just to the west of the built-up area of Abu El-Fadil to the north-east corner of the lands of Beer Ya'aqov. (The boundary line should be so demarcated as to allow direct access from the Arab State to the airport.) Thence the boundary line follows the western and southern boundaries of Ramle village, to the north-east corner of El Na'ana village, thence in a straight line to the southernmost point of El Barriya, along the eastern boundary of that village and the southern boundary of 'Innaba village. Thence it turns north to follow the southern side of the Jaffa-Jerusalem road until El-Qubab, whence it follows the road to the boundary of Abu-Shusha. It runs along the eastern boundaries of Abu Shusha, Seidun, Hulda to the southernmost point of Hulda, thence westwards in a straight line to the north-eastern corner of Umm Kalkha, thence following the northern boundaries of Umm Kalkha, Qazaza and the northern and western boundaries of Mukhezin to the Gaza District boundary and thence runs across the village lands of El-Mismiya El-Kabira, and Yasur to the southern point of intersection, which is midway between the built-up areas of Yasur and Batani Sharqi.

From the southern point of intersection the boundary lines run north-westwards between the villages of Gan Yavne and Barqa to the sea at a point half way between Nabi Yunis and Minat El-Qila, and south-eastwards to a point west of Qastina, whence it turns in a south-westerly direction, passing to the east of the built-up areas of Es Sawafir Esh Sharqiya and 'Ibdis. From the south-east corner of 'Ibdis village it runs to a point southwest of the built-up area of Beit 'Affa, crossing the Hebron-El-Majdal road just to the west of the built-up area of 'Iraq Suweidan. Thence it proceeds southward along the western village boundary of El-Faluja to the Beersheba Sub-District boundary. It then runs across the tribal lands of 'Arab El-Jubarat to a point on the boundary between the Sub-Districts of Beersheba and Hebron north of Kh. Khuweilifa, whence it proceeds in a south-westerly direction to a point on the Beersheba-Gaza main road two kilometres to the north-west of the town. It then turns south-eastwards to reach Wadi Sab' at a point situated one kilometer to the west of it. From here it turns north-eastwards and proceeds along Wadi Sab' and along the Beersheba-Hebron road for a distance of one kilometer, whence it turns eastwards and runs in a straight line to Kh. Kuseifa to join the Beersheba-Hebron Sub-District boundary. It then follows the Beersheba-Hebron boundary eastwards to a point north of Ras Ez-Zuweira, only departing from it so as to cut across the base of the indentation between vertical grid lines 150 and 160.

About five kilometres north-east of Ras Ez-Zuweira it turns north, excluding from the Arab State a strip along the coast of the Dead Sea not more than seven kilometres in depth, as far as 'Ein Geddi, whence it turns due east to join the Transjordan frontier in the Dead Sea.

The northern boundary of the Arab section of the coastal plain runs from a point between Minat El-Qila and Nabi Yunis, passing between the built-up areas of Gan Yavne and Barqa to the point of intersection. From here it turns south-westwards, running across the lands of Batani Sharqi, along the eastern boundary of the lands of Beit Daras and across the lands of Julis, leaving the built-up areas of Batani Sharqi and Julis to the westwards, as far as the north-west corner of the lands of Beit-Tima. Thence it runs east of El-Jiya across the village lands of El-Barbara along the eastern boundaries of the villages of Beit Jirja, Deir Suneid and Dimra. From the south-east corner of

Dimra the boundary passes across the lands of Beit Hanun, leaving the Jewish lands of Nir-Am to the eastwards. From the south-east corner of Beit Hanun the line runs south-west to a point south of the parallel grid line 100, then turns north-west for two kilometres, turning again in a southwesterly direction and continuing in an almost straight line to the north-west corner of the village lands of Kirbet Ikhza'a. From there it follows the boundary line of this village to its southernmost point. It then runs in a southerly direction along the vertical grid line 90 to its junction with the horizontal grid line 70. It then turns south-eastwards to Kh. El-Ruheiba and then proceeds in a southerly direction to a point known as El-Baha, beyond which it crosses the Beersheba-EI 'Auja main road to the west of Kh. El-Mushrifa. From there it joins Wadi El-Zaiyatin just to the west of El-Subeita. From there it turns to the north-east and then to the south-east following this Wadi and passes to the east of 'Abda to join Wadi Nafkh. It then bulges to the south-west along Wadi Nafkh, Wadi 'Ajrim and Wadi Lassan to the point where Wadi Lassan crosses the Egyptian frontier.

The area of the Arab enclave of Jaffa consists of that part of the town-planning area of Jaffa which lies to the west of the Jewish quarters lying south of Tel-Aviv, to the west of the continuation of Herzl street up to its junction with the Jaffa-Jerusalem road, to the south-west of the section of the Jaffa-Jerusalem road lying south-east of that junction, to the west of Miqve Yisrael lands, to the northwest of Holon local council area, to the north of the line linking up the north-west corner of Holon with the northeast corner of Bat Yam local council area and to the north of Bat Yam local council area. The question of Karton quarter will be decided by the Boundary Commission, bearing in mind among other considerations the desirability of including the smallest possible number of its Arab inhabitants and the largest possible number of its Jewish inhabitants in the Jewish State.

B. THE JEWISH STATE

The north-eastern sector of the Jewish State (Eastern Galilee) is bounded on the north and west by the Lebanese frontier and on the east by the frontiers of Syria and Trans-jordan. It includes the whole of the Huleh Basin, Lake Tiberias, the whole of the Beisan Sub-District, the boundary line being extended to the crest of the Gilboa mountains and the Wadi Malih. From there the Jewish State extends north-west, following the boundary described in respect of the Arab State. The Jewish section of the coastal plain extends from a point between Minat El-Qila and Nabi Yunis in the Gaza Sub-District and includes the towns of Haifa and Tel-Aviv, leaving Jaffa as an enclave of the Arab State. The eastern frontier of the Jewish State follows the boundary described in respect of the Arab State.

The Beersheba area comprises the whole of the Beersheba Sub-District, including the Negeb and the eastern part of the Gaza Sub-District, but excluding the town of Beersheba and those areas described in respect of the Arab State. It includes also a strip of land along the Dead Sea stretching from the Beersheba-Hebron Sub-District boundary line to 'Ein Geddi, as described in respect of the Arab State.

C. THE CITY OF JERUSALEM

The boundaries of the City of Jerusalem are as defined in the recommendations on the City of Jerusalem. (See Part III, section B, below).

PART III. - CITY OF JERUSALEM[5]

A. SPECIAL REGIME

The City of Jerusalem shall be established as a corpus separatum under a special international regime and shall be administered by the United Nations. The Trusteeship Council shall be designated to discharge the responsibilities of the Administering Authority on behalf of the United Nations.

B. BOUNDARIES OF THE CITY

The City of Jerusalem shall include the present municipality of Jerusalem plus the surrounding villages and towns, the most eastern of which shall be Abu Dis; the most southern, Bethlehem; the most western, 'Ein Karim (including also the built-up area of Motsa); and the most northern Shu'fat, as indicated on the attached sketch-map (annex B).

C. STATUTE OF THE CITY

The Trusteeship Council shall, within five months of the approval of the present plan, elaborate and approve a detailed statute of the City which shall contain, inter alia, the substance of the following provisions:

1. Government machinery; special objectives. The Administering Authority in discharging its administrative obligations shall pursue the following special objectives:

    a. To protect and to preserve the unique spiritual and religious interests located in the city of the three great monotheistic faiths throughout the world, Christian, Jewish and Moslem; to this end to ensure that order and peace, and especially religious peace, reign in Jerusalem;

    b. To foster cooperation among all the inhabitants of the city in their own interests as well as in order to encourage and support the peaceful development of the mutual relations between the two Palestinian peoples throughout the Holy Land; to promote the security, well-being and any constructive measures of development of the residents having regard to the special circumstances and customs of the various peoples and communities.

2. Governor and Administrative staff. A Governor of the City of Jerusalem shall be appointed by the Trusteeship Council and shall be responsible to it. He shall be selected on the basis of special qualifications and without regard to nationality. He shall not, however, be a citizen of either State in Palestine.

    The Governor shall represent the United Nations in the City and shall exercise on their behalf all powers of administration, including the conduct of external affairs. He shall be assisted by an administrative staff classed as international officers in the meaning of Article 100 of the Charter and chosen whenever practicable from the residents of the city and of the rest of Palestine on a non-discriminatory basis. A detailed plan for the organization of the administration of the city shall be submitted by the Governor to the Trusteeship Council and duly approved by it.

3. Local autonomy

   a. The existing local autonomous units in the territory of the city (villages, townships and municipalities) shall enjoy wide powers of local government and administration.

   b. The Governor shall study and submit for the consideration and decision of the Trusteeship Council a plan for the establishment of special town units consisting, respectively, of the Jewish and Arab sections of new Jerusalem. The new town units shall continue to form part the present municipality of Jerusalem.

4. Security measures

   a. The City of Jerusalem shall be demilitarized; neutrality shall be declared and preserved, and no para-military formations, exercises or activities shall be permitted within its borders.

   b. Should the administration of the City of Jerusalem be seriously obstructed or prevented by the non-cooperation or interference of one or more sections of the population the Governor shall have authority to take such measures as may be necessary to restore the effective functioning of administration.

   c. To assist in the maintenance of internal law and order, especially for the protection of the Holy Places and religious buildings and sites in the city, the Governor shall organize a special police force of adequate strength, the members of which shall be recruited outside of Palestine. The Governor shall be empowered to direct such budgetary provision as may be necessary for the maintenance of this force.

5. Legislative Organization.
   A Legislative Council, elected by adult residents of the city irrespective of nationality on the basis of universal and secret suffrage and proportional representation, shall have powers of legislation and taxation. No legislative measures shall, however, conflict or interfere with the provisions which will be set forth in the Statute of the City, nor shall any law, regulation, or official action prevail over them. The Statute shall grant to the Governor a right of vetoing bills inconsistent with the provisions referred to in the preceding sentence. It shall also empower him to promulgate temporary ordinances in case the Council fails to adopt in time a bill deemed essential to the normal functioning of the administration.

6. Administration of Justice.
   The Statute shall provide for the establishment of an independent judiciary system, including a court of appeal. All the inhabitants of the city shall be subject to it.

7. Economic Union and Economic Regime
   The City of Jerusalem shall be included in the Economic Union of Palestine and be bound by all stipulations of the undertaking and of any treaties issued therefrom, as well as by the

decisions of the Joint Economic Board. The headquarters of the Economic Board shall be established in the territory City. The Statute shall provide for the regulation of economic matters not falling within the regime of the Economic Union, on the basis of equal treatment and non-discrimination for all members of thc United Nations and their nationals.

8. Freedom of Transit and Visit: Control of residents.
Subject to considerations of security, and of economic welfare as determined by the Governor under the directions of the Trusteeship Council, freedom of entry into, and residence within the borders of the City shall be guaranteed for the residents or citizens of the Arab and Jewish States. Immigration into, and residence within, the borders of the city for nationals of other States shall be controlled by the Governor under the directions of the Trusteeship Council.

9. Relations with Arab and Jewish States. Representatives of the Arab and Jewish States shall be accredited to the Governor of the City and charged with the protection of the interests of their States and nationals in connection with the international administration of thc City.

10. Official languages.
Arabic and Hebrew shall be the official languages of the city. This will not preclude the adoption of one or more additional working languages, as may be required.

11. Citizenship.
All the residents shall become ipso facto citizens of the City of Jerusalem unless they opt for citizenship of the State of which they have been citizens or, if Arabs or Jews, have filed notice of intention to become citizens of the Arab or Jewish State respectively, according to Part 1, section B, paragraph 9, of this Plan.
The Trusteeship Council shall make arrangements for consular protection of the citizens of the City outside its territory.

12. Freedoms of citizens

   a. Subject only to the requirements of public order and morals, the inhabitants of the City shall be ensured the enjoyment of human rights and fundamental freedoms, including freedom of conscience, religion and worship, language, education, speech and press, assembly and association, and petition.

   b. No discrimination of any kind shall be made between the inhabitants on the grounds of race, religion, language or sex.

   c. All persons within the City shall be entitled to equal protection of the laws.

   d. The family law and personal status of the various persons and communities and their religious interests, including endowments, shall be respected.

   e. Except as may be required for the maintenance of public order and good government, no measure shall be taken to obstruct or interfere with the enterprise of religious or charitable bodies of all faiths or to discriminate against any representative or member of these bodies on the ground of his religion or nationality.

f. The City shall ensure adequate primary and secondary education for the Arab and Jewish communities respectively, in their own languages and in accordance with their cultural traditions.
The right of each community to maintain its own schools for the education of its own members in its own language, while conforming to such educational requirements of a general nature as the City may impose, shall not be denied or impaired. Foreign educational establishments shall continue their activity on the basis of their existing rights.

g. No restriction shall be imposed on the free use by any inhabitant of the City of any language in private intercourse, in commerce, in religion, in the Press or in publications of any kind, or at public meetings.

13. Holy Places

a. Existing rights in respect of Holy Places and religious buildings or sites shall not be denied or impaired.

b. Free access to the Holy Places and religious buildings or sites and the free exercise of worship shall be secured in conformity with existing rights and subject to the requirements of public order and decorum.

c. Holy Places and religious buildings or sites shall be preserved. No act shall be permitted which may in any way impair their sacred character. If at any time it appears to the Governor that any particular Holy Place, religious building or site is in need of urgent repair, the Governor may call upon the community or communities concerned to carry out such repair. The Governor may carry it out himself at the expense of the community or communities concerned if no action is taken within a reasonable time.

d. No taxation shall be levied in respect of any Holy Place, religious building or site which was exempt from taxation on the date of the creation of the City. No change in the incidence of such taxation shall be made which would either discriminate between the owners or occupiers of Holy Places, religious buildings or sites or would place such owners or occupiers in a position less favourable in relation to the general incidence of taxation than existed at the time of the adoption of the Assembly's recommendations.

14. Special powers of the Governor in respect of the Holy Places, religious buildings and sites in the City and in any part of Palestine.

a. The protection of the Holy Places, religious buildings and sites located in the City of Jerusalem shall be a special concern of the Governor.

b. With relation to such places, buildings and sites in Palestine outside the city, the Governor shall determine, on the ground of powers granted to him by the Constitution of both States, whether the provisions of the Constitution of the Arab and Jewish States in Palestine dealing therewith and the religious rights appertaining thereto are being properly applied and respected.

c. The Governor shall also be empowered to make decisions on the basis of existing rights in cases of disputes which may arise between the different religious communities or the rites of a religious community in respect of the Holy Places, religious buildings and sites in any part of Palestine.
In this task he may be assisted by a consultative council of representatives of different denominations acting in an advisory capacity.

D. DURATION OF THE SPECIAL REGIME

The Statute elaborated by the Trusteeship Council the aforementioned principles shall come into force not later than 1 October 1948. It shall remain in force in the first instance for a period of ten years, unless the Trusteeship Council finds it necessary to undertake a re-examination of these provisions at an earlier date. After the expiration of this period the whole scheme shall be subject to examination by the Trusteeship Council in the light of experience acquired with its functioning. The residents the City shall be then free to express by means of a referendum their wishes as to possible modifications of regime of the City.

PART IV. CAPITULATIONS

States whose nationals have in the past enjoyed in Palestine the privileges and immunities of foreigners, including the benefits of consular jurisdiction and protection, as formerly enjoyed by capitulation or usage in the Ottoman Empire, are invited to renounce any right pertaining to them to the re-establishment of such privileges and immunities in the proposed Arab and Jewish States and the City of Jerusalem.

Adopted at the 128th plenary meeting:

In favour: 33
Australia, Belgium, Bolivia, Brazil, Byelorussian S.S.R., Canada, Costa Rica, Czechoslovakia, Denmark, Dominican Republic, Ecuador, France, Guatemala, Haiti, Iceland, Liberia, Luxemburg, Netherlands, New Zealand, Nicaragua, Norway, Panama, Paraguay, Peru, Philippines, Poland, Sweden, Ukrainian S.S.R., Union of South Africa, U.S.A., U.S.S.R., Uruguay, Venezuela.

Against: 13
Afghanistan, Cuba, Egypt, Greece, India, Iran, Iraq, Lebanon, Pakistan, Saudi Arabia, Syria, Turkey, Yemen.

Abstained: 10
Argentina, Chile, China, Colombia, El Salvador, Ethiopia, Honduras, Mexico, United Kingdom, Yugoslavia.

(1) See Official Records of the General Assembly, Second Session Supplement No. 11,Volumes l-lV.

* At its hundred and twenty-eighth plenary meeting on 29 November 1947 the General Assembly, in accordance with the terms of the above resolution, elected the following members of the United Nations Commission on Palestine: Bolivia, Czechoslovakia, Denmark, Panama, and Philippines.

(2) This resolution was adopted without reference to a Committee.

(3) The following stipulation shall be added to the declaration concerning the Jewish State: "In the Jewish State adequate facilities shall be given to Arabic-speaking citizens for the use of their language, either orally or in writing, in the legislature, before the Courts and in the administration."

(4) In the declaration concerning the Arab State, the words "by an Arab in the Jewish State" should be replaced by the words "by a Jew in the Arab State."

(5) On the question of the internationalization of Jerusalem, see also General Assembly resolutions 185 (S-2) of 26 April 1948; 187 (S-2) of 6 May 1948, 303 (lV) of 9 December 1949, and resolutions of the Trusteeship Council (Section IV).

DECLARATION OF ESTABLISHMENT OF STATE OF ISRAEL

14 May 1948

ERETZ-ISRAEL [(Hebrew) - the Land of Israel] was the birthplace of the Jewish people. Here their spiritual, religious and political identity was shaped. Here they first attained to statehood, created cultural values of national and universal significance and gave to the world the eternal Book of Books.

After being forcibly exiled from their land, the people kept faith with it throughout their Dispersion and never ceased to pray and hope for their return to it and for the restoration in it of their political freedom.

Impelled by this historic and traditional attachment, Jews strove in every successive generation to re-establish themselves in their ancient homeland. In recent decades they returned in their masses. Pioneers, ma'pilim [(Hebrew) - immigrants coming to Eretz-Israel in defiance of restrictive legislation] and defenders, they made deserts bloom, revived the Hebrew language, built villages and towns, and created a thriving community controlling its own economy and culture, loving peace but knowing how to defend itself, bringing the blessings of progress to all the country's inhabitants, and aspiring towards independent nationhood.

In the year 5657 (1897), at the summons of the spiritual father of the Jewish State, Theodore Herzl, the First Zionist Congress convened and proclaimed the right of the Jewish people to national rebirth in its own country.

This right was recognized in the Balfour Declaration of the 2nd November, 1917, and re-affirmed in the Mandate of the League of Nations which, in particular, gave international sanction to the historic connection between the Jewish people and Eretz-Israel and to the right of the Jewish people to rebuild its National Home.

The catastrophe which recently befell the Jewish people - the massacre of millions of Jews in Europe - was another clear demonstration of the urgency of solving the problem of its homelessness by re-establishing in Eretz-Israel the Jewish State, which would open the gates of the homeland wide to every Jew and confer upon the Jewish people the status of a fully privileged member of the comity of nations.

Survivors of the Nazi holocaust in Europe, as well as Jews from other parts of the world, continued to migrate to Eretz-Israel, undaunted by difficulties, restrictions and dangers, and never ceased to assert their right to a life of dignity, freedom and honest toil in their national homeland.

In the Second World War, the Jewish community of this country contributed its full share to the struggle of the freedom- and peace-loving nations against the forces of Nazi wickedness and, by the blood of its soldiers and its war effort, gained the right to be reckoned among the peoples who founded the United Nations.

On the 29th November, 1947, the United Nations General Assembly passed a resolution calling for the establishment of a Jewish State in Eretz-Israel; the General Assembly required the inhabitants of Eretz-Israel to take such steps as were necessary on their part for the implementation of that resolution. This recognition by the United Nations of the right of the Jewish people to establish their State is irrevocable.

This right is the natural right of the Jewish people to be masters of their own fate, like all other nations, in their own sovereign State.

ACCORDINGLY WE, MEMBERS OF THE PEOPLE'S COUNCIL, REPRESENTATIVES OF THE JEWISH COMMUNITY OF ERETZ-ISRAEL AND OF THE ZIONIST MOVEMENT, ARE HERE ASSEMBLED ON THE DAY OF THE TERMINATION OF THE BRITISH MANDATE OVER ERETZ-ISRAEL AND, BY VIRTUE OF OUR NATURAL AND HISTORIC RIGHT AND ON THE STRENGTH OF THE RESOLUTION OF THE UNITED NATIONS GENERAL ASSEMBLY, HEREBY DECLARE THE ESTABLISHMENT OF A JEWISH STATE IN ERETZ-ISRAEL, TO BE KNOWN AS THE STATE OF ISRAEL.

WE DECLARE that, with effect from the moment of the termination of the Mandate being tonight, the eve of Sabbath, the 6th Iyar, 5708 (15th May, 1948), until the establishment of the elected, regular authorities of the State in accordance with the Constitution which shall be adopted by the Elected Constituent Assembly not later than the 1st October 1948, the People's Council shall act as a Provisional Council of State, and its executive organ, the People's Administration, shall be the Provisional Government of the Jewish State, to be called "Israel."

THE STATE OF ISRAEL will be open for Jewish immigration and for the Ingathering of the Exiles; it will foster the development of the country for the benefit of all its inhabitants; it will be based on freedom, justice and peace as envisaged by the prophets of Israel; it will ensure complete equality of social and political rights to all its inhabitants irrespective of religion, race or sex; it will guarantee freedom of religion, conscience, language, education and culture; it will safeguard the Holy Places of all religions; and it will be faithful to the principles of the Charter of the United Nations.

THE STATE OF ISRAEL is prepared to cooperate with the agencies and representatives of the United Nations in implementing the resolution of the General Assembly of the 29th November, 1947, and will take steps to bring about the economic union of the whole of Eretz-Israel.

WE APPEAL to the United Nations to assist the Jewish people in the building-up of its State and to receive the State of Israel into the comity of nations.

WE APPEAL - in the very midst of the onslaught launched against us now for months - to the Arab inhabitants of the State of Israel to preserve peace and participate in the upbuilding of the State on the basis of full and equal citizenship and due representation in all its provisional and permanent institutions.

WE EXTEND our hand to all neighbouring states and their peoples in an offer of peace and good neighbourliness, and appeal to them to establish bonds of cooperation and mutual help with the sovereign Jewish people settled in its own land. The State of Israel is prepared to do its share in a common effort for the advancement of the entire Middle East.

WE APPEAL to the Jewish people throughout the Diaspora to rally round the Jews of Eretz-Israel in the tasks of immigration and upbuilding and to stand by them in the great struggle for the realization of the age-old dream - the redemption of Israel.

PLACING OUR TRUST IN THE "ROCK OF ISRAEL", WE AFFIX OUR SIGNATURES TO THIS PROCLAMATION AT THIS SESSION OF THE PROVISIONAL COUNCIL OF STATE, ON THE SOIL OF THE HOMELAND, IN THE CITY OF TEL-AVIV, ON THIS SABBATH EVE, THE 5TH DAY OF IYAR, 5708 (14TH MAY,1948).

David Ben-Gurion

Daniel Auster
Mordekhai Bentov
Yitzchak Ben Zvi
Eliyahu Berligne
Fritz Bernstein
Rabbi Wolf Gold
Meir Grabovsky
Yitzchak Gruenbaum
Dr. Abraham Granovsky
Eliyahu Dobkin
Meir Wilner-Kovner
Zerach Wahrhaftig
Herzl Vardi
Rachel Cohen
Rabbi Kalman Kahana
Saadia Kobashi
Rabbi Yitzchak Meir Levin
Meir David Loewenstein
Zvi Luria
Golda Myerson
Nachum Nir
Zvi Segal
Rabbi Yehuda Leib Hacohen Fishman
David Zvi Pinkas
Aharon Zisling
Moshe Kolodny
Eliezer Kaplan
Abraham Katznelson
Felix Rosenblueth
David Remez
Berl Repetur
Mordekhai Shattner
Ben Zion Sternberg
Bekhor Shitreet
Moshe Shapira
Moshe Shertok

* Published in the Official Gazette, No. 1 of the 5th, Iyar, 5708 (14th May, 1948).

U.N. SECURITY COUNCIL RESOLUTION 242

November 22, 1967

The Security Council,

Expressing its continuing concern with the grave situation in the Middle East,

Emphasizing the inadmissibility of the acquisition of territory by war and the need to work for a just and lasting peace in which every State in the area can live in security,

Emphasizing further that all Member States in their acceptance of the Charter of the United Nations have undertaken a commitment to act in accordance with Article 2 of the Charter,

- Affirms that the fulfillment of Charter principles requires the establishment of a just and lasting peace in the Middle East which should include the application of both the following principles:

- Withdrawal of Israeli armed forces from territories occupied in the recent conflict;

- Termination of all claims or states of belligerency and respect for and acknowledgement of the sovereignty, territorial integrity and political independence of every State in the area and their right to live in peace within secure and recognized boundaries free from threats or acts of force;

- Affirms further the necessity

- For guaranteeing freedom of navigation through international waterways in the area;

- For achieving a just settlement of the refugee problem;

- For guaranteeing the territorial inviolability and political independence of every State in the area, through measures including the establishment of demilitarized zones;

- Requests the Secretary General to designate a Special Representative to proceed to the Middle East to establish and maintain contacts with the States concerned in order to promote agreement and assist efforts to achieve a peaceful and accepted settlement in accordance with the provisions and principles in this resolution;

- Requests the Secretary-General to report to the Security Council on the progress of the efforts of the Special Representative as soon as possible.

U.N. SECURITY COUNCIL RESOLUTION 338

October 22, 1973

The Security Council,

- Calls upon all parties to present fighting to cease all firing and terminate all military activity immediately, no later than 12 hours after the moment of the adoption of this decision, in the positions after the moment of the adoption of this decision, in the positions they now occupy;

- Calls upon all parties concerned to start immediately after the cease-fire the implementation of Security Council Resolution 242 (1967) in all of its parts;

- Decides that, immediately and concurrently with the cease-fire, negotiations start between the parties concerned under appropriate auspices aimed at establishing a just and durable peace in the Middle East.

ISRAEL-PLO RECOGNITION - EXCHANGE OF LETTERS BETWEEN PM RABIN AND CHAIRMAN ARAFAT

9 September 1993

1. LETTER FROM YASSER ARAFAT TO PRIME MINISTER RABIN:

September 9, 1993
Yitzhak Rabin
Prime Minister of Israel

Mr. Prime Minister,

The signing of the Declaration of Principles marks a new era in the history of the Middle East. In firm conviction thereof, I would like to confirm the following PLO commitments:

The PLO recognizes the right of the State of Israel to exist in peace and security.

The PLO accepts United Nations Security Council Resolutions 242 and 338.

The PLO commits itself to the Middle East peace process, and to a peaceful resolution of the conflict between the two sides and declares that all outstanding issues relating to permanent status will be resolved through negotiations.

The PLO considers that the signing of the Declaration of Principles constitutes a historic event, inaugurating a new epoch of peaceful coexistence, free from violence and all other acts which endanger peace and stability. Accordingly, the PLO renounces the use of terrorism and other acts of violence and will assume responsibility over all PLO elements and personnel in order to assure their compliance, prevent violations and discipline violators.

In view of the pormise of a new era and the signing of the Declaration of Principles and based on Palestinian acceptance of Security Council Resolutions 242 and 338, the PLO affirms that those articles of the Palestinian Covenant which deny Israel's right to exist, and the provisions of the Covenant which are inconsistent with the commitments of this letter are now inoperative and no longer valid. Consequently, the PLO undertakes to submit to the Palestinian National Council for formal approval the necessary changes in regard to the Palestinian Covenant.

Sincerely,

Yasser Arafat
Chairman
The Palestine Liberation Organization

2. LETTER FROM YASSER ARAFAT TO NORWEGIAN FOREIGN MINISTER:

September 9, 1993
His Excellency
Johan Jorgen Holst
Foreign Minister of Norway

Dear Minister Holst,
I would like top confirm to you that, upon the signing of the Declaration of Principles, the PLO encourages and calls upon the Palestinian people in the West Bank and Gaza Strip to take part in the steps leading to the normalization of life, rejecting violence and terrorism, contributing to peace and stability and participating actively in shaping reconstruction, economic develoment and cooperation.
Sincerely,

Yasser Arafat
Chairman
The Palestine Liberation Organization

3. LETTER FROM PRIME MINISTER RABIN TO YASSER ARAFAT:

September 9, 1993
Yasser Arafat
Chairman
The Palestinian Liberation Organization

Mr. Chairman,
In response to your letter of September 9, 1993, I wish to confirm to you that, in light of the PLO commitments included in your letter, the Government of Israel has decided to recognize the PLO as the representative of the Palestinian people and commence negotiations with the PLO within the Middle East peace process.

Yitzhak Rabin
Prime Minister of Israel

DECLARATION OF PRINCIPLES ON INTERIM SELF-GOVERNMENT ARRANGEMENTS

September 13, 1993

The Government of the State of Israel and the P.L.O. team (in the Jordanian-Palestinian delegation to the Middle East Peace Conference) (the "Palestinian Delegation"), representing the Palestinian people, agree that it is time to put an end to decades of confrontation and conflict, recognize their mutual legitimate and political rights, and strive to live in peaceful coexistence and mutual dignity and security and achieve a just, lasting and comprehensive peace settlement and historic reconciliation through the agreed political process. Accordingly, the, two sides agree to the following principles:

ARTICLE I

AIM OF THE NEGOTIATIONS

The aim of the Israeli-Palestinian negotiations within the current Middle East peace process is, among other things, to establish a Palestinian Interim Self-Government Authority, the elected Council (the "Council"), for the Palestinian people in the West Bank and the Gaza Strip, for a transitional period not exceeding five years, leading to a permanent settlement based on Security Council Resolutions 242 and 338.

It is understood that the interim arrangements are an integral part of the whole peace process and that the negotiations on the permanent status will lead to the implementation of Security Council Resolutions 242 and 338.

ARTICLE II

FRAMEWORK FOR THE INTERIM PERIOD

The agreed framework for the interim period is set forth in this Declaration of Principles.

ARTICLE III

ELECTIONS

1. In order that the Palestinian people in the West Bank and Gaza Strip may govern themselves according to democratic principles, direct, free and general political elections will be held for the Council under agreed supervision and international observation, while the Palestinian police will ensure public order.

2. An agreement will be concluded on the exact mode and conditions of the elections in accordance with the protocol attached as Annex I, with the goal of holding the elections not later than nine months after the entry into force of this Declaration of Principles.

3. These elections will constitute a significant interim preparatory step toward the realization of the legitimate rights of the Palestinian people and their just requirements.

ARTICLE IV

JURISDICTION

Jurisdiction of the Council will cover West Bank and Gaza Strip territory, except for issues that will be negotiated in the permanent status negotiations. The two sides view the West Bank and the Gaza Strip as a single territorial unit, whose integrity will be preserved during the interim period.

ARTICLE V

TRANSITIONAL PERIOD AND PERMANENT STATUS NEGOTIATIONS

1. The five-year transitional period will begin upon the withdrawal from the Gaza Strip and Jericho area.

2. Permanent status negotiations will commence as soon as possible, but not later than the beginning of the third year of the interim period, between the Government of Israel and the Palestinian people representatives.

3. It is understood that these negotiations shall cover remaining issues, including: Jerusalem, refugees, settlements, security arrangements, borders, relations and cooperation with other neighbors, and other issues of common interest.

4. The two parties agree that the outcome of the permanent status negotiations should not be prejudiced or preempted by agreements reached for the interim period.

ARTICLE VI

PREPARATORY TRANSFER OF POWERS AND RESPONSIBILITIES

1. Upon the entry into force of this Declaration of Principles and the withdrawal from the Gaza Strip and the Jericho area, a transfer of authority from the Israeli military government and its Civil Administration to the authorised Palestinians for this task, as detailed herein, will commence. This transfer of authority will be of a preparatory nature until the inauguration of the Council.

2. Immediately after the entry into force of this Declaration of Principles and the withdrawal from the Gaza Strip and Jericho area, with the view to promoting economic development in the West Bank and Gaza Strip, authority will be transferred to the Palestinians on the following spheres: education and culture, health, social welfare, direct taxation, and tourism. The Palestinian side will commence in building the Palestinian police force, as agreed upon. Pending the inauguration of the Council, the two parties may negotiate the transfer of additional powers and responsibilities, as agreed upon.

ARTICLE VII

Interim Agreement

1. The Israeli and Palestinian delegations will negotiate an agreement on the interim period (the "Interim Agreement")

2. The Interim Agreement shall specify, among other things, the structure of the Council, the number of its members, and the transfer of powers and responsibilities from the Israeli military government and its Civil Administration to the Council. The Interim Agreement shall also specify the Council's executive authority, legislative authority in accordance with Article IX below, and the independent Palestinian judicial organs.

3. The Interim Agreement shall include arrangements, to be implemented upon the inauguration of the Council, for the assumption by the Council of all of the powers and responsibilities transferred previously in accordance with Article VI above.

4. In order to enable the Council to promote economic growth, upon its inauguration, the Council will establish, among other things, a Palestinian Electricity Authority, a Gaza Sea Port Authority, a Palestinian Development Bank, a Palestinian Export Promotion Board, a Palestinian Environmental Authority, a Palestinian Land Authority and a Palestinian Water Administration Authority, and any other Authorities agreed upon, in accordance with the Interim Agreement that will specify their powers and responsibilities.

5. After the inauguration of the Council, the Civil Administration will be dissolved, and the Israeli military government will be withdrawn.

ARTICLE VIII

PUBLIC ORDER AND SECURITY

In order to guarantee public order and internal security for the Palestinians of the West Bank and the Gaza Strip, the Council will establish a strong police force, while Israel will continue to carry the responsibility for defending against external threats, as well as the responsibility for overall security of Israelis for the purpose of safeguarding their internal security and public order.

ARTICLE IX

LAWS AND MILITARY ORDERS

1. The Council will be empowered to legislate, in accordance with the Interim Agreement, within all authorities transferred to it.

2. Both parties will review jointly laws and military orders presently in force in remaining spheres.

ARTICLE X

JOINT ISRAELI-PALESTINIAN LIAISON COMMITTEE

In order to provide for a smooth implementation of this Declaration of Principles and any subsequent agreements pertaining to the interim period, upon the entry into force of this Declaration of Principles, a Joint Israeli-Palestinian Liaison Committee will be established in order to deal with issues requiring coordination, other issues of common interest, and disputes.

ARTICLE XI

ISRAELI-PALESTINIAN COOPERATION IN ECONOMIC FIELDS

Recognizing the mutual benefit of cooperation in promoting the development of the West Bank, the Gaza Strip and Israel, upon the entry into force of this Declaration of Principles, an Israeli-Palestinian Economic Cooperation Committee will be established in order to develop and implement in a cooperative manner the programs identified in the protocols attached as Annex III and Annex IV .

ARTICLE XII

LIAISON AND COOPERATION WITH JORDAN AND EGYPT

The two parties will invite the Governments of Jordan and Egypt to participate in establishing further liaison and cooperation arrangements between the Government of Israel and the Palestinian representatives, on the one hand, and the Governments of Jordan and Egypt, on the other hand, to promote cooperation between them. These arrangements will include the constitution of a Continuing Committee that will decide by agreement on the modalities of admission of persons displaced from the West Bank and Gaza Strip in 1967, together with necessary measures to prevent disruption and disorder. Other matters of common concern will be dealt with by this Committee.

ARTICLE XIII

REDEPLOYMENT OF ISRAELI FORCES

1. After the entry into force of this Declaration of Principles, and not later than the eve of elections for the Council, a redeployment of Israeli military forces in the West Bank and the Gaza Strip will take place, in addition to withdrawal of Israeli forces carried out in accordance with Article XIV.

2. In redeploying its military forces, Israel will be guided by the principle that its military forces should be redeployed outside populated areas.

3. Further redeployments to specified locations will be gradually implemented commensurate with the assumption of responsibility for public order and internal security by the Palestinian police force pursuant to Article VIII above.

ARTICLE XIV

ISRAELI WITHDRAWAL FROM THE GAZA STRIP AND JERICHO AREA

Israel will withdraw from the Gaza Strip and Jericho area, as detailed in the protocol attached as Annex II.

ARTICLE XV

RESOLUTION OF DISPUTES

1. Disputes arising out of the application or interpretation of this Declaration of Principles. or any subsequent agreements pertaining to the interim period, shall be resolved by negotiations through the Joint Liaison Committee to be established pursuant to Article X above.

2. Disputes which cannot be settled by negotiations may be resolved by a mechanism of conciliation to be agreed upon by the parties.

3. The parties may agree to submit to arbitration disputes relating to the interim period, which cannot be settled through conciliation. To this end, upon the agreement of both parties, the parties will establish an Arbitration Committee.

ARTICLE XVI

ISRAELI-PALESTINIAN COOPERATION CONCERNING REGIONAL PROGRAMS

Both parties view the multilateral working groups as an appropriate instrument for promoting a "Marshall Plan", the regional programs and other programs, including special programs for the West Bank and Gaza Strip, as indicated in the protocol attached as Annex IV .

ARTICLE XVII

MISCELLANEOUS PROVISIONS

1. This Declaration of Principles will enter into force one month after its signing.

2. All protocols annexed to this Declaration of Principles and Agreed Minutes pertaining thereto shall be regarded as an integral part hereof.

Done at Washington, D.C., this thirteenth day of September, 1993.
For the Government of Israel
For the P.L.O.
Witnessed By:
The United States of America
The Russian Federation

ANNEX I

PROTOCOL ON THE MODE AND CONDITIONS OF ELECTIONS

1. Palestinians of Jerusalem who live there will have the right to participate in the election process, according to an agreement between the two sides.

2. In addition, the election agreement should cover, among other things, the following issues:

    a. the system of elections;

    b. the mode of the agreed supervision and international observation and their personal composition; and

    c. rules and regulations regarding election campaign, including agreed arrangements for the organizing of mass media, and the possibility of licensing a broadcasting and TV station.

3. The future status of displaced Palestinians who were registered on 4th June 1967 will not be prejudiced because they are unable to participate in the election process due to practical reasons.

ANNEX II

PROTOCOL ON WITHDRAWAL OF ISRAELI FORCES FROM THE GAZA STRIP AND JERICHO AREA

1. The two sides will conclude and sign within two months from the date of entry into force of this Declaration of Principles, an agreement on the withdrawal of Israeli military forces from the Gaza Strip and Jericho area. This agreement will include comprehensive arrangements to apply in the Gaza Strip and the Jericho area subsequent to the Israeli withdrawal.

2. Israel will implement an accelerated and scheduled withdrawal of Israeli military forces from the Gaza Strip and Jericho area, beginning immediately with the signing of the agreement on the Gaza Strip and Jericho area and to be completed within a period not exceeding four months after the signing of this agreement.

3. The above agreement will include, among other things:

    a. Arrangements for a smooth and peaceful transfer of authority from the Israeli military government and its Civil Administration to the Palestinian representatives.

    b. Structure, powers and responsibilities of the Palestinian authority in these areas, except: external security, settlements, Israelis, foreign relations, and other mutually agreed matters.

    c. Arrangements for the assumption of internal security and public order by the Palestinian police force consisting of police officers recruited locally and from abroad holding Jordanian passports and Palestinian documents issued by Egypt). Those who will participate in the Palestinian police force coming from abroad should be trained as police and police officers.

d. A temporary international or foreign presence, as agreed upon.

e. Establishment of a joint Palestinian-Israeli Coordination and Cooperation Committee for mutual security purposes.

f. An economic development and stabilization program, including the establishment of an Emergency Fund, to encourage foreign investment, and financial and economic support. Both sides will coordinate and cooperate jointly and unilaterally with regional and international parties to support these aims.

g. Arrangements for a safe passage for persons and transportation between the Gaza Strip and Jericho area.

4. The above agreement will include arrangements for coordination between both parties regarding passages:

    a. Gaza - Egypt; and

    b. Jericho - Jordan.

5. The offices responsible for carrying out the powers and responsibilities of the Palestinian authority under this Annex II and Article VI of the Declaration of Principles will be located in the Gaza Strip and in the Jericho area pending the inauguration of the Council.

6. Other than these agreed arrangements, the status of the Gaza Strip and Jericho area will continue to be an integral part of the West Bank and Gaza Strip, and will not be changed in the interim period.

ANNEX III

PROTOCOL ON ISRAELI-PALESTINIAN COOPERATION IN ECONOMIC AND DEVELOPMENT PROGRAMS

The two sides agree to establish an Israeli-Palestinian continuing Committee for Economic Cooperation, focusing, among other things, on the following:

1. Cooperation in the field of water, including a Water Development Program prepared by experts from both sides, which will also specify the mode of cooperation in the management of water resources in the West Bank and Gaza Strip, and will include proposals for studies and plans on water rights of each party, as well as on the equitable utilization of joint water resources for implementation in and beyond the interim period.

2. Cooperation in the field of electricity, including an Electricity Development Program, which will also specify the mode of cooperation for the production, maintenance, purchase and sale of electricity resources.

3. Cooperation in the field of energy, including an Energy Development Program, which will provide for the exploitation of oil and gas for industrial purposes, particularly in the Gaza Strip and in the Negev, and will encourage further joint exploitation of other energy resources. This Program may also provide for the construction of a Petrochemical industrial complex in the Gaza Strip and the construction of oil and gas pipelines.

4. Cooperation in the field of finance, including a Financial Development and Action Program for the encouragement of international investment in the West Bank and the Gaza Strip, and in Israel, as well as the establishment of a Palestinian Development Bank.

5. Cooperation in the field of transport and communications, including a Program, which will define guidelines for the establishment of a Gaza Sea Port Area, and will provide for the establishing of transport and communications lines to and from the West Bank and the Gaza Strip to Israel and to other countries. In addition, this Program will provide for carrying out the necessary construction of roads, railways, communications lines, etc.

6. Cooperation in the field of trade, including studies, and Trade Promotion Programs, which will encourage local, regional and inter-regional trade, as well as a feasibility study of creating free trade zones in the Gaza Strip and in Israel, mutual access to these zones, and cooperation in other areas related to trade and commerce.

7. Cooperation in the field of industry, including Industrial Development Programs, which will provide for the establishment of joint Israeli- Palestinian Industrial Research and Development Centers, will promote Palestinian-Israeli joint ventures, and provide guidelines for cooperation in the textile, food, pharmaceutical, electronics, diamonds, computer and science-based industries.

8. A program for cooperation in, and regulation of, labor relations and cooperation in social welfare issues.

9. A Human Resources Development and Cooperation Plan, providing for joint Israeli-Palestinian workshops and seminars, and for the establishment of joint vocational training centers, research institutes and data banks.

10. An Environmental Protection Plan, providing for joint and/or coordinated measures in this sphere.

11. A program for developing coordination and cooperation in the field of communication and media.

12. Any other programs of mutual interest.

ANNEX IV

PROTOCOL ON ISRAELI-PALESTINIAN COOPERATION CONCERNING REGIONAL DEVELOPMENT PROGRAMS

1. The two sides will cooperate in the context of the multilateral peace efforts in promoting a Development Program for the region, including the West Bank and the Gaza Strip, to be initiated by the G-7. The parties will request the G-7 to seek the participation in this program of other interested states, such as members of the Organisation for Economic Cooperation and Development, regional Arab states and institutions, as well as members of the private sector.

2. The Development Program will consist of two elements:

   a. an Economic Development Program for the 'West Bank and the Gaza Strip.

   b. a Regional Economic Development Program.

   A. The Economic Development Program for the West Bank and the Gaza strip will consist of the following elements:

      1. A Social Rehabilitation Program, including a Housing and Construction Program.

      2. A Small and Medium Business Development Plan.

      3. An Infrastructure Development Program (water, electricity, transportation and communications, etc.)

      4. A Human Resources Plan.

      5. Other programs.

   B. The Regional Economic Development Program may consist of the following elements:

      1. The establishment of a Middle East Development Fund, as a first step, and a Middle East Development Bank, as a second step.

      2. The development of a joint Israeli-Palestinian-Jordanian Plan for coordinated exploitation of the Dead Sea area.

      3. The Mediterranean Sea (Gaza) - Dead Sea Canal.

      4. Regional Desalinization and other water development projects.

      5. A regional plan for agricultural development, including a coordinated regional effort for the prevention of desertification.

      6. Interconnection of electricity grids.

      7. Regional cooperation for the transfer, distribution and industrial exploitation of gas, oil and other energy resources.

8. A Regional Tourism, Transportation and Telecommunications Development Plan.

9. Regional cooperation in other spheres.

3. The two sides will encourage the multilateral working groups, and will coordinate towards their success. The two parties will encourage intersessional activities, as well as pre-feasibility and feasibility studies, within the various multilateral working groups.

AGREED MINUTES TO THE DECLARATION OF PRINCIPLES ON INTERIM SELF-GOVERNMENT ARRANGEMENTS

A. GENERAL UNDERSTANDINGS AND AGREEMENTS

Any powers and responsibilities transferred to the Palestinians pursuant to the Declaration of Principles prior to the inauguration of the Council will be subject to the same principles pertaining to Article IV, as set out in these Agreed Minutes below.

B. SPECIFIC UNDERSTANDINGS AND AGREEMENTS

Article IV

It is understood that:

1. Jurisdiction of the Council will cover West Bank and Gaza Strip territory, except for issues that will be negotiated in the permanent status negotiations: Jerusalem, settlements, military locations, and Israelis.

2. The Council's jurisdiction will apply with regard to the agreed powers, responsibilities, spheres and authorities transferred to it.

Article VI (2)

It is agreed that the transfer of authority will be as follows:

1. The Palestinian side will inform the Israeli side of the names of the authorised Palestinians who will assume the powers, authorities and responsibilities that will be transferred to the Palestinians according to the Declaration of Principles in the following fields: education and culture, health, social welfare, direct taxation, tourism, and any other authorities agreed upon.

2. It is understood that the rights and obligations of these offices will not be affected.

3. Each of the spheres described above will continue to enjoy existing budgetary allocations in accordance with arrangements to be mutually agreed upon. These arrangements also will provide for the necessary adjustments required in order to take into account the taxes collected by the direct taxation office.

4. Upon the execution of the Declaration of Principles, the Israeli and Palestinian delegations will immediately commence negotiations on a detailed plan for the transfer of authority on the above offices in accordance with the above understandings.

Article VII (2)
The Interim Agreement will also include arrangements for coordination and cooperation.

Article VII (5)
The withdrawal of the military government will not prevent Israel from exercising the powers and responsibilities not transferred to the Council.

Article VIII
It is understood that the Interim Agreement will include arrangements for cooperation and coordination between the two parties in this regard. It is also agreed that the transfer of powers and responsibilities to the Palestinian police will be accomplished in a phased manner, as agreed in the Interim Agreement.

Article X
It is agreed that, upon the entry into force of the Declaration of Principles, the Israeli and Palestinian delegations will exchange the names of the individuals designated by them as members of the Joint Israeli-Palestinian Liaison Committee.

It is further agreed that each side will have an equal number of members in the Joint Committee. The Joint Committee will reach decisions by agreement. The Joint Committee may add other technicians and experts, as necessary. The Joint Committee will decide on the frequency and place or places of its meetings.

Annex II
It is understood that, subsequent to the Israeli withdrawal, Israel will continue to be responsible for external security, and for internal security and public order of settlements and Israelis. Israeli military forces and civilians may continue to use roads freely within the Gaza Strip and the Jericho area.

Done at Washington, D.C., this thirteenth day of September, 1993.

For the Government of Israel
For the P.L.O.
Witnessed By:
The United States of America
The Russian Federation

ISRAELI-PALESTINIAN INTERIM AGREEMENT ON THE WEST BANK AND THE GAZA STRIP

Washington, D.C., September 28, 1995

The Government of the State of Israel and the Palestine Liberation Organization (hereinafter "the PLO"), the representative of the Palestinian people;

PREAMBLE

WITHIN the framework of the Middle East peace process initiated at Madrid in October 1991;

REAFFIRMING their determination to put an end to decades of confrontation and to live in peaceful coexistence, mutual dignity and security, while recognizing their mutual legitimate and political rights;

REAFFIRMING their desire to achieve a just, lasting and comprehensive peace settlement and historic reconciliation through the agreed political process;

RECOGNIZING that the peace process and the new era that it has created, as well as the new relationship established between the two Parties as described above, are irreversible, and the determination of the two Parties to maintain, sustain and continue the peace process;

RECOGNIZING that the aim of the Israeli-Palestinian negotiations within the current Middle East peace process is, among other things, to establish a Palestinian Interim Self-Government Authority, i.e. the elected Council (hereinafter "the Council" or "the Palestinian Council"), and the elected Ra'ees of the Executive Authority, for the Palestinian people in the West Bank and the Gaza Strip, for a transitional period not exceeding five years from the date of signing the Agreement on the Gaza Strip and the Jericho Area (hereinafter "the Gaza-Jericho Agreement") on May 4, 1994, leading to a permanent settlement based on Security Council Resolutions 242 and 338;

REAFFIRMING their understanding that the interim self-government arrangements contained in this Agreement are an integral part of the whole peace process, that the negotiations on the permanent status, that will start as soon as possible but not later than May 4, 1996, will lead to the implementation of Security Council Resolutions 242 and 338, and that the Interim Agreement shall settle all the issues of the interim period and that no such issues will be deferred to the agenda of the permanent status negotiations;

REAFFIRMING their adherence to the mutual recognition and commitments expressed in the letters dated September 9, 1993, signed by and exchanged between the Prime Minister of Israel and the Chairman of the PLO;

DESIROUS of putting into effect the Declaration of Principles on Interim Self-Government Arrangements signed at Washington, D.C. on September 13, 1993, and the Agreed Minutes thereto (hereinafter "the DOP") and in particular Article III and Annex I concerning the holding of direct, free and general political elections for the Council and the Ra'ees of the Executive Authority in order that the Palestinian people in the West Bank, Jerusalem and the Gaza Strip may democratically elect accountable representatives;

RECOGNIZING that these elections will constitute a significant interim preparatory step toward the realization of the legitimate rights of the Palestinian people and their just requirements and will provide a democratic basis for the establishment of Palestinian institutions;

REAFFIRMING their mutual commitment to act, in accordance with this Agreement, immediately, efficiently and effectively against acts or threats of terrorism, violence or incitement, whether committed by Palestinians or Israelis;

FOLLOWING the Gaza-Jericho Agreement; the Agreement on Preparatory Transfer of Powers and Responsibilities signed at Erez on August 29, 1994 (hereinafter "the Preparatory Transfer Agreement"); and the Protocol on Further Transfer of Powers and Responsibilities signed at Cairo on August 27, 1995 (hereinafter "the Further Transfer Protocol"); which three agreements will be superseded by this Agreement;

HEREBY AGREE as follows:

CHAPTER I - THE COUNCIL

ARTICLE I

Transfer of Authority

1. Israel shall transfer powers and responsibilities as specified in this Agreement from the Israeli military government and its Civil Administration to the Council in accordance with this Agreement. Israel shall continue to exercise powers and responsibilities not so transferred.
2. Pending the inauguration of the Council, the powers and responsibilities transferred to the Council shall be exercised by the Palestinian Authority established in accordance with the Gaza-Jericho Agreement, which shall also have all the rights, liabilities and obligations to be assumed by the Council in this regard. Accordingly, the term "Council" throughout this Agreement shall, pending the inauguration of the Council, be construed as meaning the Palestinian Authority.
3. The transfer of powers and responsibilities to the police force established by the Palestinian Council in accordance with Article XIV below (hereinafter "the Palestinian Police") shall be accomplished in a phased manner, as detailed in this Agreement and in the Protocol concerning Redeployment and Security Arrangements attached as Annex I to this Agreement (hereinafter "Annex I").
4. As regards the transfer and assumption of authority in civil spheres, powers and responsibilities shall be transferred and assumed as set out in the Protocol Concerning

Civil Affairs attached as Annex III to this Agreement (hereinafter "Annex III").

5. After the inauguration of the Council, the Civil Administration in the West Bank will be dissolved, and the Israeli military government shall be withdrawn. The withdrawal of the military government shall not prevent it from exercising the powers and responsibilities not transferred to the Council.
6. A Joint Civil Affairs Coordination and Cooperation Committee (hereinafter "the CAC"), Joint Regional Civil Affairs Subcommittees, one for the Gaza Strip and the other for the West Bank, and District Civil Liaison Offices in the West Bank shall be established in order to provide for coordination and cooperation in civil affairs between the Council and Israel, as detailed in Annex III.
7. The offices of the Council, and the offices of its Ra'ees and its Executive Authority and other committees, shall be located in areas under Palestinian territorial jurisdiction in the West Bank and the Gaza Strip.

ARTICLE II

Elections

1. In order that the Palestinian people of the West Bank and the Gaza Strip may govern themselves according to democratic principles, direct, free and general political elections will be held for the Council and the Ra'ees of the Executive Authority of the Council in accordance with the provisions set out in the Protocol concerning Elections attached as Annex II to this Agreement (hereinafter "Annex II").
2. These elections will constitute a significant interim preparatory step towards the realization of the legitimate rights of the Palestinian people and their just requirements and will provide a democratic basis for the establishment of Palestinian institutions.
3. Palestinians of Jerusalem who live there may participate in the election process in accordance with the provisions contained in this Article and in Article VI of Annex II (Election Arrangements concerning Jerusalem).
4. The elections shall be called by the Chairman of the Palestinian Authority immediately following the signing of this Agreement to take place at the earliest practicable date following the redeployment of Israeli forces in accordance with Annex I, and consistent with the requirements of the election timetable as provided in Annex II, the Election Law and the Election Regulations, as defined in Article I of Annex II.

ARTICLE III

Structure of the Palestinian Council

1. The Palestinian Council and the Ra'ees of the Executive Authority of the Council constitute the Palestinian Interim Self-Government Authority, which will be elected by the Palestinian people of the West Bank, Jerusalem and the Gaza Strip for the transitional period agreed in Article I of the DOP.
2. The Council shall possess both legislative power and executive power, in accordance with Articles VII and IX of the DOP. The Council shall carry out and be responsible for all the legislative and executive powers and responsibilities transferred to it under this Agreement. The exercise of legislative powers shall be in accordance with Article XVIII of this Agreement (Legislative Powers of the Council).

3. The Council and the Ra'ees of the Executive Authority of the Council shall be directly and simultaneously elected by the Palestinian people of the West Bank, Jerusalem and the Gaza Strip, in accordance with the provisions of this Agreement and the Election Law and Regulations, which shall not be contrary to the provisions of this Agreement.
4. The Council and the Ra'ees of the Executive Authority of the Council shall be elected for a transitional period not exceeding five years from the signing of the Gaza-Jericho Agreement on May 4, 1994.
5. Immediately upon its inauguration, the Council will elect from among its members a Speaker. The Speaker will preside over the meetings of the Council, administer the Council and its committees, decide on the agenda of each meeting, and lay before the Council proposals for voting and declare their results.
6. The jurisdiction of the Council shall be as determined in Article XVII of this Agreement (Jurisdiction).
7. The organization, structure and functioning of the Council shall be in accordance with this Agreement and the Basic Law for the Palestinian Interim Self-government Authority, which Law shall be adopted by the Council. The Basic Law and any regulations made under it shall not be contrary to the provisions of this Agreement.
8. The Council shall be responsible under its executive powers for the offices, services and departments transferred to it and may establish, within its jurisdiction, ministries and subordinate bodies, as necessary for the fulfillment of its responsibilities.
9. The Speaker will present for the Council's approval proposed internal procedures that will regulate, among other things, the decision-making processes of the Council.

ARTICLE IV

Size of the Council

The Palestinian Council shall be composed of 82 representatives and the Ra'ees of the Executive Authority, who will be directly and simultaneously elected by the Palestinian people of the West Bank, Jerusalem and the Gaza Strip.

ARTICLE V

The Executive Authority of the Council

1. The Council will have a committee that will exercise the executive authority of the Council, formed in accordance with paragraph 4 below (hereinafter "the Executive Authority").
2. The Executive Authority shall be bestowed with the executive authority of the Council and will exercise it on behalf of the Council. It shall determine its own internal procedures and decision making processes.
3. The Council will publish the names of the members of the Executive Authority immediately upon their initial appointment and subsequent to any changes.
4. a. The Ra'ees of the Executive Authority shall be an ex officio member of the Executive Authority.
   b. All of the other members of the Executive Authority, except as provided in subparagraph c. below, shall be members of the Council, chosen and proposed to the Council by the Ra'ees of the Executive Authority and approved by the Council.

c. The Ra'ees of the Executive Authority shall have the right to appoint some persons, in number not exceeding twenty percent of the total membership of the Executive Authority, who are not members of the Council, to exercise executive authority and participate in government tasks. Such appointed members may not vote in meetings of the Council.

d. Non-elected members of the Executive Authority must have a valid address in an area under the jurisdiction of the Council.

ARTICLE VI

Other Committees of the Council

1. The Council may form small committees to simplify the proceedings of the Council and to assist in controlling the activity of its Executive Authority.
2. Each committee shall establish its own decision-making processes within the general framework of the organization and structure of the Council.

ARTICLE VII

Open Government

1. All meetings of the Council and of its committees, other than the Executive Authority, shall be open to the public, except upon a resolution of the Council or the relevant committee on the grounds of security, or commercial or personal confidentiality.
2. Participation in the deliberations of the Council, its committees and the Executive Authority shall be limited to their respective members only. Experts may be invited to such meetings to address specific issues on an ad hoc basis.

ARTICLE VIII

Judicial Review

Any person or organization affected by any act or decision of the Ra'ees of the Executive Authority of the Council or of any member of the Executive Authority, who believes that such act or decision exceeds the authority of the Ra'ees or of such member, or is otherwise incorrect in law or procedure, may apply to the relevant Palestinian Court of Justice for a review of such activity or decision.

ARTICLE IX

Powers and Responsibilities of the Council

1. Subject to the provisions of this Agreement, the Council will, within its jurisdiction, have legislative powers as set out in Article XVIII of this Agreement, as well as executive powers.
2. The executive power of the Palestinian Council shall extend to all matters within its jurisdiction under this Agreement or any future agreement that may be reached between the two Parties during the interim period. It shall include the power to formulate and conduct Palestinian policies and to supervise their implementation, to issue any rule or regulation under powers given in approved legislation and administrative decisions necessary for the realization of Palestinian self-government, the power to employ staff, sue and be sued and conclude contracts, and the power to keep and administer registers and records of the population, and issue certificates, licenses and documents.

3. The Palestinian Council's executive decisions and acts shall be consistent with the provisions of this Agreement.
4. The Palestinian Council may adopt all necessary measures in order to enforce the law and any of its decisions, and bring proceedings before the Palestinian courts and tribunals.
5. a. In accordance with the DOP, the Council will not have powers and responsibilities in the sphere of foreign relations, which sphere includes the establishment abroad of embassies, consulates or other types of foreign missions and posts or permitting their establishment in the West Bank or the Gaza Strip, the appointment of or admission of diplomatic and consular staff, and the exercise of diplomatic functions.
   b. Notwithstanding the provisions of this paragraph, the PLO may conduct negotiations and sign agreements with states or international organizations for the benefit of the Council in the following cases only:
      (l) economic agreements, as specifically provided in Annex V of this Agreement:
      (2) agreements with donor countries for the purpose of implementing arrangements for the provision of assistance to the Council,
      (3) agreements for the purpose of implementing the regional development plans detailed in Annex IV of the DOP or in agreements entered into in the framework of the multilateral negotiations, and
      (4) cultural, scientific and educational agreements. Dealings between the Council and representatives of foreign states and international organizations, as well as the establishment in the West Bank and the Gaza Strip of representative offices other than those described in subparagraph 5.a above, for the purpose of implementing the agreements referred to in subparagraph 5.b above, shall not be considered foreign relations.
6. Subject to the provisions of this Agreement, the Council shall, within its jurisdiction, have an independent judicial system composed of independent Palestinian courts and tribunals.

CHAPTER 2 - REDEPLOYMENT AND SECURITY ARRANGEMENTS

ARTICLE X

Redeployment of Israeli Military Forces

1. The first phase of the Israeli military forces redeployment will cover populated areas in the West Bank - cities, towns, villages, refugee camps and hamlets - as set out in Annex I, and will be completed prior to the eve of the Palestinian elections, i. e., 22 days before the day of the elections.
2. Further redeployments of Israeli military forces to specified military locations will commence after the inauguration of the Council and will be gradually implemented commensurate with the assumption of responsibility for public order and internal security by the Palestinian Police, to be completed within 18 months from the date of the inauguration of the Council as detailed in Articles XI (Land) and XIII (Security), below and in Annex I.

3. The Palestinian Police shall be deployed and shall assume responsibility for public order and internal security for Palestinians in a phased manner in accordance with XIII (Security) below and Annex I.
4. Israel shall continue to carry the responsibility for external security, as well as the responsibility for overall security of Israelis for the purpose of safeguarding their internal security and public order.
5. For the purpose of this Agreement, "Israeli military forces" includes Israel Police and other Israeli security forces.

ARTICLE XI

Land

1. The two sides view the West Bank and the Gaza Strip as a single territorial unit, the integrity and status of which will be preserved during the interim period.
2. The two sides agree that West Bank and Gaza Strip territory, except for issues that will be negotiated in the permanent status negotiations, will come under the jurisdiction of the Palestinian Council in a phased manner, to be completed within 18 months from the date of the inauguration of the Council, as specified below:
   a. Land in populated areas (Areas A and B), including government and Al Waqf land, will come under the jurisdiction of the Council during the first phase of redeployment.
   b. All civil powers and responsibilities, including planning and zoning, in Areas A and B, set out in Annex III, will be transferred to and assumed by the Council during the first phase of redeployment.
   c. In Area C, during the first phase of redeployment Israel will transfer to the Council civil powers and responsibilities not relating to territory, as set out in Annex III.
   d. The further redeployments of Israeli military forces to specified military locations will be gradually implemented in accordance with the DOP in three phases, each to take place after an interval of six months, after the inauguration of the Council, to be completed within 18 months from the date of the inauguration of the Council.
   e. During the further redeployment phases to be completed within 18 months from the date of the inauguration of the Council, powers and responsibilities relating to territory will be transferred gradually to Palestinian jurisdiction that will cover West Bank and Gaza Strip territory, except for the issues that will be negotiated in the permanent status negotiations.
   f. The specified military locations referred to in Article X, paragraph 2 above will be determined in the further redeployment phases, within the specified time-frame ending not later than 18 months from the date of the inauguration of the Council, and will be negotiated in the permanent status negotiations.
3. For the purpose of this Agreement and until the completion of the first phase of the further redeployments:
   a. "Area A" means the populated areas delineated by a red line and shaded in brown on attached map No. 1;
   b. "Area B" means the populated areas delineated by a red line and shaded in yellow on attached map No. 1, and the built-up area of the hamlets listed in Appendix 6 to Annex I, and

c. "Area C" means areas of the West Bank outside Areas A and B, which, except for the issues that will be negotiated in the permanent status negotiations, will be gradually transferred to Palestinian jurisdiction in accordance with this Agreement.

ARTICLE XII

Arrangements for Security and Public Order

1. In order to guarantee public order and internal security for the Palestinians of the West Bank and the Gaza Strip, the Council shall establish a strong police force as set out in Article XIV below. Israel shall continue to carry the responsibility for defense against external threats, including the responsibility for protecting the Egyptian and Jordanian borders, and for defense against external threats from the sea and from the air, as well as the responsibility for overall security of Israelis and Settlements, for the purpose of safeguarding their internal security and public order, and will have all the powers to take the steps necessary to meet this responsibility.
2. Agreed security arrangements and coordination mechanisms are specified in Annex I.
3. A Joint Coordination and Cooperation Committee for Mutual Security Purposes (hereinafter "the JSC"), as well as Joint Regional Security Committees (hereinafter "RSCs") and Joint District Coordination Offices (hereinafter "DCOs"), are hereby established as provided for in Annex I.
4. The security arrangements provided for in this Agreement and in Annex I may be reviewed at the request of either Party and may be amended by mutual agreement of the Parties. Specific review arrangements are included in Annex I.
5. For the purpose of this Agreement, "the Settlements" means, in the West Bank the settlements in Area C; and in the Gaza Strip - the Gush Katif and Erez settlement areas, as well as the other settlements in the Gaza Strip, as shown on attached map No. 2.

ARTICLE XIII

Security

1. The Council will, upon completion of the redeployment of Israeli military forces in each district, as set out in Appendix 1 to Annex I, assume the powers and responsibilities for internal security and public order in Area A in that district.
2. a. There will be a complete redeployment of Israeli military forces from Area B. Israel will transfer to the Council and the Council will assume responsibility for public order for Palestinians. Israel shall have the overriding responsibility for security for the purpose of protecting Israelis and confronting the threat of terrorism.

   b. In Area B the Palestinian Police shall assume the responsibility for public order for Palestinians and shall be deployed in order to accommodate the Palestinian needs and requirements in the following manner:

      (1) The Palestinian Police shall establish 25 police stations and posts in towns, villages, and other places listed in Appendix 2 to Annex I and as delineated on map No. 3. The West Bank RSC may agree on the establishment of additional police stations and posts, if required.

      (2) The Palestinian Police shall be responsible for handling public order incidents in which only Palestinians are involved.

(3) The Palestinian Police shall operate freely in populated places where police stations and posts are located, as set out in paragraph b(1) above.

(4) While the movement of uniformed Palestinian policemen in Area B outside places where there is a Palestinian police station or post will be carried out after coordination and confirmation through the relevant DCO, three months after the completion of redeployment from Area B, the DCOs may decide that movement of Palestinian policemen from the police stations in Area B to Palestinian towns and villages in Area B on roads that are used only by Palestinian traffic will take place after notifying the DCO.

(5) The coordination of such planned movement prior to confirmation through the relevant DCO shall include a scheduled plan, including the number of policemen, as well as the type and number of weapons and vehicles intended to take part. It shall also include details of arrangements for ensuring continued coordination through appropriate communication links, the exact schedule of movement to the area of the planned operation, including the destination and routes thereto, its proposed duration and the schedule for returning to the police station or post.

The Israeli side of the DCO will provide the Palestinian side with its response, following a request for movement of policemen in accordance with this paragraph, in normal or routine cases within one day and in emergency cases no later than 2 hours.

(6) The Palestinian Police and the Israeli military forces will conduct joint security activities on the main roads as set out in Annex I.

(7) The Palestinian Police will notify the West Bank RSC of the names of the policemen, number plates of police vehicles and serial numbers of weapons, with respect to each police station and post in Area B.

(8) Further redeployments from Area C and transfer of internal security responsibility to the Palestinian Police in Areas B and C will be carried out in three phases, each to take place after an interval of six months, to be completed 18 months after the inauguration of the Council, except for the issues of permanent status negotiations and of Israel's overall responsibility for Israelis and borders.

(9) The procedures detailed in this paragraph will be reviewed within six months of the completion of the first phase of redeployment.

ARTICLE XIV

The Palestinian Police

1. The Council shall establish a strong police force. The duties, functions, structure, deployment and composition of the Palestinian Police, together with provisions regarding its equipment and operation, as well as rules of conduct, are set out in Annex I.
2. The Palestinian police force established under the Gaza-Jericho Agreement will be fully integrated into the Palestinian Police and will be subject to the provisions of this Agreement.
3. Except for the Palestinian Police and the Israeli military forces, no other armed forces shall be established or operate in the West Bank and the Gaza Strip.

4. Except for the arms, ammunition and equipment of the Palestinian Police described in Annex I, and those of the Israeli military forces, no organization, group or individual in the West Bank and the Gaza Strip shall manufacture, sell, acquire, possess, import or otherwise introduce into the West Bank or the Gaza Strip any firearms, ammunition, weapons, explosives, gunpowder or any related equipment, unless otherwise provided for in Annex I.

ARTICLE XV

Prevention of Hostile Acts

1. Both sides shall take all measures necessary in order to prevent acts of terrorism, crime and hostilities directed against each other, against individuals falling under the other's authority and against their property and shall take legal measures against offenders.
2. Specific provisions for the implementation of this Article are set out in Annex I.

ARTICLE XVI

Confidence Building Measures

With a view to fostering a positive and supportive public atmosphere to accompany the implementation of this Agreement, to establish a solid basis of mutual trust and good faith, and in order to facilitate the anticipated cooperation and new relations between the two peoples, both Parties agree to carry out confidence building measures as detailed herewith:

1. Israel will release or turn over to the Palestinian side, Palestinian detainees and prisoners, residents of the West Bank and the Gaza Strip. The first stage of release of these prisoners and detainees will take place on the signing of this Agreement and the second stage will take place prior to the date of the elections. There will be a third stage of release of detainees and prisoners. Detainees and prisoners will be released from among categories detailed in Annex VII (Release of Palestinian Prisoners and Detainees). Those released will be free to return to their homes in the West Bank and the Gaza Strip.
2. Palestinians who have maintained contact with the Israeli authorities will not be subjected to acts of harassment, violence, retribution or prosecution. Appropriate ongoing measures will be taken, in coordination with Israel, in order to ensure their protection.
3. Palestinians from abroad whose entry into the West Bank and the Gaza Strip is approved pursuant to this Agreement, and to whom the provisions of this Article are applicable, will not be prosecuted for offenses committed prior to September 13, 1993.

CHAPTER 3 - LEGAL AFFAIRS

ARTICLE XVII

Jurisdiction

1. In accordance with the DOP, the jurisdiction of the Council will cover West Bank and Gaza Strip territory as a single territorial unit, except for:
   a. issues that will be negotiated in the permanent status negotiations: Jerusalem, settlements, specified military locations, Palestinian refugees, borders, foreign relations and Israelis; and
   b. powers and responsibilities not transferred to the Council.

2. Accordingly, the authority of the Council encompasses all matters that fall within its territorial, functional and personal jurisdiction, as follows:
   a. The territorial jurisdiction of the Council shall encompass Gaza Strip territory, except for the Settlements and the Military Installation Area shown on map No. 2, and West Bank territory, except for Area C which, except for the issues that will be negotiated in the permanent status negotiations, will be gradually transferred to Palestinian jurisdiction in three phases, each to take place after an interval of six months, to be completed 18 months after the inauguration of the Council. At this time, the jurisdiction of the Council will cover West Bank and Gaza Strip territory, except for the issues that will be negotiated in the permanent status negotiations.
   Territorial jurisdiction includes land, subsoil and territorial waters, in accordance with the provisions of this Agreement.
   b. The functional jurisdiction of the Council extends to all powers and responsibilities transferred to the Council, as specified in this Agreement or in any future agreements that may be reached between the Parties during the interim period.
   c. The territorial and functional jurisdiction of the Council will apply to all persons, except for Israelis, unless otherwise provided in this Agreement.
   d. Notwithstanding subparagraph a. above, the Council shall have functional jurisdiction in Area C, as detailed in Article IV of Annex III.
3. The Council has, within its authority, legislative, executive and judicial powers and responsibilities, as provided for in this Agreement.
4. a. Israel, through its military government, has the authority over areas that are not under the territorial jurisdiction of the Council, powers and responsibilities not transferred to the Council and Israelis.
   b. To this end, the Israeli military government shall retain the necessary legislative, judicial and executive powers and responsibilities, in accordance with international law. This provision shall not derogate from Israel's applicable legislation over Israelis in personam.
5. The exercise of authority with regard to the electromagnetic sphere and air space shall be in accordance with the provisions of this Agreement.
6. Without derogating from the provisions of this Article, legal arrangements detailed in the Protocol Concerning Legal Matters attached as Annex IV to this Agreement (hereinafter "Annex IV") shall be observed. Israel and the Council may negotiate further legal arrangements.
7. Israel and the Council shall cooperate on matters of legal assistance in criminal and civil matters through a legal committee (hereinafter "the Legal Committee"), hereby established.
8. The Council's jurisdiction will extend gradually to cover West Bank and Gaza Strip territory, except for the issues to be negotiated in the permanent status negotiations, through a series of redeployments of the Israeli military forces. The first phase of the redeployment of Israeli military forces will cover populated areas in the West Bank - cities, towns, refugee camps and hamlets, as set out in Annex I - and will be completed prior to the eve of the Palestinian elections, i.e. 22 days before the day of the elections. Further redeployments of Israeli military forces to specified military locations will

commence immediately upon the inauguration of the Council and will be effected in three phases, each to take place after an interval of six months, to be concluded no later than eighteen months from the date of the inauguration of the Council.

ARTICLE XVIII

Legislative Powers of the Council

1. For the purposes of this Article, legislation shall mean any primary and secondary legislation, including basic laws, laws, regulations and other legislative acts.
2. The Council has the power, within its jurisdiction as defined in Article XVII of this Agreement, to adopt legislation.
3. While the primary legislative power shall lie in the hands of the Council as a whole, the Ra'ees of the Executive Authority of the Council shall have the following legislative powers
   a. the power to initiate legislation or to present proposed legislation to the Council;
   b. the power to promulgate legislation adopted by the Council; and
   c. the power to issue secondary legislation, including regulations, relating to any matters specified and within the scope laid down in any primary legislation adopted by the Council.
4. a. Legislation, including legislation which amends or abrogates existing laws or military orders, which exceeds the jurisdiction of the Council or which is otherwise inconsistent with the provisions of the DOP, this Agreement, or of any other agreement that may be reached between the two sides during the interim period, shall have no effect and shall be void ab initio.
   b. The Ra'ees of the Executive Authority of the Council shall not promulgate legislation adopted by the Council if such legislation falls under the provisions of this paragraph.
5. All legislation shall be communicated to the Israeli side of the Legal Committee.
6. Without derogating from the provisions of paragraph 4 above, the Israeli side of the Legal Committee may refer for the attention of the Committee any legislation regarding which Israel considers the provisions of paragraph 4 apply, in order to discuss issues arising from such legislation. The Legal Committee will consider the legislation referred to it at the earliest opportunity.

ARTICLE XIX

Human Rights and the Rule of Law

Israel and the Council shall exercise their powers and responsibilities pursuant to this Agreement with due regard to internationally-accepted norms and principles of human rights and the rule of law.

ARTICLE XX

Rights, Liabilities and Obligations

1. a. The transfer of powers and responsibilities from the Israeli military government and its civil administration to the Council, as detailed in Annex III, includes all related rights, liabilities and obligations arising with regard to acts or omissions which

occurred prior to such transfer. Israel will cease to bear any financial responsibility regarding such acts or omissions and the Council will bear all financial responsibility for these and for its own functioning.

b. Any financial claim made in this regard against Israel will be referred to the Council.

c. Israel shall provide the Council with the information it has regarding pending and anticipated claims brought before any court or tribunal against Israel in this regard.

d. Where legal proceedings are brought in respect of such a claim, Israel will notify the Council and enable it to participate in defending the claim and raise any arguments on its behalf.

e. In the event that an award is made against Israel by any court or tribunal in respect of such a claim, the Council shall immediately reimburse Israel the full amount of the award.

f. Without prejudice to the above, where a court or tribunal hearing such a claim finds that liability rests solely with an employee or agent who acted beyond the scope of the powers assigned to him or her, unlawfully or with willful malfeasance, the Council shall not bear financial responsibility.

2. a. Notwithstanding the provisions of paragraphs l.d through l.f above, each side may take the necessary measures, including promulgation of legislation, in order to ensure that such claims by Palestinians including pending claims in which the hearing of evidence has not yet begun, are brought only before Palestinian courts or tribunals in the West Bank and the Gaza Strip, and are not brought before or heard by Israeli courts or tribunals.

b. Where a new claim has been brought before a Palestinian court or tribunal subsequent to the dismissal of the claim pursuant to subparagraph a. above, the Council shall defend it and, in accordance with subparagraph l.a above, in the event that an award is made for the plaintiff, shall pay the amount of the award.

c. The Legal Committee shall agree on arrangements for the transfer of all materials and information needed to enable the Palestinian courts or tribunals to hear such claims as referred to in subparagraph b. above, and, when necessary, for the provision of legal assistance by Israel to the Council in defending such claims.

3. The transfer of authority in itself shall not affect rights, liabilities and obligations of any person or legal entity, in existence at the date of signing of this Agreement.

4. The Council, upon its inauguration, will assume all the rights, liabilities and obligations of the Palestinian Authority.

5. For the purpose of this Agreement, "Israelis" also includes Israeli statutory agencies and corporations registered in Israel.

ARTICLE XXI

Settlement of Differences and Disputes

Any difference relating to the application of this Agreement shall be referred to the appropriate coordination and cooperation mechanism established under this Agreement. The provisions of Article XV of the DOP shall apply to any such difference which is not settled through the appropriate coordination and cooperation mechanism, namely:

1. Disputes arising out of the application or interpretation of this Agreement or any related agreements pertaining to the interim period shall be settled through the Liaison Committee.
2. Disputes which cannot be settled by negotiations may be settled by a mechanism of conciliation to be agreed between the Parties.
3. The Parties may agree to submit to arbitration disputes relating to the interim period, which cannot be settled through conciliation. To this end, upon the agreement of both Parties, the Parties will establish an Arbitration Committee.

CHAPTER 4 - COOPERATION

ARTICLE XXII

Relations between Israel and the Council

1. Israel and the Council shall seek to foster mutual understanding and tolerance and shall accordingly abstain from incitement, including hostile propaganda, against each other and, without derogating from the principle of freedom of expression, shall take legal measures to prevent such incitement by any organizations, groups or individuals within their jurisdiction.
2. Israel and the Council will ensure that their respective educational systems contribute to the peace between the Israeli and Palestinian peoples and to peace in the entire region, and will refrain from the introduction of any motifs that could adversely affect the process of reconciliation.
3. Without derogating from the other provisions of this Agreement, Israel and the Council shall cooperate in combating criminal activity which may affect both sides, including offenses related to trafficking in illegal drugs and psychotropic substances, smuggling, and offenses against property, including offenses related to vehicles.

ARTICLE XXIII

Cooperation with Regard to Transfer of Powers and Responsibilities

In order to ensure a smooth, peaceful and orderly transfer of powers and responsibilities, the two sides will cooperate with regard to the transfer of security powers and responsibilities in accordance with the provisions of Annex I, and the transfer of civil powers and responsibilities in accordance with the provisions of Annex III.

ARTICLE XXIV

Economic Relations

The economic relations between the two sides are set out in the Protocol on Economic Relations signed in Paris on April 29, 1994, and the Appendices thereto, and the Supplement to the Protocol on Economic Relations all attached as Annex V, and will be governed by the relevant provisions of this Agreement and its Annexes.

ARTICLE XXV

Cooperation Programs

1. The Parties agree to establish a mechanism to develop programs of cooperation between them. Details of such cooperation are set out in Annex VI.
2. A Standing Cooperation Committee to deal with issues arising in the context of this cooperation is hereby established as provided for in Annex VI.

ARTICLE XXVI

The Joint Israeli-Palestinian Liaison Committee

1. The Liaison Committee established pursuant to Article X of the DOP shall ensure the smooth implementation of this Agreement. It shall deal with issues requiring coordination, other issues of common interest and disputes.
2. The Liaison Committee shall be composed of an equal number of members from each Party. It may add other technicians and experts as necessary.
3. The Liaison Committee shall adopt its rules of procedures, including the frequency and place or places of its meetings.
4. The Liaison Committee shall reach its decisions by agreement.
5. The Liaison Committee shall establish a subcommittee that will monitor and steer the implementation of this Agreement (hereinafter "the Monitoring and Steering Committee"). It will function as follows:
   a. The Monitoring and Steering Committee will, on an ongoing basis, monitor the implementation of this Agreement, with a view to enhancing the cooperation and fostering the peaceful relations between the two sides.
   b. The Monitoring and Steering Committee will steer the activities of the various joint committees established in this Agreement (the JSC, the CAC, the Legal Committee, the Joint Economic Committee and the Standing Cooperation Committee) concerning the ongoing implementation of the Agreement, and will report to the Liaison Committee.
   c. The Monitoring and Steering Committee will be composed of the heads of the various committees mentioned above.
   d. The two heads of the Monitoring and Steering Committee will establish its rules of procedures, including the frequency and places of its meetings.

ARTICLE XXVII

Liaison and Cooperation with Jordan and Egypt

1. Pursuant to Article XII of the DOP, the two Parties have invited the Governments of Jordan and Egypt to participate in establishing further liaison and cooperation arrangements between the Government of Israel and the Palestinian representatives on the one hand, and the Governments of Jordan and Egypt on the other hand, to promote cooperation between them. As part of these arrangements a Continuing Committee has been constituted and has commenced its deliberations.
2. The Continuing Committee shall decide by agreement on the modalities of admission of persons displaced from the West Bank and the Gaza Strip in 1967, together with necessary measures to prevent disruption and disorder.
3. The Continuing Committee shall also deal with other matters of common concern.

ARTICLE XXVIII

Missing Persons

1. Israel and the Council shall cooperate by providing each other with all necessary assistance in the conduct of searches for missing persons and bodies of persons which have not been recovered, as well as by providing information about missing persons.
2. The PLO undertakes to cooperate with Israel and to assist it in its efforts to locate and to return to Israel Israeli soldiers who are missing in action and the bodies of soldiers which have not been recovered.

CHAPTER 5 - MISCELLANEOUS PROVISIONS

ARTICLE XXIX

Safe Passage between the West Bank and the Gaza Strip

Arrangements for safe passage of persons and transportation between the West Bank and the Gaza Strip are set out in Annex I.

ARTICLE XXX

Passages

Arrangements for coordination between Israel and the Council regarding passage to and from Egypt and Jordan, as well as any other agreed international crossings, are set out in Annex I.

ARTICLE XXXI

Final Clauses

1. This Agreement shall enter into force on the date of its signing.
2. The Gaza-Jericho Agreement, except for Article XX (Confidence-Building Measures), the Preparatory Transfer Agreement and the Further Transfer Protocol will be superseded by this Agreement.
3. The Council, upon its inauguration, shall replace the Palestinian Authority and shall assume all the undertakings and obligations of the Palestinian Authority under the Gaza-Jericho Agreement, the Preparatory Transfer Agreement, and the Further Transfer Protocol.
4. The two sides shall pass all necessary legislation to implement this Agreement.
5. Permanent status negotiations will commence as soon as possible, but not later than May 4, 1996, between the Parties. It is understood that these negotiations shall cover remaining issues, including: Jerusalem, refugees, settlements, security arrangements, borders, relations and cooperation with other neighbors, and other issues of common interest.
6. Nothing in this Agreement shall prejudice or preempt the outcome of the negotiations on the permanent status to be conducted pursuant to the DOP. Neither Party shall be deemed, by virtue of having entered into this Agreement, to have renounced or waived any of its existing rights, claims or positions.
7. Neither side shall initiate or take any step that will change the status of the West Bank and the Gaza Strip pending the outcome of the permanent status negotiations.
8. The two Parties view the West Bank and the Gaza Strip as a single territorial unit, the

integrity and status of which will be preserved during the interim period.

9. The PLO undertakes that, within two months of the date of the inauguration of the Council, the Palestinian National Council will convene and formally approve the necessary changes in regard to the Palestinian Covenant, as undertaken in the letters signed by the Chairman of the PLO and addressed to the Prime Minister of Israel, dated September 9, 1993 and May 4, 1994.
10. Pursuant to Annex I, Article IX of this Agreement, Israel confirms that the permanent checkpoints on the roads leading to and from the Jericho Area (except those related to the access road leading from Mousa Alami to the Allenby Bridge) will be removed upon the completion of the first phase of redeployment.
11. Prisoners who, pursuant to the Gaza-Jericho Agreement, were turned over to the Palestinian Authority on the condition that they remain in the Jericho Area for the remainder of their sentence, will be free to return to their homes in the West Bank and the Gaza Strip upon the completion of the first phase of redeployment.
12. As regards relations between Israel and the PLO, and without derogating from the commitments contained in the letters signed by and exchanged between the Prime Minister of Israel and the Chairman of the PLO, dated September 9, 1993 and May 4, 1994, the two sides will apply between them the provisions contained in Article XXII, paragraph 1, with the necessary changes.
13. a. The Preamble to this Agreement, and all Annexes, Appendices and maps attached hereto, shall constitute an integral part hereof.

    b. The Parties agree that the maps attached to the Gaza-Jericho Agreement as:

    a. map No. 1 (The Gaza Strip), an exact copy of which is attached to this Agreement as map No. (in this Agreement "map No. 2");

    b. map No. 4 (Deployment of Palestinian Police in the Gaza Strip), an exact copy of which is attached to this Agreement as map No. 5 (in this Agreement "map No. 5"); and

    c. map No. 6 (Maritime Activity Zones), an exact copy of which is attached to this Agreement as map No. 8 (in this Agreement "map No. 8"; are an integral part hereof and will remain in effect for the duration of this Agreement.
14. While the Jeftlik area will come under the functional and personal jurisdiction of the Council in the first phase of redeployment, the area's transfer to the territorial jurisdiction of the Council will be considered by the Israeli side in the first phase of the further redeployment phases.

Done at Washington DC, this 28th day of September, 1995.
For the Government of
the State of Israel
For the PLO

Witnessed by:

The United States of America	The Hashemite Kingdom of Jordan
The Russian Federation	The Kingdom of Norway
The Arab Republic of Egypt	The European Union

ABOUT THE AUTHORS

Prof. Shlomo Avineri, professor of political science at the Hebrew University of Jerusalem, is a graduate of the Hebrew University and the London School of Economics. He served as director-general of the Israel Foreign Ministry in the first term of Prime Minister Yitzhak Rabin, and in 1996 was awarded the Israel Prize, the country's highest civilian decoration. His books on Marx, Hegel, and Zionism have been translated into many languages.

Ambassador Alan Baker, director of the Institute for Contemporary Affairs at the Jerusalem Center for Public Affairs, is one of Israel's leading international law experts. He served as the legal adviser and deputy director-general of the Israel Foreign Ministry from 1996 to 2004, followed by four years (2004-2008) as Israel's ambassador to Canada.

In addition to his membership of the Israel Bar, Ambassador Baker is a member of the International Law Association, the International Institute of Humanitarian Law, and the International Association of Jewish Lawyers and Jurists, and serves as a member of Israel's panel of arbitrators at the Permanent Court of Arbitration (The Hague). He is a partner in the Tel Aviv law firm Moshe, Bloomfield, Kobo, Baker & Co.

Prof. Alan M. Dershowitz is the Felix Frankfurter Professor of Law at Harvard Law School. A graduate of Brooklyn College and Yale Law School, he joined the Harvard Law School faculty at the age of twenty-five. He has published more than one hundred articles in periodicals such as the *New York Times Magazine*, the *Washington Post*, the *Wall Street Journal*, the *Harvard Law Review*, the *Yale Law Journal*, and others, and more than three hundred of his articles have appeared in syndication in fifty national daily newspapers.

Prof. Dershowitz has also written, taught, and lectured about history, philosophy, psychology, literature, mathematics, theology, music, and sports.

Dan Diker, a respected Middle East affairs specialist and analyst, serves as secretary-general of the World Jewish Congress. He previously served as Middle East policy adviser to the WJC since June 2009 and WJC director of strategic affairs since June 2010. From 2006 to 2010, he served as the director of the Institute for Contemporary Affairs at the Jerusalem Center for Public Affairs, where he also was senior foreign policy analyst since 2002. Before joining the Jerusalem Center, he was Knesset Affairs reporter for Channel 1 English News, and he provides political commentary for international news networks CNN, BBC, and Fox, and the Arab networks *Alhurrah* and *Al Jazeera*.

Prof. Ruth Gavison is Haim H. Cohn Professor (emerita) of Human Rights at the Faculty of Law of the Hebrew University of Jerusalem. She is the founder and president of Metzilah: Center for Liberal, Jewish, and Zionist Thought, and a longtime member of the Association for Civil Rights in Israel, where she served as chairperson and president. She was also a member of a number of public commissions, including the Winograd Commission that examined the Second Lebanon War.

In 2003 Prof. Gavison published, with R. Yaacov Medan, *A New Covenant on State and Religion Issues among Jews in Israel*, for which they won the Avi Chai Prize in 2001. She is also a recipient of the EMET Prize for Law (2003) and of the Israel Prize in Law (2011).

Sir Martin Gilbert is Winston Churchill's official biographer, and a leading historian of the modern world. He is the author of eighty-two books, among them the single-volume *Churchill: A Life*, his twin histories *First World War* and *Second World War*, a comprehensive *History of Israel*, and his three-volume work, *A History of the Twentieth Century* (also published in a single, condensed volume). He is an Honorary Fellow of Merton College, Oxford, and a Distinguished Fellow of Hillsdale College, Michigan.

His book *The Holocaust: The Jewish Tragedy* (published in the United States as *The Holocaust: A History of the Jews of Europe during the Second World War*) is a classic work on the subject.

Dr. Dore Gold, president of the Jerusalem Center for Public Affairs, served as Israel's ambassador to the United Nations (1997-1999). Previously he served as foreign policy adviser to then-Prime Minister Benjamin Netanyahu, at which time he served as an envoy to Jordan, Egypt, the Palestinian Authority and the Gulf states. He was involved in the negotiations over the 1998 Wye Agreement, the 1997 Hebron Protocol, and in 1996 concluded the negotiations with the United States, Lebanon, Syria, and France for the creation of the Monitoring Group for Southern Lebanon. In 1991 he served as an adviser to the Israeli delegation to the Madrid Peace Conference.

Dr. Gold is the author of *Hatred's Kingdom: How Saudi Arabia Supports the New Global Terrorism*; *Tower of Babble: How the United Nations Has Fueled Global Chaos*; *The Fight for Jerusalem: Radical Islam, the West, and the Future of the Holy City*; and *The Rise of Nuclear Iran: How Tehran Defies the West.*

Ruth Lapidoth is Greenblatt Professor Emeritus of the Hebrew University of Jerusalem, and senior researcher at the Jerusalem Institute for Israel Studies. She has written extensively on international law, the law of the sea, autonomy, and Jerusalem. In addition to her academic career, she has been active in the diplomatic field. She was a member of Israel's delegation to the United Nations and to several international conferences. She was the legal adviser to Israel's Ministry of Foreign Affairs (1979-1981). Since 1989 she has been a member of the list of arbitrators of the Permanent Court of Arbitration at the Hague.

Prof. Lapidoth is the 2000 recipient of the Prominent Woman in International Law award of the WILIG Group of the American Society of International Law. In 2001 she received the Gass Award for her contribution to Jerusalem studies. The Israel Bar Association honored her in 2003, and in 2006 she received the Israel Prize for excellence in legal research.

Prof. Nicholas Rostow is a Distinguished Research Professor at the National Defense University and senior director of the university's Center for Strategic Research (which is within the university's Institute for Strategic Studies). He has served in senior positions in the U.S. government, Massachusetts state government, and as university counsel and vice-chancellor for legal affairs and tenured full professor at the State University of New York. He earned his BA in 1972, PhD (history) in 1979, and JD in 1982 at Yale University. His publications are in the fields of diplomatic history, international and national security law, and national security policy.

Col. (ret.) Pnina Sharvit-Baruch retired in 2009 from the Israel Defense Forces (IDF) at the rank of colonel after serving as head of the International Law Department since 2003 and after twenty years as an officer in this department. In that capacity she advised the IDF, the Defense Ministry, and the Justice Ministry on legal aspects relating to the laws of war, targeting and operational law in armed conflicts and in counterterrorism operations, and the laws of occupation. She also served as legal adviser to the Israeli negotiation teams in the Israeli-Palestinian track and the Israeli-Syrian track of the peace negotiations between 1993-2009.

After retiring, Col. (ret.) Sharvit Baruch serves as a teaching professor of public international law at the Law Faculty of Tel Aviv University. She holds an LL.B. degree (magna cum laude) and an LL.M. degree (magna cum laude), both from Tel Aviv University.

Dr. Stanley A. Urman, founding executive director of Justice for Jews from Arab Countries (JJAC), received his PhD in global affairs from Rutgers University in 2010. He has assumed senior management positions in both the Jewish and non-Jewish worlds including, among others, as executive director of the American Sephardi Federation, the Center for Middle East Peace and Economic Development (2000-2007), the Canadian Human Rights Foundation (1982-1989), and the Canadian Jewish Congress (1976-1982).

About the Jerusalem Center for Public Affairs

Websites: English - www.jcpa.org | Hebrew - www.jcpa.org.il

The Jerusalem Center for Public Affairs is a leading independent research institute specializing in public diplomacy and foreign policy. Founded in 1976, the Center has produced hundreds of studies and initiatives by leading experts on a wide range of strategic topics. Dr. Dore Gold, Israel's former ambassador to the UN, has headed the Jerusalem Center since 2000.

Jerusalem Center Programs:

Global Law Forum – A ground-breaking program that undertakes studies and advances policy initiatives to protect Israel's legal rights in its conflict with the Palestinians, the Arab world, and radical Islam. (www.globallawforum.org)

Defensible Borders Initiative – A major security and public diplomacy initiative that analyzes current terror threats and Israel's corresponding territorial requirements, particularly in the strategically vital West Bank, that Israel must maintain to fulfill its existential security and defense needs. (www.defensibleborders.org)

Jerusalem in International Diplomacy – Dr. Dore Gold analyzes the legal and historic rights of Israel in Jerusalem and exposes the dangers of compromise that will unleash a new *jihadist* momentum in his book *The Fight for Jerusalem: Radical Islam, the West, and the Future of the Holy City* (Regnery, 2007). Adv. Justus Reid Weiner looks at *Illegal Construction in Jerusalem: A Variation on an Alarming Global Phenomenon* (2003). Researcher Nadav Shragai assesses the imminent security threats to Israel's capital resulting from its potential division, and offers alternative strategies for managing Jerusalem's demographic challenge in his monograph *The Dangers of Dividing Jerusalem* (2008).

Iran and the New Threats to the West – Preparation of a legal document jointly with leading Israeli and international scholars and public personalities on the initiation of legal proceedings against Iranian President Mahmoud Ahmadinejad for incitement to commit genocide and participate in genocide. This program also features major policy studies by security and academic experts on Iran's use of terror proxies and allies in the regime's war against the West and its race for regional supremacy.

Institute for Contemporary Affairs (ICA) – A diplomacy program, founded in 2002 jointly with the Wechsler Family Foundation, that presents Israel's case on current issues through high-level briefings by government and military leaders to the foreign diplomatic corps and foreign press, as well as production and dissemination of information materials.

Global Terrorism – Using previously unpublished documents, Jerusalem Center President Dore Gold explored the influence of Saudi Wahhabism on 9/11 in the *New York Times* bestseller *Hatred's Kingdom: How Saudi Arabia Supports the New Global Terrorism* (Regnery, 2003).

Anti-Semitism After the Holocaust – Initiated and directed by Dr. Manfred Gerstenfeld, this program includes conferences, seminars, and publications discussing restitution, the academic boycott, Holocaust denial, and anti-Semitism in the Arab world, European countries, and the post-Soviet states. (www.jewishaffairs.org)

New Models for Economic Growth in Israel – This comprehensive, 10-year project has studied the application and impact of privatization policy and other financial innovations in Israel. Sponsored by the Milken Institute, the project includes nine published volumes in Hebrew and English.

Jerusalem Center Serial Publications:

Jerusalem Viewpoints – providing in-depth analysis of changing events in Israel and the Middle East since 1977.
Jerusalem Issue Briefs – insider briefings by top-level Israeli government officials, military experts, and academics, as part of the Center's Institute for Contemporary Affairs.
Daily Alert – a daily digest of hyperlinked news and commentary on Israel and the Middle East from the world and Hebrew press.
Post-Holocaust and Anti-Semitism – a monthly publication examining anti-Semitism after the Holocaust.
Jewish Political Studies Review – a scholarly journal founded in 1989.

Jerusalem Center Websites

www.jcpa.org (English)
www.jcpa.org.il (Hebrew)
www.jcpa-lecape.org (French)
www.jer-zentrum.org (German)

The World Jewish Congress is the international parliament of the Jewish people representing the vital interests of Jewish communities around the world. The WJC is headed by its President Ronald S. Lauder, former U.S. ambassador to Austria, and its Secretary-General Dan Diker.

Founded in Geneva in 1936 to unite the Jewish people and mobilize the world against the Nazi onslaught, the WJC is the representative body of Jewish communities and organizations in over eighty countries from Argentina to Zimbabwe across six continents.

The WJC works to:

- Secure the rights and safety of Jews and Jewish communities around the world
- Intensify the bonds among world Jewry and strengthen the ties of solidarity among Jewish communities everywhere
- Act in coordination with and on behalf of Jewish communities before governmental, intergovernmental, and other international authorities on matters concerning the Jewish people
- Cooperate with all peoples on the basis of universal ideals of peace, freedom, and justice

The WJC is supported by those communities and individual members who, as concerned Jewish citizens, want their voices to be heard on matters of importance to the Jewish people.

With headquarters in New York and Jerusalem, the WJC has affiliate offices around the world including Brussels, Budapest, Buenos Aires, Geneva, Johannesburg, Moscow, Ottawa, Paris, and Sydney.

The Jerusalem headquarters is also the host of the WJC Research Institute and the Israel Council on Foreign Relations.

As a global leader, the WJC received special credentials and recognition at the United Nations making it unique among worldwide organizations as it enjoys a diplomatic seat in the UN and within many of its institutions, commissions, and sub-bodies.

As we have been for nearly three-quarters of a century, the World Jewish Congress continues to be the permanent address of world Jewry.